BLACK SHEEP

Roger Jose

NICHOLAS JOSE

BLACK SHEEP

JOURNEY TO BORROLOOLA

PROFILE BOOKS

First published in Great Britain in 2002 by
Profile Books Ltd
58A Hatton Garden
London EC1N 8LX
www.profilebooks.co.uk

10 9 8 7 6 5 4 3 2 1

Typeset in Minion by MacGuru
info@macguru.org.uk

Printed and bound in Great Britain by
Clays, Bungay, Suffolk

A CIP catalogue record for this book is available from the British Library.

ISBN 1 86197 373 X

For my father, Bob Jose, who flew over
Borroloola with 13 Squadron,
Royal Australian Airforce in 1945

CONTENTS

AUSTRALIA'S FARTHEST SHORE

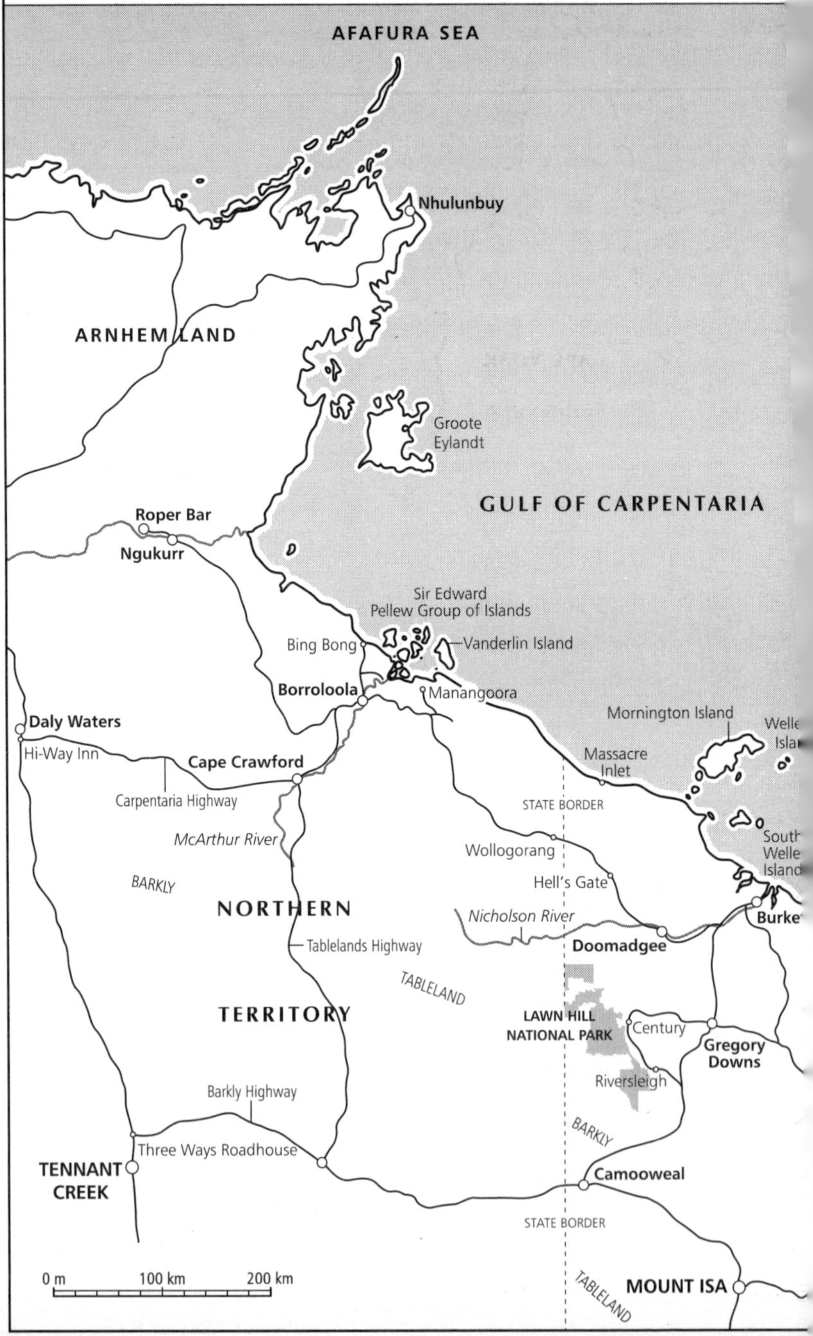

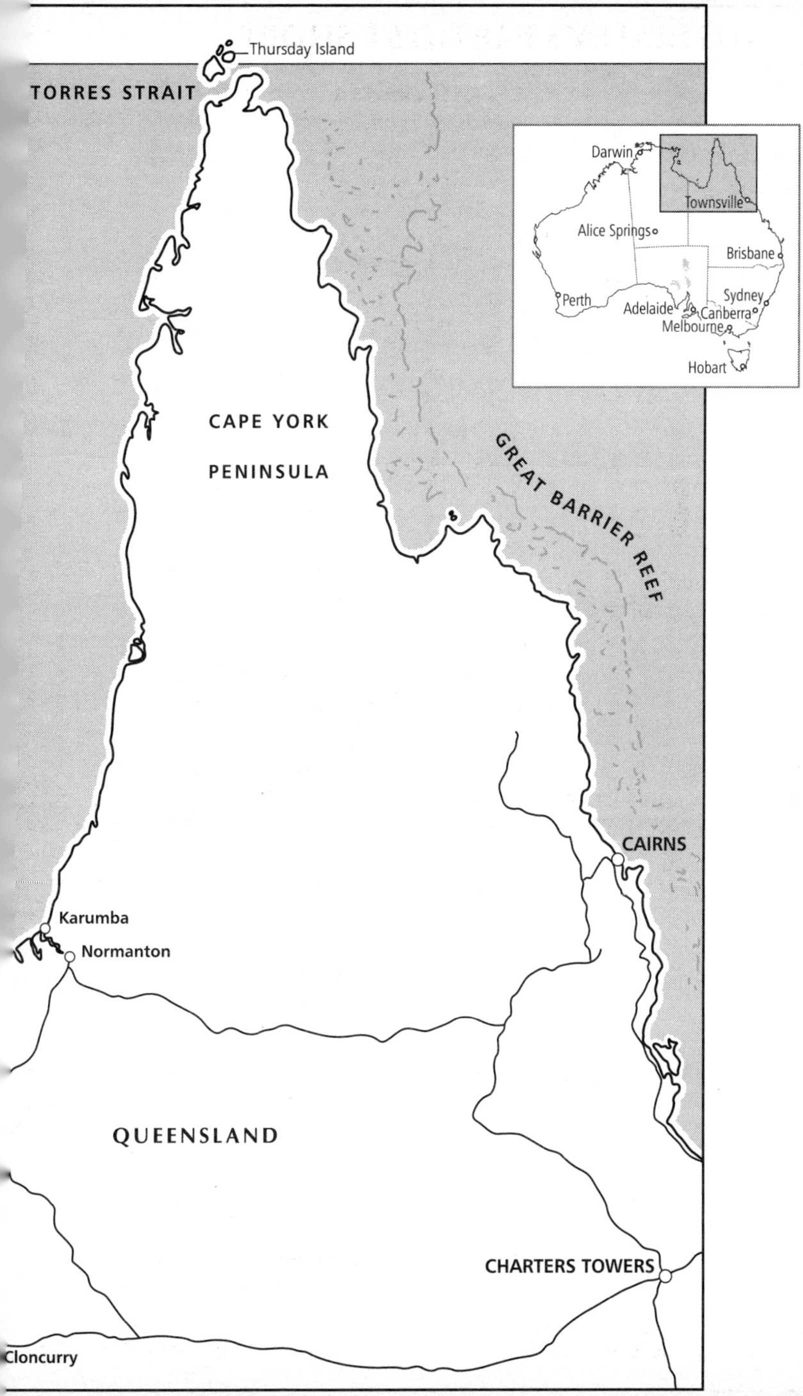
Thursday Island
TORRES STRAIT
Darwin
Townsville
Alice Springs
Brisbane
Perth
Sydney
Adelaide
Canberra
Melbourne
Hobart
CAPE YORK
PENINSULA
GREAT BARRIER REEF
CAIRNS
Karumba
Normanton
QUEENSLAND
CHARTERS TOWERS
Cloncurry

Marndaa marndaa,
Ngali-wingkayani,
Ki-nganjinya ki-awarala,
Jali-wingkaya.

By foot,
Walking,
We two are about to go.
In this relation country of mine.
In this country,
We two are walking.

Yanyuwa song

PROLOGUE

LOST STEPS

Our mystery relative lived with his Aboriginal wife in an upside-down water tank in a place called Borroloola. That was about as far beyond the pale as you could go. He used to push his wife along in a wheelbarrow because she was too fat to walk.

I was a child when I first heard of Roger Jose. There was a photograph of him in a magazine – an old man with a prophet's beard and funny clothes standing outside a strange corrugated-iron dwelling in the middle of nowhere. His name provoked the laughter of grown-ups as any connection with him was dismissed out of hand. Borroloola was a wild little outpost in tropical Australia where no one had ever been, and Roger Jose was an embarrassment to the family.

Adelaide, South Australia, on the other hand, where I grew up, was a city of churches and manicured gardens with a Mediterranean climate, Athenian aspirations and a Spartan moralism. It was a whited sepulchre of a place, known for its sandstone and progressivism, and a famous arts festival. Our family was respectable. The men were doctors or professionals of other kinds. We had the consciousness of lineage, however tenuous, that occurs in provincial, colonial societies when uprooted people who have made themselves a new place in the world devise an ancestry to go with it. My great-grandfather, George Herbert Jose, avid amateur genealogist, traced our name back almost to the Domesday Book.

Herbert, as he was called, was the Anglican Dean of Adelaide, a benign, well-regarded man with a firmly Masonic line on the sectarian arguments of the established church. His elder brother, Arthur Wilberforce Jose, was more bohemian and had been the first Jose to emigrate to Australia, from Bristol. Arthur became a literary gentleman in Sydney, correspondent for *The Times* of London and editor of the *Australian Encyclopedia.* A pioneering historian and an Empire man, he would be remembered as 'the Macaulay of Australia'.[1] Arthur and Herbert were joined by a younger brother, Aubrey, who came to Adelaide in 1901 as tutor to the children of Hallam Tennyson, the late poet laureate's son, state governor at the time.

The Jose brothers survived in Australia as professional men without ever quite entering the local gentry – a status mostly bought through land-grabbing and real estate. In a country founded on transportation, exile and dispossession, there were surprising anxieties about social standing and respectability, although people prefer not to think that way. When it came to sheep and goats, or white sheep and black sheep, lines were drawn. If Roger Jose was indeed who he said he was, he would have been the unknown son of one of those three brothers – my grandfather's brother or first cousin. With relief it was declared that there was nowhere on the family tree he could have fallen off.

But there were few details. I don't know whether that was a consequence of indifference or rather a wilful family forgetting designed to make Roger Jose more of a tall story and less of a problem. For me his image became a kernel of fascinated, energetic speculation.

In 1963, the year he died, Roger Jose appeared in a documentary made by the young David Attenborough on an expedition to the Northern Territory. He was presented as one of the hermits of Borroloola and a bush philosopher of some distinction. Attenborough called him 'noble-looking'.[2] Douglas Lockwood, the Darwin journalist who helped Attenborough with his visit, said, 'Roger Jose taught me more about simplicity and humility than any other man'.[3] Another witness said he was 'the most remarkable person I ever met'.[4] Yet the family to which he claimed to belong had no wish to claim him in return.

Borroloola was quite out of reach in those days. It's easier to get to now, although still out of the way. Maybe because more people are going there, Roger Jose is surfacing again in travel literature and local histories. A recent guidebook celebrates 'Roger Jose ... rumoured (probably incorrectly) to be the son of an Anglican Dean of Adelaide'.[5] It's an extraordinary survival for someone who did his best to make himself lost to the world.

Nearly half a century after I heard of him, I went in search

of Roger Jose – the name by which he is remembered in Borroloola. Never as Roger or Jose, but as 'Roger Jose', as you might speak of Robin Hood or Rip Van Winkle or Crocodile Dundee or the Green Man. I did not realise how much more I would be seeking. In my quest for his true family I would journey not only to remote Borroloola, but far into the Gulf Country of northern Australia, travelling through a highly contested land where old fights continue and yet a dream still hovers of dignified independence, with like and unlike in harmonious co-existence.

Getting there, all the clichés proved true. It's vast, flat country, in all shades of red, often monotonous, occasionally dramatic, 'a land half-made' in the words of the national poet, Banjo Paterson, author of 'Waltzin' Matilda', who visited a century ago. But that is only the surface. The land *is* made, by stories of such fraying scope and complexity that they become tellable only by taking the most wandering of pathways.

Some sentences from *The Lost Steps* come to mind, that great jungle odyssey by the Cuban novelist Alejo Carpentier. He writes: 'New worlds had to be lived before they could be analysed. Those who lived there did not do so out of any intellectual conviction; they simply thought this, and not the other, was the good life.'[6] That applies to the people I am going to meet on the way to and from Borroloola.

I

BOOZE AND BLOOD

They say it's as far as you can go in Australia without a passport. On a national remoteness index it's the remotest place in the country after somewhere in the desert where there's no settlement at all. A thousand kilometres from Darwin on the Northern Territory side of the Queensland border, and another 1,000 kilometres from the mining town of Mount Isa, which is already 1,000 kilometres inland from the populated east coast, it is out of reach of the centres of Australian life. It has about the same latitude as Lusaka and La Paz and, going north, the same longitude as Osaka and Khabarovsk in Siberia. It's almost as close to the equator as Bangkok. I'm sure it's not visible from space.

Borroloola. The word drips from the tongue like honey. Mellifluous. Redolent of bees in pollen. Maybe that explains why it stuck in my memory, with Roger Jose's name flown from its mast like a pirate's flag. The town sits upstream from where the wild waters of the McArthur River debouch into the Gulf of Carpentaria. The river flows during the winter Dry and bursts its banks in the summer Wet – November to

March. At its tidal limit there's a rocky bar where Aboriginal people have been crossing for centuries. The water is fresh and game abounds as bush tucker – or used to. Downstream the river widens into a salty estuary thick with mangroves and crocodiles. Further up the banks turn to rugged gorges. The place where the unpredictable river could be forded was a camp and ceremony ground for Aboriginal people. When the original people were wiped out by the depredations of colonialism, responsibility for the land passed to kin and neighbours, whose descendants make up most of today's community of about 1,200 people.

Borroloola has had about the worst press of any place in Australia. Its beginnings were rough for Aboriginal people and tough as far as the white man was concerned. In 1886 it got its notorious tribute as 'the resort of the scum of Northern Australia'. For most of the century that followed it retained that reputation. The *Lonely Planet* guide describes it as 'a dirty, unpleasant place – part town, part rubbish dump – with expensive accommodation and no redeeming features'. The guidebook urges travellers to hurry on, warning that the road out is no better, 'a potholed, decaying beef road with blind rises and few places to overtake', which makes even the leaving an ordeal. It echoes an old complaint about the town before the road went through, when it was cut off from the outside world for weeks at a time. Locals said that the only way out was to die. Ernestine Hill, an itinerant journalist who first visited in the 1930s, called Borroloola 'the hardest place in Australia to get to, and the most difficult to get away from'. The policeman remembered it as an unpopular posting, 'a dead-end place, on the road to nowhere'. It was Australia's loneliest ghost town, the place where roads turn back, the end of the line.[1]

The first European to document a journey through the Gulf Country was Ludwig Leichhardt, who followed existing Aboriginal footpaths to cross the McArthur River at the ford near Borroloola in 1845. The obsessive naturalist was finding a way through to the north coast from south-eastern Australia. He disappeared out there. Forty years later a wild white man emerged from the bush being carried by two Aboriginal women and speaking German. Before his identity could be confirmed he was killed by a white shooting party who mistook him for a black. Maybe he was one of Leichhardt's men. A tree carved with the letter L is displayed in the Old Police Station Museum at Borroloola today, another relic of Leichhardt's last expedition.

In *Tales from the Austral Tropics*, the explorer-novelist Ernest Favenc wrote of an ancient Dutchman who, discovered in an inland gorge, revealed the secret and curse of a paradise of gold. Favenc imagined a ghostly castaway from one of the Dutch East India Company's ships that explored the Gulf of Carpentaria in the seventeenth century. Variants of the Flying Dutchman and the Wandering Jew recur in this unwritten terrain, where objective reporting shades into a more fantastical gothic topography, as fact and story feed each other. Later the Prussian tragedy of Leichhardt would inspire Patrick White's epic novel *Voss*.

When the Overland Telegraph was going through from Adelaide to Darwin in 1870–72 – 36,000 poles and 5,000 kilometres of singing copper wire – Borroloola became a depot for bringing materials in by sea that were then hauled by bullock team to the line 400 kilometres away. Borroloola dreamed of becoming a major port, thriving on the cattle industry, mineral riches and the trade that would flourish between Australia and the Asian lands to the north. But the dream was an illusion. Arriving in Borroloola in 1919 after four years away at the war in Europe, bush yarn-spinner Bill Harney found merely 'a decadent river port for small craft in the Gulf of Carpentaria' and no more.[2]

To the west the telegraph line followed the route from south to north that John McDouall Stuart had forged in 1860, straight as a rule on a map. But the land tracks and water routes that link Borroloola with other camps and stations across the region follow Aboriginal contours to this day. From the late 1860s drovers came through with cattle from Queensland to stock the Northern Territory, inspired by Stuart's optimistic report of country 'of the finest description for pastoral purposes', and later went as far as the Kimberley in the top corner of Western Australia.[3] They watered their stock where they crossed the McArthur River, at the bar near Borroloola. When the gold rush came to fields around Pine Creek, south of Darwin, in the 1870s and 1880s, prospectors, many of them Chinese, followed the same cattle route in their rush across from the east, again retracing those old Aboriginal paths.

Borroloola's isolation ended when the all-weather road was finally put through in 1968, sealing part of the route with tar. It is marketed to tourists now as the Savannah Way, recommended for the caravanserai of young backpackers and elderly Australians from Down South, the blond nomads and grey panthers whose recreational vehicles proceed in file down the strip of bitumen during the holiday season.

Not all the old pathways are so honoured. There is another pattern of tracks that looks more like the broken map of lines on a hand. It has the living, breathing rhythm of land and water, connecting memory and history with the present world, with a seasonal sense of change and continuity, moving out from the mainland, along the shores of river and Gulf, and out across the islands. It involves working and wandering, 'sitting down', as Aboriginal people say, and letting the mind roam. By seasonal I don't only mean summer and winter, the Wet and the Dry, but also the larger weather of time, of generations, of changing perspectives and attitudes. It's a pattern that is less concerned with putting Borroloola on the road to somewhere else than with the net of local interactions that makes the place what it is, and what it will be.

But let's not get too fancy about Borroloola.

Like more illustrious places, Borroloola has a myth of origin. It became a white man's watering hole when it had been a place of water for Aboriginal people from time immemorial.

Ginger Riley Munduwalawala, The Four Archers and Garimala, *1989*

A Scot named Billy McLeod sailed across the Gulf of Carpentaria in 1883 with a 400-gallon tank of rum which he unloaded under a banyan tree on the bank of the McArthur River. The river may have been named by Leichhardt after wool and rum pioneers in faraway Sydney, the Macarthurs, who sponsored his expedition. (The spelling of place names was often wobbly.) The grog was intended to waylay drovers bringing cattle through on the Gulf Track. When the local

Aboriginal people 'challenged the Scotsman's right of tenure', McLeod 'proved it with a shot-gun', according to one account.

A year after the giant rum keg was unloaded there, a part-Maori smuggler called Black Jack Reid crossed from Thursday Island off the tip of Cape York Peninsula on the other side of the Gulf with an illegal cargo in his schooner and baptised the place. 'A few days after we arrived,' an old-timer remembered, 'the *Good Intent* came up the river and made fast at the landing … Her notorious owner [was] Maori Jack Reid. His first mate was a big buck American nigger. We never heard his name, but christened him "Smoked Beef" … Reid boasted openly that on the way up the river had he got a chance he would have shot "Smoked Beef", his mate, so that he could give him a clean receipt for his wages. "Smoked Beef" heard of it and the result of an Oklahoma cyclone was nothing compared to what "Smoked Beef" did to Reid and his shanty … So Borroloola was born.'[4]

Maori Reid was a blackbirder, the name given to the slave traders who provided cheap Melanesian and Polynesian labour for the sugar plantations of northern Queensland. He and his crew

> used to raid villages on [Pacific] islands, or coax a crowd of islanders on to their vessel for trade, set sail, and when out at sea cull out all the able bodied natives and make the unfit 'walk the plank' … [Reid] loaded up a lot of provisions, not forgetting a big supply of whisky – square bottles, with

> green labels, named 'Come Hither'. Good God, what a havoc that terrible stuff did! It made a jack rabbit fight a bulldog. A man who got a few shots of that stuff under his belt would charge hell with a bucket of water! … Eager hands soon helped him unload his cargo especially when they knew that whisky was part of [it] and then the orgy started. What a christening Borroloola got!

The old-timer's account of the town's beginnings is blunt but as selective as any novelist's: we can only guess what we're not being told. The motive, years after the event, is to engrave the teller's own version of things – heightened, apologetic, exculpatory. Few of us, it seems, are capable of holding on to the undoctored truth.

'We were one of the first mobs to form the herd of the McArthur … We had a rough time, blacks as thick as hair on a dog, on the route, burning the country behind and ahead of us, and at Skeleton Creek driving six of our horses away in the night and spearing them … [A cattle man] was, with a blackboy, speared up the river on the opposite side of town, both being killed in broad daylight in sight of a mob of cattle and men tailing them … Borroloola came to light under tempestuous times.'

The town had earned its reputation as a Wild West sort of place. It was surveyed in 1885 and by the next year the essentials were in place – a police station, a store and a pub. In the gold-rush days of 1886, 1,500 people passed through with 3,000 horses. For a while Borroloola was a rations and transport hub. The first race meeting was held and the McArthur River Jockey Club was formed. Then, in 1895, to raise the cultural tone of the place, the McArthur River Institute was established. But the gold ran out and the cattle bonanza faded. The Gulf turned out to be less than ideal cattle country. Herds were stricken with tick fever. Asian markets failed to materialise and domestic markets were small or too far away. The decade of the nineties proved catastrophic. Borroloola's glory days were over before they began.

When Baldwin Spencer and Francis Gillen visited Borroloola to study the local Aboriginal people in 1901, the only non-Aboriginal residents were the policeman, the publican, the storekeeper, a gardener and a Chinese tailor. Gillen wrote in his diary that 'the ghastly uninteresting reality is worse than anything we anticipated'. The white population was down to three by the next year and more or less stayed that way.

Some of the blame can be sheeted home to the administration. South Australia had annexed the Northern Territory in 1863 against the view of the Colonial Office that it was 'perfectly preposterous' for the northern parts of Australia to 'be governed from Adelaide from which they are separated by the whole breadth of the continent'.[5] In the 1840s South Australia was the first Australian colony to experience a mineral boom. Rich from copper, its graziers and speculators were expansive in their lust for land and easily swayed by glowing reports of prospects up north. But the colony over-

Police Station, Borroloola, 1901–1904

reached itself. It would have made better sense for all of tropical Australia to be run as one entity east to west, but that was not how people saw the continent. Development north of Capricorn suffered from ignorance and indifference, with Borroloola as an outermost limit. Eventually South Australia admitted defeat and in 1911 transferred responsibility for the Northern Territory to the newly federated Commonwealth government. The Territory owed South Australia more than £6 million, which included what had been spent on two ends of a transcontinental railway. (The track languished unfinished until 2001, when work began again.)

'The inescapable conclusion is that [South Australia's] fundamental blunder lay in annexing the Northern Territory in the first place,' judges the historian Ross Duncan.[6] I wonder if a veil was drawn over the fiasco after that; if Adelaide turned her back. Certainly, growing up there, I had no sense of a connection, historical or otherwise, with the tropical north. The desert pressed down on the temperate belt of orchards, vineyards and granaries that surrounded our oasis city, kept green on precarious supplies of water. The train north, named the Ghan after the Afghans who had run camel trains on the route, headed up the tracks beyond the red Flinders Ranges across the dry country to Alice Springs and stopped. There was an extended boundary beyond that, a desiccation, a dissipation, an unravelling – if you wanted to disappear, that's where you would go. Unlike grand bluestone Adelaide, there was no permanence up yonder. When Darwin was bombed by the Japanese in February 1942, most of the civilian population had bailed out back to Adelaide. The north was an outpost for fighting an offshore war. The casualties from those bombings have never been counted absolutely because the records of who lived there were unreliable. It happened again when Cyclone Tracy blew Darwin away on Christmas Day 1974. And if Darwin was like that, how much more so was Borroloola, administered after Adelaide relinquished it by a federal government located in remotest Melbourne and later in the new capital, Canberra?

In 1912 Borroloola received a grand visit from the Governor-General of the Commonwealth of Australia, who must have been bemused by what he saw of civilisation's trappings: a pub, a store and a police station. The Aboriginal population may have been around 300 at the time, allowing for seasonal variation as people moved about their country. The settlement drew people who were struggling to survive the rupture of their customary way of life. Borroloola was an old camping place, after all. The handful of European residents, including the so-called hermits, were actually sustained by a substantial population of Aboriginal people. 'To this day,' notes geographer-historian Richard Baker, 'Europeans have outnumbered Aboriginal people on probably only two occasions. This occurred for the first time very briefly in 1886, when large numbers of gold-diggers passed through ... Aboriginal people would not have been outnumbered again until the government-sponsored Borroloola centenary celebrations in 1985 resulted in a weekend influx of Europeans.'[7]

Government officials filled their reports with statistics, but were content to let numbers blur when it came to Aboriginal people. In the administrator's report for 1925–26 the population of the Northern Territory is given as '2,345 European and 1,040 coloured [mostly Chinese], exclusive of Aboriginals ...', while it is proudly noted that the cattle herds had increased to 970,342 head. Elsewhere the same report estimates that there were 'approximately 10,000 Aboriginals living in the coastal belt, and about the same number in other portions of the Territory'. Aboriginal people, who were mostly out bush, could not be counted with the actuarial precision of livestock tallies. Besides, cattle and horses were property. The Protector of Aborigines, Cecil Cook, noted that 'the figures are in many instances, owing to the nomadic nature of the Aboriginals, only an estimate, but it is hoped that by correcting the returns annually, a fairly reliable estimate will be obtained'. For the wider administrative district centred on Borroloola, the 1926–27 figures are given as 800 adults and 380 children, with 12 'half-caste' adults and 9 children, a total of 1,201 (of an overall total for the Territory of 20,542). By way of comparison, the 1996 census gives the population of the Northern Territory as 195,101, with 46,277 people identifying themselves as of Aboriginal descent. Aboriginal figures have doubled while non-Aboriginal people have increased fifty-fold. The occupation looks like being permanent.

Protector Cook concludes his report with a Panglossian turn: 'The treatment of Aboriginals during the year has been satisfactory. In such an immense area, it is impossible, of course, to supervise the daily action of isolated men and there may be instances of petty tyrannies. The Aboriginals, however, are now getting wise enough to know that they have a protecting power to whom they can appeal, and as there have been no reports of ill-treatment of Aboriginals, it is safe to assume that such ill-treatment does not exist.'

That was a year before the infamous massacre at Coniston, north-west of Alice Springs, in 1928, when 70 Aboriginal people of the Walpiri nation were slaughtered by police and others in officially sanctioned revenge killings. Twenty years earlier the Eastern & African Cold Storage Supply Company Ltd had taken up a vast tract of land for cattle north of the Roper River on the Gulf of Carpentaria and organised shooting parties to eliminate people who were brusquely designated 'hostile blacks'. Aboriginal people were spearing cattle because they saw it as their hunting right. They were raiding the intruders' camps as a guerrilla tactic to drive the white pastoralists away. The company's response amounted to an attempt at ethnic cleansing, intending the genocide of the entire local population. At great cost, however, the Aboriginal resistance succeeded. The company went bankrupt, abandoning its ambitious Arafura Station. Of 20,000 cattle introduced, fewer than half were recovered. Andrew McMillan relates the story as told by Yolngu people in his close-up, loving book *An Intruder's Guide to East Arnhem Land*: 'The hunting parties had dispersed survivors far and wide, creating devastating social upheaval; they'd wiped out entire clans leaving the country they'd held responsibility for in limbo. Inter-clan feuds would flare as opposing elders tried to exert ceremonial and political control over the vacated lands and waters and dreamings.'[8] Oral history is the main source for terrible events that were kept under wraps by their perpetrators. South of the Roper River in Borroloola other massacres are remembered where, again on the pretext of reprisal for cattle spearing, hundreds of Aboriginal people were slain as the cattle stations were opened up. The details have never been officially recorded.

The Protector's interest in statistics suggests a dawning realisation that Aboriginal people, for whom the dying pillow had been smoothed in the confident expectation of the demise of their race, were not in fact disappearing, especially in the north. The fascination in the post-war period with the hermits of Borroloola can be seen in the same anxious light, made sharper by the sense that embattled English-speaking Australia had just had a lucky escape from the Asiatic hordes. The war in the Pacific drew new attention to Australia's patchy defensibility. Ernestine Hill writes of Borroloola in 1945: 'The population today is little more than four old men, and a policeman to keep them in order, surrounded by about 10,000 myall blacks.'[9] 'Myall' meant 'wild', a euphemism for uncivilised, unassimilated, untamed. In fact, very few of the local Aboriginal people fitted that description.

The police officers stationed at Borroloola kept a daily journal that also shows a preoccupation with numbers and property. They would regularly count and list their police horses, which they did for neither Aboriginal people nor others. Europeans are referred to by given names and surnames, and often titles, such as Mr or Mrs. Aboriginal people are given English first names only, often nicknames or diminutives, with sometimes an attempt to render their proper Aboriginal-language clan name alongside if the entry concerns an important matter. The police horses are referred to by name as well: Virgil, Tradition, Coronation, Sweetness. Sometimes the horses shared the residents' names, Aboriginal and non-Aboriginal alike: Maggie, Biddy, Blittner (after Freddy Blittner, a local character) and Roger, after Roger Jose. To judge by the space and care allotted in these journals, the horses often meant more to those isolated constables than their human charges. In February 1927 an officer notes that one of his horses has a crocodile bite on a fleshy part of the shank that should heal. A month later comes the plaintive follow-up: 'Police Horse Bondi who was torn with Alligator is very poor & is suffering in my opinion of Wasting Disease.' The horse died.

B'rroLOOLAH – as it is pronounced by locals – had a bad reputation. One of its nicknames was the 'Loo, or the Other 'Loo, the first one being Sydney's Woolloomooloo, the neighbourhood hewn from rock by Australia's early convicts, refuge of street gangs and den of unruliness and vice from the 1860s to, well, today, despite every effort at gentrification. I walk through its dodgy streets when I go to Sydney's Mitchell Library to do my research. Borroloola can sometimes sound like a reinvention, a century later, of the penal colony at Sydney Cove that started modern Australia. The difference is that those whitefellas found their way to Borroloola voluntarily. If they weren't all crims, they were all escaping something.

That has been true in different ways for Aboriginal people there too. They were left relatively alone by missionaries and other officers of the state, for better or worse. Ted Harvey, a welfare officer in the town in the 1950s, commented that in Borroloola, compared to other places, 'there was no [paved] road, there were no tourists, there were no bad influences, there was no grog'.[10] Isolation depends on your orientation. Remote from the population centres of Australia's south, maybe, but close to the busy, populous archipelagos to Australia's north. Closer, in fact, to the great world.

Today the area's remoteness is a tourist attraction, which ironically may cause the isolation to disappear as more and more visitors come to look. Thirty kilometres downriver from the town, at what used to be a popular Aboriginal fishing ground, the Borroloola Boat & Fishing Club has staked its claim. In a few years it has grown into a residential lager camp with 3,000 members (said to be whites only) and with links to the Northern Territory's conservative Country Liberal Party, who hope the influx will tilt the balance their way in future elections.

'Too many tourists,' complains one Aboriginal woman, 'you never see me go out fishing, I'm frightened ... Might get shot or something.' A Vietnamese mudcrabber claimed to have been shot at with a semi-automatic by someone from the fishing club recently. If the club is a law unto itself, it has ambitions to become a prospering town, under the macho name of King Ash Bay – as Borroloola once aspired in the heyday of its frontier past. So bets are on. The area is a paradise for anglers who like the sport of pulling in big, wild, fighting barramundi. But as fishing stocks are depleted under the pressure of numbers, this paradise may well be lost too and the latest boom-time dreams for the McArthur River will fade away like all the rest, letting isolation return.[11]

'If they want money,' declared a visiting official of the denizens of Borroloola in 1886, 'they don't stand on much ceremony about getting a man half drunk, taking him into the scrub, bashing his head against a post, giving him one or two kicks in the ribs, robbing him of all his cheques and leaving him to come to as best he can. If they want horses they take the first they come across, what beef they require they kill anywhere … they steal anything they can lay hands on.'[12]

Unlawful possession of beef is the most common crime in the old police records for Borroloola. Cattle-stealing, known as cattle-duffing or poddy-dodging – rounding up someone else's clean-skin cattle and branding them as your own – was a way of doing business in the early days, particularly for battlers on smaller properties along the coast, who took cattle from the much larger company-owned stations on the Tableland. Even now residents of the town are quick to complain about thievery, pointing the finger not only at Aboriginal kids but also at the tourists in the caravan parks.

The Wild West image glosses over what those wild times were really about. 'War been fight here, everywhere people ought to know … war yes,' as one man phrases it. 'Shoot everybody.' Droving cattle into new country, crossing the McArthur River at Borroloola, bringing in rum, the overlanders were frontline troops in an undeclared war. Aboriginal people fought back.

Ironically, when conflict scaled down, with the new order imposed by force, Aboriginal people – the very people who had been dispersed – could be recognised as a useful, even necessary labour force. In his report for 1915–17, J. A. Gilruth, the Northern Territory administrator, writes frankly of the need for the local black slaves: 'The great increase in the white population of Darwin has resulted in the demand for Aboriginal assistance in households exceeding the supply, though the officers of the Department have done everything possible to assist housewives anxious to obtain this, the only, class of domestic assistance available.'

At the same time Gilruth draws a draconian line against miscegenation, revealing the psychopathology of dependency: 'illicit intercourse between white and native … has in some measure been overcome by the drastic regulations referred to by the Chief Protector [in his rules for segregation].' He waxes eloquent, flying a wobbly scientific kite that is tangled around a rigid need to assert white superiority, even as he acknowledges reliance:

> That the Aboriginal is not the degraded human being, and of the low order of intelligence that is so commonly asserted, I am more and more convinced … the blackfellow who is not demoralised by the European, who comprehends what his employer wishes, and is treated firmly yet sympathetically, displays an intelligence and a loyalty of no mean order … Their value in the penetration and exploration of this vast empty land, waterless for enormous stretches in the interior, has not been sufficiently recognised. Today it is rare that one meets a white traveller or resident in the bush who has not the assistance of, at least, one Aboriginal, and even the small miner working his own claim is almost invariably assisted by Aborigines, to whom at times he trusts, in a degree, his life.
>
> Notwithstanding these observations, it is true occasional individual or group actions of lawlessness against

> whites have to be recorded. The majority are traceable to primary wrongdoing on the part of the white – frequently to interference with females, the native code regarding which is strict, and the penalty often death. More rarely ... it is attributable to the malign influence of another 'semi-civilised' native ... The Aboriginal ... never develops beyond the schoolboy stage, and must be dealt with as an adolescent, not an adult.

Those sentences signal the cursed relations between settlers and indigenous people in my country, a relationship that mars Australia's history even as it defines it.

Yet in isolated Borroloola, with only a few non-Aboriginals remaining for most of the twentieth century, things had a chance to work out somewhat differently – and I think perhaps they have. That included assumptions about how Aboriginal and non-Aboriginal people could interact. One former policeman recalled that 'the Aboriginals Ordinance provided heavy penalties for white men convicted of keeping Aboriginal women as mistresses ... But this law had rarely been enforced at Borroloola.' There were a few notorious crime cases, but by 1948 things had quietened down so much, or the town's attractions had so declined, that the visiting superintendent of police recommended closing down the police station. There were not many more than 30 Aboriginal people residing in town during the Dry, and six or seven ageing white men. There had been some trouble with the constable, who was reported as 'drinking excessively' and 'somewhat doubtful in the performance of his duties'. The fault lay 'with whoever moved such a young inexperienced Constable to the place … I do not consider taking any disciplinary action (there is an insufficiency of evidence, anyhow)', the superintendent writes, 'but to move the Constable and his wife and young child away from such a desolated locality' and not replace him. 'It seems to me that it is a waste to maintain a policeman at Borroloola – unless he is to be viewed as an "old men's home" keeper.'

The decision drew the ire of Roger Jose who wrote a letter of protest in his bold cursive handwriting, dated Borroloola, 10 December 1948:

> To His Excellency, The Administrator N.T., Honoured Sir: May I respectfully claim your attention to the matter herein. It now seems very probably that the local Police Station is to be closed, and at a most difficult time i.e. in the 'Wet'. Being strictly reasonable Sir: is this not most inconvenient and rather hard on the residents, the nearest Police Station being 180 miles away, at Anthony's Lagoon. Apart from the actual possible need of protection, there is a good deal of civil business transacted at a rural Police Station i.e. burning [dingo] scalps, issuing licences, permits, way-bills, medical attention within reason and many little duties, which will only be appreciated at their full value when ceased. Many of the residents have already expressed their chagrin and stated their willingness to sign a petition conveying their feelings in the matter to Yourself; my reason for

> not forwarding this now, is the fact that many of the men in the outlying district are not yet aware of the proposed change; but I am quite confident of their support from their attitude when it was first mooted some time ago. Sir: it is fervently hoped you will give this important matter your deepest consideration; and may I respectfully inquire in closing pro.tem. the proposed alternative measure.
>
> Hopefully and very respectfully yours
>
> Roger Jose[13]

The petition might not have included many names, but in this emphatic letter is heard the voice of a tiny community fighting for its life, tones familiar today from protests at small-town closures of post offices and banks and other services. In the querulous epistolary rhetoric we hear the authentic voice of Roger Jose, self-appointed scribe of the people.

A month later he was fobbed off with an unequivocal reply and the police station was closed. 'In my considered opinion it is to the benefit of everyone,' wrote the administrator, ignoring the town's protests. Borroloola became a ration depot for Aboriginal welfare. By 1956, notes the resident welfare officer, the Aboriginal population was 200 during the Wet and 80 during the Dry. He adds that 'there are four other white residents who may be considered as permanent. Two of these [including Roger Jose] are married to natives.' The officer was interceding with his superior to be able to stay on.

'I like the natives here and am keenly interested in them and their problems. It is my desire that I may be permitted to remain here ...' But someone else thought otherwise. Hard to get to it may have been, but Borroloola was also a place that at least a few people found hard to leave.[14]

I am still on the way, not there yet, but sifting through papers and books and manuscripts, hearing other people's voices, piecing together a sense of what such a place might mean, a pinprick on the map that looms large in the imagination as a setting for a black sheep. I'm coming to understand that there's no Roger Jose without Borroloola. This peculiar place, as far from the white man's world as he could go, made him its most peculiar son.

I drive to Borroloola from Darwin in a rented off-road Toyota, accompanied by my friend Bob from New York. Seven hours south down the Stuart Highway we take a left at the Hi-Way Inn, a service station where I fill up on diesel and pick up a couple of cassette tapes for the journey. Nat King Cole, The Shirelles. There isn't much choice. When I pay with my credit card, the lady notices that my card is the next number in the series from hers. Uncanny. What's the significance of that? A sign that connections are there if you look for them?

It's a land of unexplained disappearances and unsolved murders. The day after we pass, the Stuart Highway is closed by police. A van had been stopped in the middle of the night, a British backpacker tied up, a shot fired and her boyfriend's blood found on the road. The young woman got away and hid in the bush while a man with a moustache stalked her with his dog. Failing to find her, he drove off into the darkness, leaving no trail. Neither boyfriend, assailant nor dog has been heard from since.

The road is a single strip no wider than a country lane, heading across sparse, scrubby, orange country into smoke. There are termite mounds all the way, changing in size and colour and architectural style. I think of Angkor Wat, Chartres, Gaudí's unfinished Sagrada Familia in Barcelona, Guggenheim Frank Lloyd Wright, Bilbao Gehry. No other landscape can be so changed by the natural presence of one creature, dominating this vast terrain with their constructions. They look like fields of endless tomb monuments, except they are so exuberant in their repetitive, competitive artistry. The termite mounds might be an installation of disguised robotic receptors for aliens already well advanced in their campaign. But something makes them humorous, like an almighty three-dimensional dot painting, mocking human pretensions. If they were no more than turd piles, Bob and I would still look at them with fascinated respect and take photographs. You can almost hear them laughing back at us, these cartoon termitaries, these antbeds.

After weeks of rainless Dry the dead grass is burning close to the road. All around the trees are blackened. In some spots new sprouts are already uncurling. The termite mounds, ash-grey here and about a metre in height, withstand fire as well as flood. Where the fires are recent the landscape is an eerie monochrome, the eucalypt leaves still hanging from the boughs, browned like potato crisps. The smoke blows across the road and flames run in little lines along fallen branches, chased by the wind. The grass is reduced to sooty tufts in black soil. Soon the black cockatoos come, with the red flash in their tail, shrieking at the fragrance that rises like incense smoke from the pungent burning wood. They pick over the hearts of seeds that have burst in the heat.

Shapes loom on the roadside, legs in the air like upended tables, round as hot-air balloons, the same bleached colour as the scorched leaves. It takes time to see them for what they are – dead cattle, bloated to twice their normal size, each one as big as our white truck. They look more like sputniks that have crashed to earth, their antennae reaching out to a mother-ship that has let them go, yet rotund and taut enough to lift off as smoke blows across them from the black earth. We are so startled by this surreal vision that we don't know what to do. Bob, rousing himself from the jetlag caused by 40 hours in planes and airports from New York via Sydney to Darwin, with *Artificial Intelligence* at an air-conditioned multiplex during the Los Angeles layover, breaks into raucous laughter. He has no idea where he is. It could be a Damien Hirst art installation but in our bewilderment we miss the photo opportunity and drive on. A twister of smoke is ahead down the straight flat road.

The three bloated beasts died in a crush when the last wagon of a road-train whiplashed out of control. They will either burn or burst and feed the crows and then the ants. Soon their pale Brahman hides will be pressed to the bitumen, all that's left.

The fire is a walking fire, burning slowly enough to walk beside, a fire that cleans up and renews the land. Walking beside the slow-burning flame is like being a tightrope walker on a slackened rope. So we hear when we reach the next pitstop, Heartbreak Hotel, the only premises at Cape Crawford. That's where the Tableland drops down to spinifex plains and a bluff of rock protrudes from the line of hills into low-lying emptiness. There is no cape and no water. A good name is often all you need. Borroloola.

II

NO HUMBUG

The first time I mentioned Roger Jose it was as if I had mentioned Santa Claus. The old woman shrieked with laughter. She came from Borroloola but was living in Darwin now. 'That old man, I remember him, he was a good old man,' she said, giving me the names of some people I could ask about him. She told me the first person I should talk to was Roy Hammer and I wrote his name down. She laughed with high-pitched hilarity, as you might at Jerry Lewis or Jim Carrey. Roger Jose may have been a good man, but he was obviously very funny too.

On the database in the State Library of New South Wales I found a dozen or so references to Borroloola, mostly to the on-again, off-again Aboriginal land claims of the last 25 years, to Aboriginal language material and to the town's appalling health issues. Roger Jose, who died in 1963, is a sideshow to all this. But he was the focal point for a number of celebrity visitors to the town in the decades after the Second World War, of whom David Attenborough, with short back and sides and a lank blond fringe, was the biggest fish.

A conversation with Roger Jose in which he shared his pearls of wisdom was worth taking back to civilisation. Not everyone was convinced, but impressions were mostly favourable. The trouble is, one account bleeds into another; a fragment of memory is spliced to a rumour, and stories grow, even as the fact-checkers busy themselves over particular points.

I joined this industrious band of burrowers. From Sydney, armed with references to obscure newspaper articles that the library did not have, I contacted the Northern Territory Archives and the local genealogical society. I tracked down phone numbers of officials who had worked in Borroloola in the old days and talked to them – there were still a few alive. Then I found myself in Darwin.

I come not as an expert, neither a historian nor an anthropologist nor a linguist, nor as someone hired to do a job. I am driven by curiosity. As usual after reading about something I want to go there, to rivet my imagination to the circumstances of time and place and people. Once, when I was researching a hybrid Chinese rose, I made the journey to Mauritius in the Indian Ocean where the rose was first found growing and walked right around the island of Rodrigues in search of it.

Many Australians have never been to Darwin, or only to touch down when flights stop there to refuel. That's as true of people from Adelaide who face a long drive up the tedious, arduous Stuart Highway. Darwin is not much written about either. It's a staging post, a stepping-off point. I like it. It's young and friendly and people know how to do their work.

Yet it's not what you see. Something's concealed. People are there for tangled reasons that have a day-time and a night-time side.

The Northern Territory Library in Darwin is housed in the brand-new parliament building, a white extravagance in contemporary Brunei-style architecture (money and tropical-colonial references), gazing out over the tourmaline waters of the Arafura Sea. The newspaper reading area, where local investors come to check the financial markets, opens on to a terrace wafted with balmy breezes soothing any losses. The library occupies temporary space. So far the Northern Territory, not a fully fledged state, has only a lower house of parliament. The chamber the library inhabits is reserved for the upper house, which so far doesn't exist. When the Northern Territory parliament's ambition for two houses is eventually realised, the library will move on, no doubt to less opulent accommodation. I am sidetracked by many fascinating things there, but find little about Roger Jose.

I do better down the street in the drab upstairs rooms that house the local archive. In white gloves I handle the leather-bound worm-eaten journals from the Borroloola police station. On almost every day for more than half a century the local policeman was required to write an entry, recording conditions, comings and goings, police matters and other things of note, including, wittingly or unwittingly, his own state of mind. The characters and fortunes of the officers varied in that lonely place as much as their handwriting, but write they did, even when they had to apologise for 'smudge caused by perspiration on arm' when the heat and humidity soared in an era without air-conditioning, electricity, running water or other amenities of modern life. Because Borroloola was small and not much happened, the record is comprehensive once you become familiar with its euphemisms and shorthand. It gives a picture of life in a forgotten tropical port that Joseph Conrad could have been proud of. I read of peace proclaimed with Germany in November 1918 and Roger Jose coming in from the bush and a few days later taking the lugger *Iolanthe* out across the Gulf to Thursday Island. I read of a photographer arriving in town by pushbike in 1919 with a cine-camera. I read of Aboriginal women being brought to the police station with venereal disease and leprosy, and of part-Aboriginal children being escorted to mission stations, following the practice of removing paler-skinned children from their mothers. I read of riotous behaviour and theft of goat meat and hard labour for Aboriginal prisoners, clearing weeds or cutting timber. I read of Bill Harney reported for trying to get 'an Aboriginal girl ... aged 9 or 10 years old for immoral purposes' in 1922. I read of Freddy Blittner going out to the islands by canoe in search of sandalwood. One night he was so drunk when he left the hotel that he climbed on to a crocodile rather than his boat to cross the river home – and lived to tell the tale, earning the title 'Freshwater Admiral'. A seasoned bushman, Blittner could fight with Aboriginal weapons and curse fluently in the language – so well that his death, when it did occur, was attributed to Aboriginal sorcery. I read of Roger Jose coming into town in 1927 with 'his wife (lubra) per foot one horse'. I read of him labouring and labouring, cutting ironwood posts for stock-yards, clearing sandbars from the river channel, felling trees for the airstrip and filling in washed-away roads, until he disappears into the bush.

I see Roger Jose's probate document, based on his death certificate. His length of residence in Australia is given as life. His marriage to Maggie, described as 'full-blood', in Darwin in 1926 is listed, and his marriage, on Maggie's death in 1957, to her sister Biddy, who had lived with them, is there too. He is said to have been 67 when he died intestate in Borroloola, leaving a shotgun valued at £10 and £15 of other property, including the tank house that went to Biddy.

The people at the archives warn me that Borroloola can be a dangerous place. This accords with what I have heard in Sydney from journalists who have reported from there in recent times. There was a ghastly killing of a woman by a gang of drunken young men. I was told I could pass through but would not want to stay there. In Darwin I'm staying with a friend from Adelaide, a doctor who has worked in Borroloola. He tells me about the famous sign at the entrance to the pub: NO HUMBUG, NO GUNJA, NO FIGHTING, NO DRUNKS. 'Humbug' is the word used in Aboriginal English for harassment – for money, favours or sex. He tells me to stick to the front bar.

Humbugging is what I'm doing to people who might help in my quest for Roger Jose.

'Woz'up?' asks my doctor mate, who has worked in the Territory for a long time. He quizzes me on what I'm looking for. He's a big, good-looking man in a loud shirt with a love of making music and a hungry humour for life. When I phoned to say I was coming to stay, my calls were not returned. The silence turned out to mean that he and his wife had been summoned away to tragedy – his parents-in-law had died in a car crash on their annual pilgrimage north up the long road from Adelaide to Darwin. The house when I arrived was empty. Palm fronds rotting in the swimming pool and laundry piled unwashed in the machine were signs of the family's abrupt evacuation. His wife was the adopted daughter of the couple who died. As well as having two children themselves, my friend and his wife, when they were living in London, adopted two other children. The family was strong and now the boy from London had a Darwin Aboriginal woman as his partner and was responsible for her family too. When I caught up with my doctor friend he said one of the things he learned from working with Aboriginal people was the importance of family and the complexity of information that families carried. It was like a contemporary version of kinship systems, not strictly biological but dependent on who was acknowledged as family with due ritual and ceremony. The reckoning of grief he was going through for his parents-in-law became another sort of ritual, informed by that understanding of family relationships.

He was suspicious of the missionary motives that many non-Aboriginal people bring to Aboriginal communities, where they come to work or learn, looking for something for themselves. But he understood the need for connection, its possibility and value, across the widest gulfs. He wondered where I fitted in. I told him that Roger Jose, my putative kin, a labourer who lived 'blackfella', in the policeman's disapproving words, might turn out to be the most exemplary of forebears, a neglected visionary. I wanted the connection because I wanted to join myself to someone who had earned his belonging in this country.

My friend said it was an age thing, that kids are only interested in where they're going to and have no interest in where they've come from, but that at some point in life the urge comes to revisit the past and reorder it. Where you're going turns into where you've come from.

The people who make the Northern Territory's genealogical society such a frantically thriving concern are mostly retired people, elderly volunteers, in a pattern repeated around the world, where genealogy, that unlikely beneficiary of the Internet, is a consuming passion of those with time to pursue it. But of the millions of hits that besieged the British census for 1901 when it went online, many came from young people curious about family secrets, curious about continuity and identity, curious about the web of generation. Perhaps it is a response to anxieties of not belonging, a way of moving the story on. In settler societies, such as the United States, Canada, New Zealand and Australia, local history flourishes at community level, tracing and dignifying often unremarkable events. Pedigrees are established, hard-won from original displacement, in backwaters from the main sweep of history elsewhere. The orphan is legitimated and given a home.

I smile in my own case. It has taken me half a lifetime to strike out for Borroloola. I'm doing it after I've been almost everywhere else. Inveterate traveller, I had to see the Taj Mahal and the Wailing Wall and the Great Pyramids and the Forbidden City and the Chrysler Building and the Golden Gate Bridge and the Sistine Chapel and Universal Studios, not to mention returning to within the sound of Bow bells in London, place of my birth, before my curiosity about a hermit in Borroloola, a reputed relative, became a compulsion. I take those other journeys and contexts with me as I contemplate the existence of a man who turned his back on it all.

'Too easy,' says the doctor, making a phone call to the Borroloola elder on my behalf. She cackles and I'm tickled pink. He winks at me. 'Whatever floats your boat.'

Nat King Cole sings 'Nature Boy' like a god. Bob sits beside me navigating from a map he downloaded before he left New York. Heartbreak Hotel advertises helicopter rides to the Lost City. Which Lost City is it? Apparently this one is just off the road, a formation of crumbling sandstone pillars on high ground. The Territory has a dozen Lost Cities and still counting, named by visitors in a childish hankering for the ruins of elsewhere. But this is not Mexico or Peru. These evocative sites are natural wonders, humanised only in the splendid immateriality of language and belief. That invisible knowledge is the missing civilisation here.

A sign points east to my own Lost City – Borroloola. As

we approach over the bleached grass plains the ground turns rocky, red, grey and black, the colours of mineral-bearing ore. Hills rise, sheared by cliff faces and plunging escarpments, and the backbone of the land is laid bare in a great snaking line of ragged stone against the sky.

Suddenly, when we reach the McArthur River Mine, the road changes to a stretch of multi-lane highway. State-of-the-art road-trains barrel past, carrying lead and zinc ore to the port facility at Bing Bong. The road runs like an arrow to the coast, making it easy for fishing folk to reach the camp at King Ash Bay, giving Borroloola a wide bypass. Then at the turnoff to the town the road shrinks back to its old size and patchy condition. Waterholes are covered with waterlilies and crowded with birds. A pair of brolga, the stately, dancing birds known as native companions, step through the blackened scrub to drink, as tall as I am and a smoky grey colour that would render them invisible in early morning fog. Black and white storks, or jabiru, airborne on beating wings a couple of metres across, descend on the bare branches of a tree growing from the pond. Heron and ducks and smaller birds, some flaming emerald green, others with the punk red topknot of northern bower birds, join them in conference. I drive by on a flat road that cuts through black soil with the appearance of a wintry lowland in a Dutch painting, yet dried hard as roof tile in this hot dry season. A few thin trees mark the plain with verticals, not giving much shade.

I'm apprehensive about Borroloola. Hard to believe I'm actually so close, after a lifetime with the word round my tongue.

It's unspectacular. This straight road turns a right-angle and becomes Robinson Road, heading past some signs until low structures appear. Even before we're in the town a scratchy placard announces a heritage trail, pedestrians only, that peters out in long grass. There's no arrival, no transition. The pub on one side and the store and a payphone on the other. A few weathered people are hanging around on the green outside the store. A family car full of kids is fuelling up. The buildings are spaced and fenced and set well back from the road. There's a sense of amplitude and emptiness. Past the pub it's as if the town has already stopped again. There's a burnt-off reserve, then the caravan park. Further down the road are more houses, and some temporary dwellings put up after Cyclone Kathy in 1984 – still here. Only later do I understand that the town spreads out in different parts over a large area, reflecting division, change, destruction, fresh starts, randomness and planning that has and hasn't happened.

We pull off the road and check in at the caravan park, a kempt stretch of lawn shaded by lofty tamarind trees with an office and an ablutions block. It is actually no more expensive than a package rate at the Singapore Hilton. The owners are away in Darwin for the birth of a grandchild and a young woman from Down South, outside Adelaide, is minding the office. She says she hasn't been away from the caravan park since she arrived in Borroloola. There's a fault to the phone lines in the area and she doesn't know if any of the phones in town are working. She directs us to our deluxe cabin, a metal box with a kitchenette and a shower cubicle that has not been cleaned since the previous occupancy and a bed and a bunk and a television. We have chosen it so we can work by electric light in the evenings. It is far more luxurious than we expected. But in the end Bob is too jetlagged even to stay awake after dark and I watch television. It turns out that Borroloola gets *The Weakest Link.*

To orient ourselves we walk down to the river. It's a beautiful fast-moving body of water, olive-green, wide and wild, with trees drooping gracefully along its high banks. The river overflowed in floods in the Wet, inundating houses set well back towards the town, the water washing things off shelves on the walls. Today it is contained, sleepily imposing. Paperbark trees, roots deep in wet soil, stand watch with pale flaky skin. Their bark is like many layers of curling old paper at which you can pick and pick without ever stripping it away, like a thickness of torn manuscript. In one version of its etymology, Borroloola was named for the paperbark, trees that grow by water. But like most explanations here, the origin of the name is vague. People stood by the lagoon and when asked said 'Borroloola', perhaps answering a different question. Recommended by the town's surveyor, the name might have appealed as a riposte from the Austral tropics to Gitchigoomi, the sonorous name in *Hiawatha.* The captivating name of the first 'Loo, Woolloomooloo, turns out to be a hodge-podge of Europeanised pseudo-Aboriginality. For me Borroloola has been a place of paper, of hearsay and musty records. Now as I stand under the trees by the McArthur

River it becomes more literally a 'place of paperbarks' and takes shape in my mind.

The old pub, Tattersalls Hotel, was damaged by cyclone and fire and abandoned. The new pub dates from 1969 but most of it has been eaten by white ants and replaced. We walk into an extensive compound with open bars and iron fences all round. The sign is there on the gate: NO HUMBUG, NO GUNJA etc. Inside the front bar, there's a thin crowd in the large, airy space. The concrete floor is clean, tables ready for the dinner hour, television on, jukebox low, pool table at rest. It's before six o'clock and the pub is not living up to its reputation. A life-sized model of a white shark pierced with a spear hangs over the bar, with a canoe outrigger in which sit a couple of black plastic dolls, oars coming out of their ears. Did someone have too much gunja? The artist, a lofty black man in a big hat who doesn't drink or smoke, stands silently by. The walls are papered with other examples of local art. Paintings of spears and shields and other weapons with traditional markings on bright acrylic grounds. Curtains of cloud alive with lightning dropping over islands and dark seas populated by dugong. White trees on red earth. Painted crocodile jaws and turtle shells.

Drinks of choice are rum and Coke or light beer, XXXX Gold, drunk from bottles stuffed into foam holders. A puce-faced bloke in grimy car-wrecker's clothes bends over the bar with his empty Coke can and the barmaid fills it with rum. He buys a packet of white sliced bread to mop it up and creeps away, taking a swig as he goes and letting the neat liquor run down his chin.

After chatting at the bar a bit, I notice a familiar face come in. I recognise John Moriarty, one of Borroloola's famous sons. He lives in Sydney now where he and his wife Ros run the Balarinji Design Studio that painted two flagship Qantas jumbos with Aboriginal designs. I remember the red one, *Wunala Dreaming*, descending through the fog to land in Beijing on its inaugural flight to China when I was working there on a posting as cultural attaché at the Australian embassy. The Chinese were wild about the brilliantly painted jumbo. There's even a theory that Aboriginal designs and the patterns on ancient Chinese bronzes have common elements, a shared ancestry in the Rainbow Serpent and China's thunder-and-lightning dragon.

John Moriarty was born on the banks of the McArthur River in 1938. His father was an itinerant Irish cook. There's a photograph of him at the old pub. His mother was Aboriginal, a Mara-Kalkadoon woman. Under pressure from the welfare officer, John's mother took him to the Anglican mission school at nearby Roper River. He was there for a couple of weeks and, when she came to pick him up, he was gone. It was wartime and Aboriginal people were subject to tighter control than ever. Against his will he had been put in a truck with other boys and taken to a series of church homes and schools, far away in New South Wales and finally to Adelaide. Ten years later, as a teenager, he saw his mother again in Alice Springs. John Moriarty belongs to what are called the 'stolen generations'. He became a champion soccer player and when he was chosen to play for South Australia in 1960 he discovered he still needed permission from the Protector of Aborigines to travel interstate. His outrage helped draw him into the politics of Aboriginal rights. He went back to school, to university and on to a successful career in Aboriginal affairs. Eventually he started going back to Borroloola, reconnecting with family and being recognised by authoritative elders, such as his uncle Musso Harvey, who kept the joke name of Mussolini given him by whites. John also found out more about his Irish relations. Sorting out family was a matter of more than personal importance: 'Australians had … to come to terms with the reality that many whites had family histories that were very closely entwined with Aborigines.'[1]

John and Ros Moriarty are back in Borroloola on one of

the regular pilgrimages that help their children know the old people and connect with traditional country. Before Sydney they lived in Adelaide, and Canberra, and before that … well, it's a story of roaming across country in search of identity, opportunity and the best for the family, culminating in the commercial and cultural triumph of their design business. John tells the story himself in his autobiography *Saltwater Fella.* In that title he declares himself as belonging to this part of the world, the saltwater of the Gulf of Carpentaria and the Sir Edward Pellew Group of islands immediately across from the McArthur River's mouth.

The Moriartys were neighbours and friends of my sisters in Adelaide. It's a coincidence to meet them here in Borroloola, as if the web of connection that binds them to this place so firmly has some loose threads for me too. They are sitting at a long table under a tree, under the stars in the garden of the pub. They introduce me to their companions, their Borroloola kin, including an elder called Roy Hammer.

When he hears my name, Roy asks at once if I'm a relative of Roger Jose. 'His tank house was over there,' says Roy, 'where the caravan park is.' He extends an arm.

'That's where I'm staying,' I say.

Roy laughs. 'I knew that old man.'

The old woman in Darwin had told me that Roy Hammer was the first person I should ask about Roger Jose. Here he was, a tall lean blackfella in his sixties wearing an indigo shirt and jeans.

Roy Hammer was no stranger to the world. He had painted up in his traditional gear and marched with the Australian army to mark the anniversary of the Pacific War. He had flown to Japan in one of the Qantas planes bearing Balarinji designs. There's a photograph of him on the Gulf Region web site. He laughingly calls himself Chief Hammer, pointing out a crude effigy of the same name hanging on the wall of the pub. Authority for the Borroloola people passed to Roy Hammer when Musso Harvey died and he has worked to keep the town strong.

Within hours of arrival I have found my connection. Borroloola lives up to its reputation as a meeting place, the crossover point it has always been. It might have been a coincidence to meet the Moriartys, but where else would I be more likely to meet them than at the pub here? As John explains in *Saltwater Fella*,

> We have links from Borroloola down to the Waramunga area, near Tennant Creek [in central Australia], and they extend towards Normanton, right over to Wattie Creek, the Victoria River Downs area and round the Gulf to the northwest [in Queensland], as well as right through to the Myalli tribal group at Pine Creek [in the Top End].
>
> You get songs and ceremonies that criss-cross all that area ... Borroloola is ... a crossroads where many languages are spoken that relate to adjoining regions. And there are many songs from those areas that give it great ceremonial importance. With those songs you can go a long, long way.[2]

Water connects Borroloola to faraway places too. A network that does not take the end of land as a boundary fans out through the islands of the Gulf of Carpentaria and up the coast to Arnhem Land and across to the islands of Torres Strait and the Indonesian and Melanesian archipelagos. 'For more than 350 years the coast and its Aboriginal inhabitants have been subjected to visits by men from distant lands,' writes historian Campbell Macknight. 'Dutch, and possibly earlier voyagers, Macassans, British, French, Japanese and southern Australians. For all these people it has been a very long way to come, and this has influenced very strongly the way they have thought and behaved. Indeed for each group in a different way, this coast has seemed the most distant place to which they could come, the remotest sphere of their activity, their farthest coast.'[3]

But for Aboriginal people it was, and still is, a centre of the world. It may have been inaccessible by land from southern Australia, but it could be reached by sea-comers, and that happened long before the rest of Australia was colonised.

Macknight distinguishes a coastal strip of northern Australia about 250 kilometres wide that is tropical and monsoonal but is kept from becoming unbearably hot by the influence of the sea. The soil is poor and the aspect unpromising, with no navigable rivers to form a welcoming gateway. 'Much of the coast is low and fringed with sombre mangroves, laced with deceitful winding creeks whose contortions and sudden terminations have tried the patience of many … Behind the mangroves, bare salt flats or boggy plains stretch away to low bush', bounded on the south by a high land contour. For centuries this coast failed to attract foreign settlement, which was eventually attempted from the south in ignorance of its distinctive conditions.

One group, however, found a way of integrating that far coastline into their world. They were the Macassans. From the end of the seventeenth century, the 'energetic and adventurous nachodas, or captains of [Macassan] praus,' as Macknight describes them, came south to the Australian coast, the land they called Maregé, to trade in trepang, a humble sea-creature also known as *bêche de mer*, sea-cucumber or sea-slug, that was prized in Chinese culture as an aphrodisiac food.

I remember in Beijing seeing a geriatric veteran of the People's Liberation Army chopstick-fed slices of *haishen* – sea ginseng, as it translates – by an attendant youth. It would keep the old man going.

In the eighteenth and nineteenth centuries the shallow waters of the northern coasts of Arnhem Land and the Gulf of Carpentaria, via the middlemen of Macassar, supplied a good proportion of the huge Chinese market. The unlikely sea-slug must be added to clove, nutmeg, sandalwood and camphor, and other more fragrant products of South-East Asia sought in faraway empires, as a driver of world trade long before the concept of globalisation was devised. Consumption of *haishen* did not take off in China until the late Ming period (1368–1644). Perhaps it was the collapse and flight of the Ming dynasty, and the restriction of navigation by the Manchus who supplanted them, that caused new pathways of maritime trade to develop, reaching further afield from China than ever before. Perhaps new cravings arose for foodstuffs that became harder to get. Around the same time Taiwan was incorporated into China's orbit by Ming fugitives and the Malay taste for betelnut was passed on – a comparable delicacy.

Borroloola did not exist as a town, nor even perhaps as a name, when the Macassans first started coming. They sailed each year to the northern coasts of Australia from what is now Ujung Pandang in Sulawesi, Indonesia. They were maritime entrepreneurs with fleets of distinctive ocean-faring prau that dominated regional trade as Dutch influence receded. From the Gulf of Carpentaria they took pearls and pearl shell, turtle shell, sandalwood, minerals and trepang. In exchange they brought rice, tea, sugar, tobacco and arrack (spirits). They introduced the long-stemmed clay pipe still found in Arnhem Land. On their boats they carried dugout canoes for coming on shore which were exchanged with Aboriginal people in return for their permission and their labour in gathering trepang. The new canoes were adopted as an improvement on the local model.

Matthew Flinders found evidence of the Macassans as he charted the Gulf of Carpentaria in HMS *Investigator* in 1803. He was pleased to encounter their fleet off the coast of Arnhem Land. Thanks to the interpreting services of his Malay cook, Flinders could communicate with Pobassoo, the

Macassan commander. They went on board each other's craft and exchanged information, while watching out for guns and daggers. 'These people were Mahometans,' Flinders writes in his journal, 'and on looking into the launch, expressed great horror to see hogs there; nevertheless they had no objection to port wine, and even requested a bottle to carry away with them at sunset.' Flinders is, as ever, wryly poised in his response. He was curious as to how the trepang was treated, and was struck to discover that the Macassans had no knowledge of the British settlement at Sydney. 'My numberless questions were answered patiently, and with apparent sincerity; Pobassoo even stopped one day longer at my desire … and he begged of me an English jack, which he afterwards carried at the head of his squadron.' Flinders opened his mind to the opportunity of communion with the elderly chief – and I imagine Pobassoo remembered young Matthew.

The *Investigator*'s artist, William Westall, sketched Pobassoo and his boats. The prau struck people as admirable but unlikely craft.

> The prau has no deck but above the water hold and trepang bunker, from the poop up to the foremast, there is a floor of bamboo rods, covered with a mat roof, thus forming a sort of between-decks for the thirty or forty sailors … Above the roof are further cabins that one would easily take as chicken roosts. Add to all this a multitude of small packages, bags of rice, chests, etc. and you will perhaps get an idea of such a vessel,

Pobassoo, Macassan captain

wrote one observer. They were remarkably seaworthy for the job they were doing. The customs officer Alfred Searcy explained that 'the sail is of matting stretched on two bamboo yards of immense length and of such girth that a section would make a fair-sized bucket. These yards are suspended in a manner that admits of their being inclined in any direction – straight up, slanting or horizontal – whichever suits best for the wind.'[4]

Aboriginal rock and bark paintings show the Macassan prau sailing in, elegant craft recognisable by their large rectangular sails. The paintings suggest the importance of the annual visits of these fleets that linked mainland Australia to systems of exchange far afield. Porcelain shards and other archaeological finds suggest that trade may have been carried out between prosperous China and Aboriginal Australia for some centuries, which helps explain the presence of a mysterious Great South Land on early Chinese maps. There are no records to confirm that the heroic Chinese admiral Zheng He sailed his fleet of junks that way in the fifteenth century, but it is hard to believe that the maritime Ming did not sight Australian land on their voyages to East Africa. Aboriginal people in the area tell stories of legendary visitors who sound like Chinese, and there are said to be the remains of a stone Ming-dynasty house from as early as the fifteenth century hidden deep in an off-limits part of Arnhem Land.

At any rate, local interaction with the later Macassans was prolonged and intensive, and included intermarriage and sea journeys from Australia to other Indonesian islands and back. 'As … Aboriginal accounts of voyages with the Macassans testify,' Macknight tells us, 'the men concerned learnt a great deal about the world beyond the small society they left behind. By necessity they picked up new languages and experienced social relationships of a kind unknown at home. They observed, even if they could not fully understand, the economy and technology of South Celebes and elsewhere. The tone of their response … is familiar from a thousand stories of foreign travel.'

The Dutch governor-general noticed Australian Aboriginal people in Macassar in 1824, describing them as 'very black, tall in stature, with curly hair, not frizzy like that of the Papuan peoples, long thin legs, thick lips and, in general … quite well built.'[5]

These contacts challenge the view that Aboriginal Australia was primordially isolated from the outside world until advanced Europeans broke into its static, frozen culture, bringing catastrophe from the collision of modern with stone age. The Macassan crews were a mixed group, made up of people from throughout the Indonesian archipelago and beyond. Through them Aboriginal peoples became participants in wide economic and cultural networks of considerable sophistication and were able to respond in their own ways to the knowledge those connections brought them. They learned to co-operate with the outsiders in subtle protocols by which the trading visits were managed, customs respected and borders negotiated. The coastal peoples of northern Australia had dimensions of experience that the Europeans did not expect, including a word for white men bequeathed by the Macassans: *balanda*, or Hollander.

The people whose land includes the Sir Edward Pellew Group of islands, with its important trepang sites, and the adjacent coastline are the Yanyuwa. That land is Yanyuwa land.[6] Further north along the coast are the Mara, whose country also includes the sea. (Roy Hammer is a Mara man, a saltwater man.) Their inland neighbours, freshwater people as against the saltwater groups, are the Garawa and the Kurdanji – and once the Wilangarra. What is now the Borroloola common was originally Wilangarra land. After their demise it passed to the Binbingka, who then passed it to the Yanyuwa, who came into the settlement there with the Mara, the Garawa and the Kurdanji. They mixed, formed alliances and worked out a way to share the country within the larger pattern of kinship systems they all acknowledged. Aboriginal people constructed new communities from the decimation of the old in the wake of the colonial invasion. In this complex, drawn-out process, the adaptability and perspective learned by those particular Aboriginal peoples who had dealt with the Macassans may have been helpful. It suggested possibilities of productive co-existence that were unknown elsewhere. Perhaps a similar expertise is available in the no less difficult negotiations of today's world.

White Australia did not like these Macassan visitors. From 1907 the trade was prohibited by law and the coasts policed. The policy impacted on the coastal Aboriginal communities with their long-established dependency on the exchange and was resented as an arbitrary, incomprehensible intervention by the new power. The Macassans had treated Aboriginal people better than most white men did. Some Europeans filled the gap left in the trepanging industry, contracting Aboriginal people to collect and process trepang on a seasonal basis, very often at the old sites where camps had been established. Such work provided a new source of payment in tobacco, alcohol and other sought-after items, and a few Europeans were gradually incorporated into the local Aboriginal economy.

But they did not make a great success of it. If trepang was Australia's first export industry, it was also the first industry to be killed by government intervention.

In administrative circles in Darwin the Aboriginal people of the Gulf region got a reputation for being different – more 'virile' in the quaint language of one commentator – by virtue of their exchanges with people across the sea: stronger, more confident. That explanation was a eugenic fantasy, based on the notion that their Aboriginal blood had been improved with something better. Yet the symbolism of the crossing of land tracks and seaways is important. The coastal strip that includes Borroloola seems like the end of the line, but the boundary is porous.

I stayed in the pub until after midnight. The tennis was on, broadcast from Wimbledon, and I watched every point of the five-hour men's final, which was played that year between Australia's Pat Rafter and Goran Ivanisovic from Split in Croatia. Rafter comes from Mount Isa in Queensland – just across the state border from Borroloola and close enough to make him a local boy. He had the whole pub behind him and he played every shot until, after an interminable string of match points, he went down to the fervent young Croatian. No one begrudged Ivanisovic his victory. He was playing for a dead mate who had been killed in the vicious territorial wars in former Yugoslavia. Rafter's sad-sack grace in acknowledging that someone had to be a loser and once again that someone was him duly noted, the epic match was immediately shrugged off. In that moment of pub good-will we were reminded of the aspiration, so often betrayed, of Australia as a borderless place, and of Australians as people who can be generous towards both the triumphs and tribulations of others.

Roy Hammer is off to get some sleep. I walk down the road to the caravan park. The wide grass belts along the roadside are dark and owls call from the pale trees that lead the way into the bush. By our cabin the lemon myrtles shine in the moonlight. Their perfume brushes me as I pass. There's a light on in the cabin. Bob has emerged from New York time and is sitting up for me. The novel he's working on is called *The Witch* and as I fumble at the door he calls out in his best Hollywood crone voice: 'Is that you, Roger Jose's child?'

I inform him of the news from the pub. The corrugated-iron cabin where we are staying sits on the site of Roger Jose's tank house, under the same tamarind trees that the Macassans brought. I tell him that I've met Roy Hammer, the Borroloola elder, who used to trim those trees for Roger Jose when he was a kid, to make the new leaves grow. The old man would give young Roy rice and stew in exchange, and pay him a bounty for dingo scalps. Roger described the fence on which he hung the dingo scalps to dry as smelling like the hanging gardens of Babylon.[7]

'Yo, Roger Jose's child!'

III

'THE SURF UPON THE SHORE'

Flinders was omnipresent where I grew up. There was Flinders Park and Flinders University and the Flinders Ranges. I had my piano lessons at the back of the Flinders Street Baptist Church. But I never knew who Flinders was. The name was part of the order of things, so common that it lost its meaning. I belong to a peculiar generation of Australians that was taught almost nothing about their own country. If I was a total stranger to the Northern Territory, I knew not much more about my home town of Adelaide. We learned Australian history at school as a set of *Boys' Own* stories about which we were sceptical even then, sensing gaps in the record. As we matured we moved on to the more world-shaking stuff of epic and drama that happened in other places and times. It was left to a generation of revisionists to open up the riches of Australian history for students younger than I. Belatedly I have tried to educate myself, free of the classroom. I was blind to many obvious things – my lack of organised knowledge has spurred me on.

The coastline of South Australia was the last part of the

Australian periphery to be explored by Europeans. As far as we know it was not seen by any outsider until Matthew Flinders sailed by in the *Investigator* on his mission to chart what he called 'the unknown coast'. He wanted to see whether a major waterway might lead from there into the heart of the continent, cutting it in two. He was disappointed to find that the two large inlets petered out in muddy flats, not mouths but gulfs that he named Spencer and St Vincent after his backers in the Admiralty. Flinders gave names to many of the landmarks in the world in which I lived. He named Mount Lofty, the highest of the Adelaide Hills, near where the Tennyson children went with their tutor to a vice-regal summer retreat a century later and near where Herbert Jose, the clergyman, built his Chinese-influenced garden house. Flinders named Port Lincoln after his home county, and Yorke Peninsula, 'the very ill-shaped leg and foot' between the two gulfs, where I spent my childhood holidays, after another Admiralty lord.

The bottom end of Yorke Peninsula was another dead end. No railway line served it and the sealed road stopped. Ships no longer called at its jetties. It was a quiet, slow place that kept to itself. Squat limestone farmhouses overlooked barley fields and ti-tree scrub. The coast crumbled into calm reefs and seaweed banks and wild beaches of barrelling surf. On long summer days when the sea was a mirror and a lone voice could carry from one side of the bay to the other, you would imagine you were at the farthest edge of the earth, another land's end for those Cornishmen who had come and built those low stone dwellings. It was easy for a boy to feel that we – my sisters and our friends – were the first people ever to strip off our clothes and run down the vast white sandhills, as wide as Arabian deserts, into breaking waves that porpoises rode, with no one in sight along miles of beach, except perhaps a crayfish boat bobbing out in the blue. We gave our own names to places as if they had never been named before: the Dust Bowl, Pebble Beach, Stiffy's.

Yet to feel myself the first person there was also a kind of loneliness, a pubescent state that yearned wordlessly for connection. From the cliff top I would gaze at the sea as it bled into sky and imagine things. There had been fears of invasion even down here, from Russians, Germans, Japanese. I would look at the outline of islands on the horizon that seemed to be stepping-stones to other lands. I would imagine an intruder breaking that glassy serenity, and the people on the shore, the original people, gathering in perturbation, transfixed and alarmed, as their curiosity fought with an impulse to hide. The first ship known to appear in the bay our beach shack faced was the *Investigator*, on 19 March 1802. Flinders named it Hardwicke Bay.

Anchoring off the craggy bluff that he called Corny Point, he wrote: 'At sunset land seen from the masthead … Saw a fire upon the westernmost land which served us to steer by … At 9 hrs 40 being at no great distance from the land … furled sails. Heard the howling of dogs on shore …' So close and yet so far, the next morning Flinders was gone again, leaving the Narangga, the indigenous people of that place, in peace for a few decades more. Aboriginal people from further along the coast have a song about a big white bird that came in over the ocean, slowly stopped and folded its wings.[1]

The spot at which I used to gaze out was a few miles east of Corny Point, and the topographical features I gave names to on the maps I drew were insignificant compared to things Flinders named. That holiday world, though boundless to me, was actually quite small, but I always seemed to be seeing it for the first time. When, years later, I came to know about Flinders' relationship to the place, as the first man to look at it through a European lens, I looked more closely at his charts. Flinders was scrupulous in every particular and he hugged the coast on his voyage so he could draw his line with the extraordinary accuracy that he believed in. When for some reason he could not go in close, he dotted the line. For 20 March 1802 he wrote, 'For the general exactness of [the] chart, I can answer with tolerable confidence; having seen all that is laid down ... Throughout the whole extent of the shores the waterline was almost everywhere distinguished; the only exception [...] being, small portions at the head of Hardwicke [Bay].' That was exactly where I had looked from. Sure enough, on the famous map Flinders drew of Australia, showing one island-continent for the first time, my stretch of shore appears as a broken line. It looks like a roughly sewn hem. Flinders had taken a short cut across Hardwicke Bay without going right in. Once you got down to details and changed to the scale of a boy walking along the beach, it was still an unknown coast.

Yorke Peninsula is cold in winter, arid in summer, quite different from its tropical northern partner, the much larger Cape York Peninsula, that runs east along the Gulf of Carpentaria, a gulf equally unlike Spencer's Gulf, except that Flinders looked for passage into the heart of the continent there too. And while I stood dreaming of my unknown shore, back in 1963, Roger Jose was living out his last days on a shore he had come to know well, at the farthest end of land from me.

Matthew Flinders comes last in the line of great navigators, a chippy doctor's son who went to sea as his best chance of making a way in the world, struggling for opportunities with the great and powerful, handsomely justifying himself nine times out of ten.

And yet –

He was a brilliant cartographer, commanding the latest advances in technology to map what he saw, and he had a good eye. He was skilful in handling ships and men; determined, even obsessive, yet open to what he might find. What mattered was to possess something in words, measurements and, if possible, a name. Flinders wrote with the grace, ease and plainness that characterise his time and culture, 'the language of men' as advocated by William Wordsworth in his preface to the *Lyrical Ballads*, published in 1802, the same year as Flinders' circumnavigation of Australia. In that revolutionary and romantic time, the young commander shared the poet's sense of a new world to be found or created from nature. He would encounter domains that no Englishman had seen. Wordsworth's farewell to his fellow poet Coleridge might have gone with him:

> For thou hast sought
> The truth in solitude, and, since the days
> That gave thee liberty, full long desired,
> To serve in Nature's temple ... Fare thee well!
> Health and the quiet of a healthful mind
> Attend thee!
>
> *The Prelude* (1850), II, 460–68

Flinders passed his time on board the *Investigator* reading *Paradise Lost.* On his eventual return he might have read Jane Austen too, with whose brother Charles, another naval man, he passed a few days experimenting with magnetism.

Flinders realised his ambition to circumnavigate the continent that he named Australia, but at enormous cost. Yet even as his physical health collapsed, his 'healthful mind' sustained him, and his compulsive faith in writing: his letters, his charts and his journals.

Among the factors that compelled Flinders to a life at sea was a book, not a scientific book, but a work of imagination from a writer of an earlier generation to Wordsworth and Austen who also insisted on plain style. As a teenager Flinders had read *Robinson Crusoe*, published by Daniel Defoe in 1719, and later confessed that he was 'induced to go to sea against the wish of friends' from reading it. He was not alone. Few novels have inspired as many thoughts of real-world action as Defoe's classic – the Robinson Crusoe fantasy of escape to a desert island lives on in the history of Borroloola's hermits and is with us still. Flinders, this model of a practical man, praised for his coolness and lack of histrionics, unloved by historians for his lack of imagination, acknowledges his starting point as a story. And his achievement, apart from the practical, must be seen as the writing of his own story, writing it and getting it out, in two volumes with atlas, in 1814, the year of his early death.

As a result, Matthew Flinders seizes the imagination now. The bicentenary year of his famous voyage has produced a surge of books, exhibitions and re-enactments in tribute to him.[2] He seems like a candid young man of modern sensibility, a character in a Patrick O'Brian novel, a perfect role for the new breed of Hollywood hero. Flinders has his fans. It's a pity that his book will not have a birthday re-issue: I read him from a weighty facsimile of the original edition.

The Gulf of Carpentaria came into existence for the great world in the daily flow of Flinders' sentences. The curiosity that draws him on is palpable. His book is an answer from nature, through the medium of his pen, to Defoe's fiction. Its title encapsulates a career: *A Voyage to Terra Australis; Undertaken for the Purpose of Completing the Discovery of that Vast Country, and Prosecuted in the Years 1801, 1802, and 1803, in His Majesty's Ship the Investigator, and Subsequently in the Armed Vessel Porpoise and Cumberland Schooner. With an Account of the Shipwreck of the Porpoise, Arrival of the Cumberland at*

Mauritius, and Imprisonment of the Commander during Six Years and a Half in that Island. That is to say, the author himself.

Matthew Flinders was born in Donington, Lincolnshire, in March 1774, the same month that the British Parliament shut down the port of Boston, Massachusetts, part of the chain of events that led to the American colonies' independence from Britain. Flinders' future was to lie with the new colony founded at Sydney Cove in 1788 partly to replace America. By the time he was 17, Flinders was on a navy ship sailing for the South Seas. He was soon making reconnaissance voyages down the coast of New South Wales and by the age of 25 he had circumnavigated Tasmania, with his friend George Bass, for the first time. By 1800 he was back in England looking for a command of his own. He fell in love with Ann Chappelle, a friend from home, and wrote her rhapsodic love letters, but he was not ready to walk away from his vocation. Sir Joseph Banks emerged as a sponsor and some of the best scientists and artists in England rallied round. By 1801 Flinders found himself in charge of HMS *Investigator*, preparing a research voyage around Australia. He and Ann were married in haste. He wanted to take her with him, but Banks put a stop to that. If Ann went, Flinders would be relieved of his command once the ship got to Sydney. Flinders acquiesced and Ann stayed behind. Neither could have known of the trials ahead that would postpone their reunion for ten years. Ernestine Hill, the journalist of Borroloola, wrote a melodramatic bestseller about it, aptly titled *My Love Must Wait.*

In his portraits Flinders looks like a nervous fawn: a slight man with thin lips, his hair in tight curls. Across his forehead is the slash of a scar that in some portraits is painted out. The buttons and bows of his uniform look too big, but his eyes are bigger still, round, dark and magnifying, like optical machines that could pick up information from 360 degrees. The *Investigator* reached Cape Leeuwin, the south-western tip of Australia, in December 1801 and the work began. For much of what would follow Flinders and his men would apply their eyes to see and understand all they could.

One of the first tasks was to establish a protocol for encounters with Aboriginal people. Flinders insisted that any approach should be designed to establish friendly relations. His success in this shows up the cruder tactics of many others before and after. On an earlier voyage through Torres Strait he had witnessed bloodshed against indigenous people, awkwardly defending the captain in his report. Flinders was a man of sensibility in believing that a decent accommodation could be reached. His interest was in knowledge, not land; discovery, not domination. At port near today's Albany, he was amused at how an old Aboriginal man imitated the drill of the red-coated, white-belted marines.

For all his reluctance to leave Ann, Flinders strikes me as a solitary type. His brother Samuel, six years younger, was on the voyage, a fellow officer to whom Flinders might confide. But Samuel proved to be more trouble than he was worth. He was always getting things wrong, a careless character so different from the punctilious older brother.

Portrait of Captain Matthew Flinders

Flinders was concerned for his men, but kept his own company, although in the all-male environment of the ship he was capable of forming sentimental attachments, as he had in his younger days with George Bass. He wrote to Bass that 'there was a time, when I was so completely wrapped up in you, that no conversation but yours could give me any degree of pleasure; your footsteps upon the quarter deck over my head, took me from my book, and brought me upon deck to walk with you …'[3] The manuscript librarian at the Mitchell insists there is nothing sexual about this; Flinders was purely demonstrating his finer feelings in the gentlemanly language of the time. Perhaps Flinders felt similarly towards his and Bass's subaltern friend John Thistle, the hand-picked master on the *Investigator*. When the cherished Thistle was lost at sea with other men while going ashore in a small boat in search of drinking water, the captain was deeply upset. It was hot, the coast was arid and the waters treacherous. Flinders named it Cape Catastrophe, and nailed a plaque to a tree at a place he called Memory Cove. Of John Thistle, he wrote warmly, 'I have known him since the year 1794, and we have mostly been together since that time … For his superior merit and prudent conduct [he] was advanced from before the mast to be … a master in His Majesty's service … In a voyage like the present, his loss cannot be otherwise than severely felt.'[4]

Thereafter his affections were reserved for his cat Trim, 'this good-natured purring animal' born on board ship in 1799. Named for Uncle Toby's companion in *Tristram Shandy*,

Trim was a black cat with white paws and was with Flinders for four years before he disappeared in Mauritius, feared by his master to have been eaten by 'catophagists' out of spite. Flinders penned a moving encomium that makes Trim famous among seagoing cats: 'He would frequently place himself on the quarterdeck before the officers in the middle of their walk; and spreading out his two white hands in the posture of the *lion couchant*, oblige them to stop and admire him. They would indeed say low to each other, "See the vanity of that cat!" but they could not help admiring his graceful form and beautiful white feet. Indeed, when it is known that to the finest form ever beheld he joined extraordinary personal and mental qualifications, the impossibility that the officers could be angry with him must be evident.' Perhaps Flinders projected his own best self on to his adored feline: 'I will say for him that he never spoke ill of or objected to the pretensions of others, which is more than can be said for very many bipeds.'[5] Trim's statue, tail aloft, stands in an alcove behind the statue of his master outside the Mitchell Library in Sydney.

Before leaving the unknown coast of South Australia for the north, Flinders had an odd encounter with a rival French explorer, Nicolas Baudin, the gifted captain of *Le Géographe*, on 8 April 1802 at Encounter Bay, named for their meeting. They looked at each other's charts. Later the French would claim precedence over the British for discoveries in the area. On 8 April 1902 Hallam Tennyson unveiled a memorial at the site that read: 'These English and French Explorers Held Friendly Conference'. Perhaps the governor's children and their tutor, Aubrey Jose, were there. In another hundred years, on 8 April 2002, South Australians, including my father – the tutor's nephew's son – would gather on the same pretty shore to watch tall ships commemorate a moment of scientific sharing, of uneasy equilibrium between opposing powers.

Baudin entertained with Flinders the hypothesis that New Holland (Australia) might be divided by a strait down the middle, making it two large islands. When he eventually reached the Gulf of Carpentaria, which seemed a likely place to find a clue, Flinders kept a look-out for rivers or other water openings, but he missed the mouths of rivers that dispersed into shallow flats.

Existing Dutch charts were more than a century old. 'The real form of this Gulf,' wrote Flinders,

> remained in as great doubt with geographers, as were the manner how, and time when it acquired its name. The east side of the Gulf had been explored to the latitude of 17°, and many rivers were there marked and named; but how far the representation given of it by the Dutch was faithful, – what were the productions, and what its inhabitants – were, in a great measure, uncertain ... Of the rest of the Gulf no one could say, with any confidence, upon what authority its form had been given in the charts; so that conjecture, being at liberty to appropriate the Gulf of Carpentaria to itself, had made it the entrance to a vast arm of the sea.

That it might lead to a sea that split the landmass was a speculation Flinders laid to rest. He acknowledged his Dutch precursors: 'this coast seems to have been first described by Tasman in 1644, but was probably seen by Carpentier in 1628'.

The scientists on the *Investigator* were making useful anthropological and other observations, but the ship was leaking, so they camped off Sweers Island at the bottom of the Gulf for repairs. The carpenters gave a devastating report. The ship was decayed beyond repair, good for six months at best. The monsoons were coming and they had to get back to Sydney. Flinders' journal entry is despairing.

> From this dreadful state of the ship, I find the complete examination of this extensive country, which is one of the nearest objects to my heart, to be greatly impeded if not frustrated. I have hitherto considered, that my business is to make so accurate an examination of the shores of New Holland and New South Wales, that there shall be no necessity for any further navigator to come after me; and with this object always in view, whenever circumstances would allow it, I have ever kept close in with the land that nothing might escape our notice; much closer I believe than navigators have usually thought it necessary or safe to do; for, that we might not be deceived in the distance, I always desired to see the washing of the surf upon the shore … but with a ship which cannot encounter bad weather, – which cannot be repaired if any of the shoals or rocks, with which we are almost continually surrounded, does her bottom any injury, –

> with such a ship, I do not know how to prosecute so great an undertaking.

He is justifying himself to his masters and to posterity, but he was determined to use the time he had left.

For the next three months Flinders explored the coast up to Arnhem Land. He charted the islands he named the Sir Edward Pellew Group, after the colossal Cornish naval chief who was later his benefactor. (Pellew was famous for seizing the secret French code when he boarded the *Cléopatre* in one of the first engagements of the Napoleonic wars. The French commander, intending to swallow the code, swallowed his commission by mistake.) The *Investigator* made the first record of Aboriginal rock paintings, which were copied by William Westall, the ship's artist. Those watercolours are now in the National Library of Australia in Canberra. Some of Flinders' men were ambushed by Aboriginal people when away from the ship on patrol. One was speared and recovered; one died from sunstroke. Flinders notes that 'the more we seek after, and appear desirous of an interview, the more suspicious they become'. It is a revealing observation, perhaps assisted by Bungaree, a Sydney Aboriginal man whom Flinders had brought along on the voyage to help avoid misunderstandings with Aboriginal people – on the mistaken assumption that all Aboriginal people might speak the same language. A game of hide and seek was going on, or cat and mouse. The local people's come-hither shyness was a tactical response designed to lure the visitors into vulnerable situations or, better still, shoo them away. In February Flinders met the fleet of Macassan prau. All in all, under pressure of time, with the heat and tropical rain of the Wet season, and worsening health for many men including the captain, it was the most intense period of the voyage. Everything is being noted and analysed with all the attentiveness the mind can muster, as if it will never be seen again.

Flinders relented reluctantly. On 5 March 1803, the last day of his surveying career as it turned out, he wrote:

> should the ship prove no worse than our expectation, a heavy gale would probably founder her, and be the loss of almost the whole produce of our risks and labours, as well as the loss of our lives; and I think it more probable that she will be worse than our expectation ... It may well be said, that to leave such a coast as this without exploring it, when there is a possibility, nay perhaps a probability, that I may never again return to accomplish it, shews but very little of that genuine spirit of discovery which contemns all danger and inconvenience when put in competition with its gratification! Upon the score of duty I might (it may be said) be forgiven, but must never boast of a single spark of that ethereal fire with which the souls of Columbus and Cook were wont to burn! – I am not indeed such a Quixote in discovery as this, although, since I was able to read *Robinson Crusoe*, it has been my constant pursuit; but there is another reason remaining in aid of the first, – the

> debilitated state of my health, as well as of many others in the ship, and a lameness in both feet from incorrigible scorbutic ulcers, render me unable to go about any longer in boats, or to the mast head of the ship; both of which are absolutely necessary to any tolerable accuracy in this kind of surveying; and I suppose it is unnecessary to state, that the whole of this important part of our duty rests upon me: – For Port Jackson, then, we now steered away, with a fresh and fair wind.

He was 29. Later, recollecting in tranquillity, he added, 'The accomplishment of the survey was, in fact, an object so near to my heart, that could I have foreseen the train of ills that were to follow the decay of the *Investigator* and prevent the survey being resumed, – and had my existence depended upon the expression of a wish, I do not know that it would have received utterance; but Infinite Wisdom has, in infinite mercy, reserved the knowledge of futurity to itself.'

The *Investigator* made it back to Sydney by heading west, via Kupang in West Timor, all the way round with a depleted crew – an astonishing journey. Flinders agreed to return to England with his charts in order to organise a follow-up voyage to complete the survey. But the ship he took was wrecked on the Great Barrier Reef. After making the return trip to Sydney by sea to fetch help in rescuing survivors, Flinders continued on his way towards England in the tiny *Cumberland*, another leaky ship. Once more he passed through Torres Strait and crossed the Gulf of Carpentaria, reaching

Kupang again and then heading out across the Indian Ocean in bad weather, short of provisions and the ship taking in more and more water. He was forced to take refuge in Mauritius. Then known as Île de France, Mauritius was a French colony. When Flinders left Sydney, it was understood that Britain and Napoleon's France were no longer at war. But unknown to him, the situation had changed. Hostilities had broken out again and, arriving in Port Louis, he was in enemy territory and a Bonapartist bastion. It was no use seeking special treatment as a navigator, a man of science. Flinders was detained as a suspected spy.

At first he thought it must be a mistake and he fought intemperately with his captor, General Charles de Caen, to be released. But de Caen found incriminating remarks in Flinders' journals and would see him as nothing but a spy. Flinders' unseaworthy ship was deteriorating in the port. His papers were seized, his letters censored. After three months he was moved to house arrest where he would stay for the next six years. Never an adroit politician, he handled the situation badly. But his frustration, exacerbated by ill health, is easy to understand. As much as for his skin and his rights, he was worried about the precious charts on which his reputation would depend. After de Caen confiscated volume 3, Flinders never saw it again.

He found kindred spirits on Mauritius with whom he played his boxwood and ivory flute in musical soirées and he completed much scholarly work. Although conditions improved during those tedious years, he never overcame his bitterness towards de Caen. Banks had done all he could for Flinders in Paris, but de Caen was wary to the end. Rivalry between France and Britain over Australia continued, and Mauritius was strategically placed. In 1808 Flinders learned to his horror that Baudin's discoveries had been published, giving French names like Terre Napoléon and Golfe Joséphine to places Flinders had seen first on the South Australian coast. He felt that more was at stake in his captivity than was admitted. But by then the British blockade of French territories in the Indian Ocean was closing in, and in 1810 Flinders was released. '[A]fter a captivity of six years, five months and twenty-seven days,' he wrote, 'I at length had the inexpressible pleasure of being out of the reach of General de Caen.'

He was so changed from when he had left England 10 years earlier that his old servant felt obliged to warn Ann. Her husband's hair was white. A colleague who witnessed the reunion apologised that he 'felt so sensibly the affecting scene' that he 'could not have remained any longer in the room under any consideration'. Back home, Flinders directed all his energies to completing and publishing *A Voyage to Terra Australis*. This was another heroic effort, involving patrons, printers, booksellers, artists, engravers, scientists and his own labour in writing, fact-checking and microscopic proofreading, especially of maps. All took money he scarcely had. A finished copy of the great work was ready for Banks's perusal on 26 June 1814. Flinders died three weeks later. The edition sold out, but made a loss for his widow.

Today we read it less to admire its enduring accuracy than to appreciate it as literature. It expresses the mind of a modern man, a secular visionary, a man of facts who was also interested in translating facts into other media, making the larger picture that for him was knowledge. He had nerves, patience and intellectual courage. In the words of his biographer, 'He chose to measure an entire continent.'[6] Was that insane? A quixotic job that needed doing? No one other than Flinders would have seen it like that. He was a masterless man in a gentlemanly sort of way, a man who was happiest making his own rules, a borderless man. He suffered from the existence of arbitrary borders imposed by class, gender and politics. He was drawn to natural boundaries, where land meets sea, believing he could breach them with understanding. Mediators such as Bungaree and the unnamed Malay cook helped him know the people he encountered. He had little time for human science, for cultural relativism or the irrational divisions of creed. The natural science he favoured sought facts of universal application. He was, like Robinson Crusoe, a man on his own, attracted to extremes and often, against his will, experiencing extremes, a man at the edge who has left his namings scattered along Australia's shores.

Matthew Flinders is an apt forerunner to the European men who were looking for the end of the line and found it on the Gulf of Carpentaria, in Borroloola, where they crossed over into a world that belonged to others. Aboriginal people there remember him to this day, with mixed feelings about the attention he receives. They had been navigating that complex shore for centuries after all, mapping with their minds its ins and outs, its shallows and depths, its seasonal variations. I'm told that the Yanyuwa people of the Borroloola district are reclaiming their oral history to produce a three-volume atlas of their own, provisionally titled *Forget About Flinders.*

IV

BORDER-LAND AND COMBO-LAND

I vowed to record every detail of every impression of my time in Borroloola, every day in my journal, just like Matthew Flinders. I would sit on a hard-backed chair parked in the gravel outside the cabin with my bound red Chinese notebook on my lap and write in the morning sun.

People come by to talk. The man in the next cabin is a health worker from Darwin, a cool sort of bloke from the suburbs Down South who has come north to do something meaningful with his life. And to put something behind him. He has a dark, agitated manner, a cynical optimist who is accustomed to bashing his head against a brick wall, working to improve Aboriginal health, which in Borroloola has hit the headlines as in critical condition. The place is woefully underresourced. Half the health money from Canberra is siphoned off by Territory administrators. The rest is reserved for showpieces that tourists will see, like Jabiru in Kakadu National Park. In Borroloola one doctor serves a vast region. Pink cheeks, white beard, smiling eyes, black T-shirt over a modest beer belly, the guy from the next-door cabin knows my doctor friend in Darwin who is working for the same things from the other end. He wants to talk to me about leprosy.

All I can manage are a few notes. Information is coming in faster than I can get it down, the diarist's problem. If you spend all day writing your diary, what do you find to write about? Nor can I tell what the important information is. I'm enough of an iconologist, though, to know that the smallest things may be the most telling, the most powerful. I have my favourite quote from art historian Aby Warburg to hand: 'The good Lord lives in detail.' My difficulty is compounded by the fact that as I experience Borroloola in the present I'm experiencing it through the writings of the past at the same time. Part of Borroloola's character is that there has been nothing much except memories of what went on at some other time. Its reputation is as a place of old people. Writing in 1957, Bill Harney began a memoir of Borroloola by invoking the 'strange old white men who talked only of the past yet lived in the present, and the Aborigines who reversed the process by talking of the present yet lived in the past'.[1]

What is written preserves what was passed down in conversation. It selects and shapes a series of rambling, sharpened-up oral exchanges, remembered first hand, second hand, third hand, over many years. What is written about things here, where no one could ever check, yields to the attraction of the tall story and, crossing the line into fiction, makes it taller. People contradict, and that's just another story. I have discovered already that it's a town where people talk. Their role is to fill the visitor's ear with tales. To keep a handle on things, they become unreliable narrators. The lines of writing are like the slats of the venetian blind in our cabin, opening out on to the airy domain of the oral, filtering it at the same time. But the oral, still around to comment and correct, or to simply move things along in some new direction of contemporary appeal, has power to set the record adrift.

I write hard to keep up, putting down what my own faulty memory retains, not judging truth but the energy a phrase or an image has to enliven the shape-making mind.

Bob emerges from his work on *The Witch*, yawning, eating a sesame cracker he has brought from Chinatown in New York City. His baseball cap says 'Jello'. Maybe that's how he feels. He can smell tarragon. It's the myrtle tree exuding in the sun, with honeyeaters swinging from its weeping fronds.

For the early *balanda* visitors to the Top End of Australia, language was a lifeline. To communicate what they experienced in words lay at the core of their mission. Their own psychological survival depended on the necessity of keeping a record, on working at their journals each day. The survival of their labours relied on seeing their writing into print. It was a benign way to possess an uncharted domain and take its likeness away.

Those who wrote were often men of action, turning to words in their retirement. They tended to gild the lily, or gild over it. Their racial attitudes can be hard going for modern readers. Making allowances, I wonder how intelligent people could think the way they did without questioning it. How can I enjoy a literary gentleman's fine-sounding sentiments, penned with pulsing sensitivity in the evening, when I suspect him of having been out shooting blacks during the day? Ernest Favenc explored the Gulf Country in the 1870s and later wrote stories about it. *Tales from the Austral Tropics* (1894) is period stuff, sketching a haunted, murderous world in plain language and brisk characterisation. Aboriginal people are present but not quite visible. Any crossover is fatal. A 'nigger with white hair' is an evil omen. A gold prospector's body turns to rotting bones as an ancient spirit claims him. Those who glimpse the alleged 'missing link' between native beings and civilised intruders die of madness. Favenc satirises the virtue of those who would protect the indigenous people: the black youth who works for the parson and shares his tent turns out to be a tempting maiden, in a variation of a common outback story in which drovers travelled with a young Aboriginal woman who was dressed as and always called the 'drover's boy'. She served him sexually as well as with her skill round camp and on horseback. Favenc notes in passing the 'dispersing parties' that went out, removing blacks, often by killing them. It is likely that he took part himself. He ended his days in faraway Sydney, residing among literary folk in Darlinghurst, surrounded by portraits of explorers long dead, unrecognised as he frailly descended the stony steps of Wolloomooloo on his way to the Mitchell Library.[2]

The 'Border-Land' was Favenc's suggestive name for the country around the Gulf of Carpentaria. It was border in more ways than one: a border of land and sea, the hinterland of remote governments, where jurisdiction was wearing thin, the front line between black and white, the tropical threshold opening Australia to Asia and all that the seas could bring.

That status continues today as navy ships seek to repel invasion from the north, which comes seasonally in the form of desperate refugees crowded on to leaking boats. For a prime minister in Canberra, the northern shore makes Australia vulnerable, a soft touch; it is where the rot must be stopped. In his campaign for re-election in 2001 John Howard pushed the concept of border security: 'We will decide who comes into this country.' It's the same mentality that goes into policing a neighbourhood: the suburban attitude of Not In My Backyard. It appeals most strongly to city folk who are making their home their castle, realising their dream of a sanitised, controlled, late-model environment behind the gates of their quarter-acre estate. This time the refugees are from Afghanistan, fleeing a war, from Iraq, Iran, Pakistan, the Palestinian lands, Sri Lanka and Vietnam. They are always non-white or non-Christian. Those who believe in Australia as a fortress of hard-won middle-class prosperity demonise them as criminals and queue-jumpers, an advance guard of unstoppable hordes, trash they don't want polluting their street. The government legislates for them to be turned back to sea, where they drown, as if they were the wartime enemy in new guise. Sinking, impoverished Pacific islands are lavishly bribed to take them off our hands, as if the world stops beyond Australia's exclusion zone. In a moment of memorable ignominy in September 2001, the Australian government shunned its obligation to help 430 asylum-seekers rescued at sea by a Norwegian container ship. When the captain of the MV *Tampa* requested the nearest Australian territory to respond to his distress call, the government sent its crack troops to make sure the human cargo was shunted somewhere else, fudging legality in the process. Admittedly if those asylum seekers had been allowed in, they would probably have been locked up behind razor wire in a desert detention centre where they would have languished without explanation, perhaps for years, until the Immigration Department found a way of deporting them. Two months later John Howard won his election.

The northern coasts are that fraying border-land too, between rich and poor, between cultures and histories, the few and the many, the complacent and the driven, the light and the dark.

For 15 years from 1882, Alfred Searcy was the customs officer responsible for policing the coastline with a view to collecting fees from the Macassans and other vessels trading in and out of Northern Territory ports. 'He harassed the Macassan captains with a dash only limited in the first instance by having to pursue them in the government cutter *Flying Cloud*, a vessel reputed to sail backwards when beating into the wind,' writes Northern Territory historian, Alan Powell.[3] After his retirement back to Adelaide, Searcy was no less vigorous as a writer. *In Australian Tropics* (1907) and his other books give a rollicking account of a life up north that he was reluctant to leave. A believer in white superiority, at least in the treatment of animals, he was dismayed when his own kind stole 18 horses from Chinese competitors, hamstrung them and left them to die in agony. Of the large Chinese population he wrote, 'it was their virtues, not their vices, we had to fear'.[4] He also feared the Aboriginal population. His voyages around the coast in the 1880s took place at the time of the greatest violence between white and black in the rush to grab land for cattle; 'wild times', as Aboriginal people laconically remember it today. In Searcy's account of his hazardous voyage to Borroloola in 1886, the year after the settlement's birth, his unwillingness to engage with the local people is palpable. 'During the afternoon [as they were pulling their boat up the McArthur River] a nigger hailed us from the left-hand bank, yelling, "Borroloola, trrrr; Borroloola, trrr", and pointed in a certain direction. We were cross and tired, and would not take any notice of the black fellow ... if we had only interviewed the nigger we would have saved ourselves a fifty miles pull.'

Of Borroloola, Searcy wrote: 'the settlement was in a state of chaos, owing to the absence of police, and for hundreds of miles round ... the district was in a state of terror. This was no exaggeration, for the crimes committed were beyond description ...; in fact, this country was a sanctuary for every ruffian in Australia ... It must be remembered that in these out-back places the population was entirely floating, here today and gone tomorrow … Unless the unfortunate fellows were staunch teetotallers they had a poor chance of getting away until they had been lambed down to the last penny. Then they could go to Hades.'

Searcy does not tell us what the crimes were. But he has already made his attitudes clear. On the voyage out, the ship hit a storm. In a scene reminiscent of Joseph Conrad's *Lord Jim*, Searcy writes: 'The decks were constantly awash. When I reached the skipper he yelled in my ear, "It is all up with us, we cannot make the land." I might mention that we were nineteen all told on board, ten of whom were Europeans. The skipper and I settled that at the first sign of foundering the Europeans were to take possession of our own small boat, and in it to try and weather the gale. If the worst came to the worst it meant a fight for life, and probably bloodshed, so I saw that my revolver was in good order, and kept it at my belt the rest of the night.' The only land was at Melville Island, where 'the niggers … were fierce and treacherous'.

Searcy, another escapee from right-thinking South Australia, was a man of pluck and rough humour who told it like it was, evocatively, but without looking into himself. He was a man of his time. It was easier that way. Let's leave him in that small boat, pulling back out to sea through the crocodiles of the McArthur River: 'It was weary, weird work, the only sounds, besides the splash of our oars, being mysterious cracking noises in the mangroves, and now and again the splash of some great brute tumbling into the river. Soon after midnight we reached the open sea, but we had no idea where we were ... we could hear the alligators wallowing and bellowing on the mud-bank adjacent. It blew from every point of the compass during the night, and heavy rain fell, so it can be imagined what a time we had in the little boat. *Three Men in a Boat* were nothing to it.'[5]

By the time its short-lived boom was over, Borroloola was starting to acquire an additional reputation. It was a border-land in another sense. It had become a place for going so far that you could never go back, a place where a white man could go with an Aboriginal woman – with lasting consequences for both. It was called 'the combo's retreat'.

'Combo' is not a pretty word in Australian slang usage: 'A white man who lives with an Aboriginal woman, often within an Aboriginal community; a white man who sexually exploits Aboriginal women.'[6] Presumably it's a twist on 'combination', the same derivation that gives us a jazz combo or other musical ensemble. 'Combo' with its pejorative meaning came into existence in the 1890s, that decade of high anxiety about racial pollution. There were fears that the import of coloured labour in large numbers, particularly from China, would lower wages and squeeze out the working white man with his decent, democratic values. Those fears were fanned by press and politicians in the nationalist fervour that led up to Federation in 1901. 'The word "Combo" ... meant ... a man who associated with the Binghis [Aboriginals] above what was considered the correct thing', explained the *Bulletin* in 1912, the popular nationalist magazine that trumpeted the exclusionary policies later legislated as White Australia. A combo was 'one who, not content with having a lubra about his camp, lived for longer or shorter periods entirely in the camps of black brother – and sister'. The *Truth* put it more rabidly: 'Concupiscent combo-land. The nauseated Northern Territory.'

The stigma of the combo was not merely that he consorted with an Aboriginal woman, but that he found degrees of mutuality and equality between black and white. The combo showed that the two communities could sometimes mix contentedly. He challenged the myth of white supremacy and Aboriginal inferiority that social Darwinism had bequeathed, exposing the falsehood of the idea that the two ways of life were incompatible. Combos were despised because they undermined the orthodoxy of values the new society was determined to impose.

I'd heard 'combo' used as a way of dismissing Roger Jose. Living 'blackfella' was even worse, since it amounted to going over to the other side completely.

Blackfella, or 'blackfellow', as it used to be written, has a history of ambivalence. Nowadays it's an insiders' word, used by Aboriginal people of themselves and affectionately by their supporters. But it can carry a derogatory overtone. The term appeared in the formative years of Australian settlement when at Sydney in 1795 one Aboriginal man, who was on good terms with the English, urged them to shoot other Aboriginal men of an enemy tribe. There was a feud going on. Young Carruey, who must have been something of a charmer, had become the lover of his tribal uncle Bennelong's former wife, Gooroobooroobaallo. But she had been stolen away by a man from a different tribe and 'carried up the harbour', in revenge for which Carruey and a kinsman speared the Botany Bay man while he was asleep. He came after them and an armed ceremonial stand-off occurred. It sounds like the start of the Trojan War, when Helen of Troy was carried off by Paris and the Greek ships were launched for vengeance. David Collins, the colony's Judge-Advocate, records in his journal: 'Our friends appeared to have some apprehension of the event not proving favourable to them; for perceiving an officer there with a gun, Carruey strenuously urged him, if anything should happen to him, to shoot the Botany Bay *black fellows*' (my italics). But the English, disappointing their allies, kept out of it, and the confrontation passed with no one being wounded.[7]

'Black' had a complex knot of associations but simplified matters by categorising the natives. 'Fellow' is one of those peculiarly duplicitous English words that can mean its opposite. A fellow is a partner or, in a less trustworthy sense, an accomplice. It slides easily to the slangy 'feller' or 'fella'. 'Blackfellow' cleans up the more colloquial 'blackfella'. In Kriol, the Aboriginal pidgin of Northern Australia, 'blackfella' becomes *blek bala*, and, freed from its etymological residue, is neutral again.

Time and taste play with such sensitive words. Language sidesteps to avoid offence, then that becomes a new kind of insult. Almost all the terms are problematic. 'A blacks' camp' was how parents described an untidy bedroom when I was a child. Then black was beautiful, but that was American and didn't translate automatically to Australian Aboriginal people who define their Aboriginality less by colour than by socially recognised descent. There are names for specific Aboriginal groups, such as the Yanyuwa in Borroloola, but 'indigenous' or 'Aboriginal people' are preferred general terms nowadays. The problem is that after two centuries of conflict about just who was wanted in the Australian nation the term 'Australian' both includes and excludes. There are still people today for whom 'Australian' means predominantly Anglo-Celtic white people whose parents were born here before any 'New Australians' came as migrants after the Second World War. A common alternative to 'white people' (who from an Aboriginal perspective might be more genially called 'whitefellas') is 'Europeans'. This makes an incongruous appeal to history. Politically the colonisers were British, but they included people of many nationalities. It's an odd usage, as when you see a sign in a national park telling you that 'Europeans' brought the invasive weeds and pests. They brought the sign and the concept of a park too, and 'they', in a complex sense, are 'us'. 'Europeans' also ignores the non-Europeans, notably the people from nearby Asia who sojourned to Australia from earliest times and have settled in sizeable numbers. 'Non-Aboriginal', 'non-indigenous', but 'Eastern' rather than 'Western' and not necessarily 'colonist', 'imperialist' or 'mainstream'. The tiptoeing round language, on stilts it sometimes seems, is unavoidable and the best that can be said is that a writer's clumsy self-consciousness becomes a marker of the powerful, inadequate connection between words and the abrasiveness of actual conditions in which people still live.

In his epic novel of northern Australia, *Capricornia*, Xavier Herbert wrote melodramatically: 'Once a man went combo he could never again look with pleasure on a white woman unless he blacked her face.' To be a combo may have been a form of racial betrayal, like going native or going troppo (losing your cool in a tropical clime), yet is there not a note of envy? They are people who have thrown over the traces, men (always) who have escaped the restrictive net of civilisation with its institutionalised dos and don'ts, men who, tasting a forbidden fruit, sought to regain paradise even as they were expelled from conventional society.

In reaching across the racial divide of early Australia, the combo and his partner were moving towards a kind of freedom from prejudice, even if in most cases the imbalance of power between white man and black woman led to exploitation and neglect. The law did not like it and, to protect vulnerable Aboriginal women and girls from abuse, disease and unwelcome pregnancies, but also out of a concern for racial purity, governments legislated against it. In 1899 the *Bulletin* reported that 'the recently-introduced Queensland Aborigines Protection Act compels all and sundry (excepting station-managers of the genus "combo") to either marry or get rid of their dusky Kitties and Pollies'. By 1911 a similar act had been passed to cover the Northern Territory and a Chief Protector of Aborigines and sub-protectors appointed. 'All employment of Aborigines was subject to their control,' writes historian Alan Powell. 'Asians were not permitted to employ Aborigines at all; the Administrator had power to exclude them from any area at will – and Darwin's Chinatown was the first place to be declared a no-man's-land to blacks; the Chief Protector could prohibit whites and Asians from entering Aboriginal camps; he could take any Aborigine or half-caste into custody; and he became the legal guardian of every Aboriginal and part-Aboriginal child under the age of eighteen years.' In a further ordinance in 1918 the Chief Protector was given power 'to regulate wages and conditions for Aboriginal employees, to attempt the separation of town blacks from alcohol and opium, of white men from black women and tribal Aborigines from all whites except officials and, reluctantly, the missions'. The Chief Protector censored the films shown in the Aborigines' compound in Darwin, banning anything that 'tended to lower their respect for the white man'.[8] Black and white needed the Chief Protector's permission to marry.

One of the early Chief Protectors was Baldwin Spencer, a distinguished anthropologist who none the less reviled the Chinese. Chinese people made up half of the non-Aboriginal population of the Territory in 1911, when the Commonwealth took over administration from South Australia: '98%

[of Chinese] are low depraved beasts who want deporting', thought Spencer, disliking the way the two non-white populations related. From his perspective the Chinese were the late products of a decadent civilisation rather than the noble savages he admired. The racial construction of early-twentieth-century Australian society is starkly seen in the attitudes to Aborigines, Chinese and Europeans in the Northern Territory, where co-existence is envisaged only by means of segregation.

Yet Borroloola was something of an exception, and even if that earned it a reputation as a gathering place for scum, the scum included people who wanted to live by different rules.

How the Aboriginal Ordinance was policed can be seen from evidence given to the Borroloola Police Court in October 1948, when an itinerant called Roy Green was charged.[9] It was the evening of Ration Day, when people came into town and caroused. There was a tip-off to the police that Green had Mabel, the wife of Aboriginal tracker Donegan, down at his camp. They went to investigate. When Mabel emerged from the shadows, the constable asked where she had been.

'"With that man," said Mabel, pointing at Green, whose trousers were undone. "Did you sleep along him?" the policeman asked.

'"Yes," Mabel replied, "he been gibit scrape" (and by signs of the hand indicated sexual intercourse).'

She had been promised tobacco in exchange.

Green's version is that he was just turning in for the night when he heard voices.

'"I pulled my trousers on again and only done up one strap I walked a few yards and heard someone sing out ... I never had intercourse with a Gin and you never saw me."'

Nevertheless the defendant was fined £10 with 15 shillings costs to be paid within 24 hours. The police officer knew Roy Green from before in Alice Springs and wanted him out of town. It's easy to see how the Aboriginal Ordinance was open to abuse on all sides.

At the heart of the contempt for combos was that they ignored the line between black and white. They showed that human attachments crossed colour and caste barriers. In time the bloodlines would mix and the simple-minded distinction upon which white claims to superiority were based would disappear. When Aboriginal and European married, the Aboriginal person was brought within the European framework of law and custom as an individual in his or her own right, upsetting the premise that the Aborigines were scarcely human beings. The British occupation of Australia was justified on the grounds that no one was there, no sovereign of an organised society with whom to negotiate terms. A combo marriage made the Aboriginal partner visible. In this way it challenged not only Western prejudices and British imperial structures, but also the legitimacy of the Australian state in its formative period. The prejudice has endured, even though the word is not much used nowadays.

The writer Keith Willey remembers Borroloola in the 1970s: 'There was a convention in the bush, and it persisted until not so very long ago, that while white men might sleep with Aboriginal women, they should not live with them and, above all, never marry them. Those who transgressed were denigrated as "combos" and "gin jockeys", and generally looked down upon. But this notion did not impress Jack Mulholland, one of Borroloola's long-term white residents. When a visitor suggested he might stay to dinner ... Jack said that would be all right, but first he would have to ask Mrs Mulholland, who was a full-blood Aboriginal.

'"Bring her in too," [the white visitor] said. "I'm not proud."

'"No," Mulholland said, "but she might be."'[10]

Bill Harney gave Borroloola the name 'combo's retreat'. He was one himself. After all he had been through in Gallipoli and France, he felt happy to turn his back on so-called civilisation. '"They tell me Borroloola is a good place,"' his mate told him when he returned from the war in 1919, '"plenty of Abos and water, no flies and mobs of fish and crabs." We all felt happy at the prospects of coastal rivers, with Aborigines hunting in canoes, and us taking life easy beneath a shady tree.'[11] Borroloola was a kind of Shangri-La for Harney, who returns there again and again in his writings, usually with Aboriginal women hovering in the background to meet his needs, and Aboriginal men to work for him.

It is hard to know how to take Bill Harney. The story of his trip to a hideous war in a foreign land, an innocent abroad, and his return to his homeland to try and regain some of that innocence evokes ready sympathy. He appears to have stumbled into the imperial forces at a time when the jingoistic pressure to enlist was intense, and not generally resisted by young men keen to take the chance of seeing the world. It probably took more guts not to heed the call. Harney remembers people waving him goodbye 'on the river in the moonlight night in old Burketown … with their hurricane lanterns'.[12] They were singing *We don't want to lose you, / But we think you ought to go.* Once he was out to sea, he decided to get off. 'You can't get orf,' he was told. 'You've enlisted for the war and if you run away now, they might shoot you.'

Harney, born in outback Queensland in 1895, was 19 when he went away to war and he never responded well to army discipline. Historian Manning Clark says that Harney fought two wars, one against the enemy and one against what he found to be the inept and inhuman organisation on his own side, in which an Australian digger was low in the heap.[13] He became convinced of the futility of war. Modern technology, modern organisation and modern mass inhumanity advanced in step with the unspeakable horrors of the Great War. The experience made Harney and many like him profoundly disillusioned with the values of so-called civilisation. The trauma of the trenches made the rules of society seem rotten and irrelevant for modernist rebels in Europe and the United States. In faraway Paris, Picasso and others looked to primitive Africa for renewal. In Borroloola Bill Harney turned his back on conventional morality and entered an Aboriginal world.

'I felt a hatred for war and what it stood for. And a hatred for discipline and what it stood for. So when I come back to Australia, I got off at Melbourne and went straight through ... I rode eight hundred miles to Borroloola on a horse, to forget about it all,' he later wrote. He kept his silence about the war itself. 'In that time of stress I saw brave men go down, and memories of those days compel me to pause ...' He acknowledged that the war had led him to write his own rules.

He and a friend were swimming in a secluded pool when some Aboriginal girls appeared, laughing 'happily as they shook the water from their naked copper-skinned bodies ... They who have lived as I did over the war years can readily understand how I felt. Mixing with thousands of men during the war, I was certainly not going to be hampered by convention in this land of ancient customs and strange experiences.'[14] But the joke is on Harney. The girls are bait sent out by their old Aboriginal husband to procure food and clothing from passing strangers. It was not the last time that Harney would get himself into trouble over Aboriginal women.

Bill Harney stayed in the Borroloola area for quite a few years, making a living as a cattleman and a trepanger. He was involved in one of the biggest cattle-duffing operations that ever came to court, although he never admitted his guilt. He was a little man who pitted himself against the big absentee pastoralists. Later he worked as an enthusiastic patrol officer with the Northern Territory's Native Affairs Branch, becoming a Protector of Aborigines himself. He wrote outraged reports about the treatment of

On hot days the native women love the cool rockholes of their land

Reproduced from W. E. Harney, Life Among the Aborigines, *1957*

Aboriginal people on large company-owned cattle stations.[15] A short, fit man with piercing grey eyes and bandy, leathery legs, he was a great raconteur. He has his fans and his detractors to this day. Not for nothing does his Aboriginal name, *bilarni*, sound like 'blarney'. Helped by ghost writers and editors, he made a name for himself with an output of bush yarns that traded on insider knowledge of Aboriginal lore: 'The images will arise and so I set them down … the "blackboy" … sings his tribal songs – those plaintive themes that tell about the greatness of his race, murmuring every now and then: "Poor fellow my country, poor fellow my country!"'

Harney explains how he was educated in the 'book of the bush'.

> You see we had few books, and in our pack bags would only carry those full of meat: Shakespeare, Herodotus, Plutarch, Emerson, Marx. Each of us became a disciple of his tome and in the arguments at night would try to slay his opponent with excerpts from his book of knowledge … The campfire burns away … the Prince of Denmark gives his philosophy of life; the wise sayings of the oracle of Concord are mixed with extracts from *Das Kapital* … [Then] a cough from the bush, a signal that the nymphs of the night – the girls from the blacks' camp nearby – are here, acts as a magic spell. The sages of yore slink back into their musty covers; the bush oracles falter over their words; their minds are elsewhere … the fires die down, and Orion the mighty

> hunter in the heavens looks down upon the mighty hunters of the woods ... So closes another day.[16]

Harney acknowledges the Aboriginal people even as he appropriates from them. 'Much as they were cursed and despised, Australia owes a deep and lasting debt to these humble people of the land.' In his view it was usually the 'young native woman' who led men on into the unknown, like a siren. His writing often has the flush of soft porn. It was marketed to readers in the post-war years with voluptuous full-page photographs of naked nymphs – 'On hot days the native women love the cool rockholes of their land,' reads one caption – concealing peepshow with anthropology, rather as scholarly gentlemen felt safe in thumbing the obscene passages in Greek and Latin texts.

Yet this Falstaff of the bush knew the tough truths of what happened out there, where 'most of them left their bones': 'the war was on; the victors were this remnant at the 'Loo, "the town of old men"'. From one war Harney had gone to another that was not proclaimed. He knew he could not survive without the Aboriginal people who brought in dugong, turtle and fish and gathered lily bulbs and the fruit of cycad palms to make flour, when supplies ran low during the Wet, and the Chinese gardener who knew how to cook. 'The natives controlled our lives more than we would admit,' he concludes. Perhaps that irked him. When he left the town, he told one of Borroloola's old men, 'The black man has been living off our backs a long while. From now on, I'm going to live off his.'[17]

Harney became a celebrity guide as well as an author. His last job was as a ranger at Uluru (Ayers Rock) in central Australia.[18] In those desert years he was an interpreter of Aboriginal people at a time of growing concern for their plight. If not always an accurate ventriloquist, he was an engaging mouthpiece for people with whom he had passed years of close proximity. Yet he preferred Borroloola to the desert. It was a place for all kinds of mixing, and that suited Bill Harney:

> Trooper, and storeman, teamster, man;
> All made up in a godly plan,
>   A dinkum Boor-o-loo-la brew.
> Blackman, Malay and Chinaman too,
>   Boatman, bagman, welcome all
>   … come, for the old town calls.[19]

When food was low in the Borroloola days, Harney and his mates fell back on wild honey and lilies from the lagoon. Young Aboriginal women would dive for waterlily roots. This gave Borroloola a reputation as a place where the soles of the feet were sunburned – a local variant of lotus-eating.

'I lay back as the natives did my bidding,' Harney writes on one occasion, 'and wondered why people ever left a land as peaceful as this.' Much of Harney's writing is self-justificatory, but despite the stupors of pleasure somewhere his conscience is troubled. He saw the destruction brought to Aboriginal society. He saw the young people breaking away from the law of the elders. He was among the first popular writers to lament the violence and exploitation that Aboriginal people suffered. When he saw an old Garawa man in chains, he was ashamed 'that for this sort of thing I had gone away to the war'. He prophesies that the tables will be turned: 'A law of compensation was in operation. Whereas these old white men had, in the beginning, exploited the natives, now the black people were returning to the attack to get their own back.'[20]

One of the best stories Harney tells is of the Borroloola horse races. As in the legend of the Wandering Jew, an Irishman called Taboo Paddy had destroyed some sacred Yanyuwa objects. A curse was put on him that each time he came to Borroloola the oldest white man would die. When Taboo Paddy is rumoured to be heading to town for the races, the oldest man considers moving out. But the next oldest talks him out of such useless superstition. Then in the excitement of the meet, everyone forgets about it. Late that night didgeridoos sound from across the river. In the morning Taboo Paddy is discovered to have arrived in town without anyone noticing, the oldest man has beat it bush, and the second oldest, now the oldest white man left in town, is dead according to the curse.

Harney died alone, turning his back on the Territory at the end of his life, retreating to coastal Queensland. But he preserved 'The Combo's Anthem' that was sung round campfires to an old Irish tune. It is far from politically correct, but it sings of the lure of crossing the line:

They are comely and dark, and the glint of their eyes
Are as dew-drops that gleam on a wintry sun-rise.
And the firm rounded breasts that seductively tease
Are like seed-pods that sway from squat baobab trees.
So hail Borroloola ...!

'Each country is full of these men who laughed at society yet became the ancestors of people who are proud that their stem goes back to the original tribes,' Harney concludes.[21] In many cases it is their progeny who are taking power today.

Harney walked away from a world he could not accept, seeking refuge in a polymorphous innocence. He came to identify with Aboriginal people and it changed him. He spoke with their voice. 'That's why I go back and sit on me beaches out from Darwin. Listen to the sea coming in and get the crabs and the fish and me mates come in and we talk and everybody's happy.' A veil was torn from his eyes, but there was no revelation that came with it – only a set of questions about human nature to which there was no end:

Some husks and shells beside the grinding stones,
A painted cave, or etchings scratched on bones ...
Our laws, religion, customs, all were born
Amidst the shards and flints of mankind's dawn.
Dig deep, oh spade, beneath the pomp of kings
To search amidst the dust for great small things.[22]

Late at night in the pub I talk to a young woman. She belongs to one of the old Borroloola families. She's back in town to see her kid, from her job on the night patrol at Tennant Creek a few hundred kilometres away. Tennant Creek is a dry town. Alcohol sales are restricted. The night patrol helps to police drinking and domestic violence. It can be depressing going round at three o'clock on a cold inland night pulling people apart or rousing them and giving them a blanket. Her eyes are swimming as she tells me all this in her sleepily animated way. She's surrounded by family, brothers, sisters. She's glad to be back in town. She orders an ouzo and Coke. I'm way out of my depth, a middle-aged ghost who's already spoken for. But eyes and words can always do it. I got hooked on China by that combination, years ago, when I sat on a train and a young Chinese woman with deep shining eyes told me the terrible things she had been through during the Cultural Revolution, but that's another story. In the Borroloola pub that night I felt the same pull on me. When the eyes tell the story, I want to be part of it.

There was 'no fighting' in the pub that night, the woman said with a smile. That's what the sign on the gate insisted on, along with 'no drunks'. There were often both. Alcohol is the cause of many of Borroloola's problems, many of its deaths. A night patrol used to operate here too until its funding was cut. Paul Roy's film *A Dying Shame* (1997) shows what it can be like at closing time on a bad night. The film, a documentary on health issues, gives the last words to

Barbara McCarthy, a young local woman committed to making the town strong: 'What you see here in Borroloola is about anger, it's about shame, it's about sadness, it's about joy, and we're dealing with it the best way we know how.'

I walked home smelling the frangipani on the air, past the smooth white gums. At one o'clock in the morning when the pub closes the noise spills out into the darkness. *Farrkyeew! Faarrkyeeuw!* From my bunk in the cabin I hear whooping and shouting and swearing to shake the stars. It's familiar. The same sounds fill the small hours of Sunday mornings in inner-city Sydney where I live, as people wend homewards from the clubs and pubs of Oxford Street.

V

THE REVENGE OF THE ORAL

The story goes that a mounted trooper called Cornelius Power, posted to Borroloola in 1891, was short of reading matter. He thought the town needed something to improve itself during the confined months of the Wet. He is said to have approached Lord Hopetoun, then Governor of Victoria and later the first Governor-General of Australia, or even to have written directly to Andrew Carnegie, the Scottish-born iron and steel magnate, who had a reputation for establishing libraries, not just in Pittsburgh, where he made his money, but to the furthest reaches of the English-speaking world. In response some 3,000 volumes steamed up the McArthur River to Borroloola – a place of promise that no one knew much about, except that the craving for learning seemed to burn strongly there.

The 3,000 books were duly catalogued and a lending library set up that lasted 40 or more years, despite heat and wet and white ants. Books were carried in the swags of wandering men, debated around campfires and not always returned. The collection was housed in a narrow cell at the back of the old iron courthouse until a cyclone blew it away. Borroloola was proud of the reputation it acquired as a seat of learning on the Gulf of Carpentaria. The Carnegie Library was a mark of distinction, a precious charge. As the town slumbered through the early decades of the twentieth century, it became Borroloola's unlikely claim to fame. A man might be found dead out in the bush with a volume beside him for company. Eventually the book, at least, would find its way back.

'Town Dies, Books Live', declared Ernestine Hill in a piece she sent back to a Sydney paper in 1933, later adapted for her book *The Great Australian Loneliness.* 'Closed in by jungle and forgotten of men, I stumbled upon a library of 3000 books,' she writes, 'the finest and most comprehensive library in the North …' Peering 'through the dusty windows of the old court-house, at myriads of canvas-covered volumes, [I] could scarcely believe them true'. The library, she says, 'became a kindly light of sanity to men half-mad with loneliness'.[1]

Bill Harney discovered the library when he was in jail awaiting trial for cattle-duffing.

> We hear a lot of the great seats of learning in other countries, but I have heard little of this place of timber and iron, which for years cast its magic spell over the bushmen of the Northern Territory … I can look back on those days in that little cell as one of the turning points in my life. It was no prison to me; within its narrow walls I travelled far,

> struggling along the old silk road … with Marco Polo, sailing the Pacific with Magellan, travelling through the jungles of South America … I sailed and travelled everywhere. Then, as night fell and we couldn't read any more, we would discuss far into the night the things we had read about that day.[2]

If the war had been Harney's education into life, his months in the Borroloola lock-up in 1923 were his initiation into literature.

Aboriginal people were welcome to use the library in those days, but perhaps not many did. 'I found its tomes in blacks' camps, where the natives had used them to look at the pretty pictures,' Harney recalls. 'A splendid edition of Shakespeare had been used to light some camp-fire, and my first introduction to Plutarch was in the lavatory of the local pub. In that place of restful reading I read … until I heard shuffling footsteps without. Hastily I hid the book for future reading, and smiled to myself as I thought of the new patron cursing and swearing when he discovered he had, as the blacks say, "nothing longa finger".' Hill writes that 'a young buck of the Yanyuwa' was tasked to spray away the silverfish and keep the white ants at bay. 'He always gets the numbers mixed and the volumes wrong side up.'[3]

That decaying library seemed to contain the best of Western civilisation. In time it became associated with the great minds of the past rather than contemporary life. Like an ark, it carried the classics and the sweep of history, with the Bible, the Greeks and Shakespeare at its core, and Gibbon's *Decline and Fall of the Roman Empire*, its pages crumbling as they turned, warning that the mightiest of empires and the most advanced of civilisations were as vulnerable to defeat from their own internal corruption as at the hands of barbarians.

The settlers in remote Australia made sense of their mission by reference to the grand reach of the empire for which they were foot soldiers. Even the centres of Australian life were little more than outposts for Great Britain. Some of those far-flung men literally served London's financial interests in the cattle industry. Others were serving their own interests as ambivalent agents of civilisation. They were there as products of complex forces of geography, history, politics and economics. Books, even as they entertained, helped explain all that. No matter that the most popular books were novels. Fiction set in London or Manchester or Boston or the Mississippi held an illuminating mirror to the stranger-than-fiction situations of their own lives. One favourite was *The Red Badge of Courage*, Stephen Crane's stark tale of the American Civil War, in which a young man has his innocence stripped away in battle. Another was Eugène Sue's sexy romance, *Mysteries of Paris.*

The library became a standard topic for writers who visited Borroloola. As men of words, they were attracted by the idea of books. Douglas Lockwood reports that the library was 'built by Chinese labourers in 1886' and was Borroloola's proudest possession when Roger Jose arrived in 1916: he 'read his way along the shelves – Plutarch, Aristotle, Hippocrates, even Hansard'. In this way 'he acquired a passion not only for learning but for words,' adds David Attenborough. Passing through Borroloola to gather material for *Ghost Towns of Australia*, George Farwell records that the Carnegie Library has vanished. He says that lonely Corporal Power wrote 'to the Carnegie Trust in New York, asking for something to read. The trustees may have lacked a map of Australia or else they were impressed by such an imposing name [as Borroloola]. Perhaps they ranked it with Melbourne or Sydney. They made a rich grant … The effect on these lotus-eaters was remarkable. [But] now there is nothing left …'[4]

The idea of a vanished library haunts the imagination. The burning of the great library of Alexandria comes to mind, and the phantom books bequeathed to posterity from its flames, lost classics known only because people referred to them after they read them – like all those books you've heard about but never read. According to Plutarch, Julius Caesar burned the library to protect his fleet in 48BCE. The likelihood that this is serious exaggeration or myth has done nothing to dent the image. The Alexandrian library may have recovered from the fire, but the missing library also persists. It is not so different from that imagined by another librarian, the Argentinian writer Jorge Luis Borges, in his story 'The Library of Babel', an imaginary eternal library that might contain 'all books'. 'When it was proclaimed … men felt themselves lords of a secret, intact treasure. There was no personal or universal problem whose eloquent solution did not exist.' But in that infinity of books the solution can never be found. While the human species moves towards extinction, the library survives, infinite but useless. The reverse process happened in Borroloola.

There's a sense, though, that the library was wasted there, that the Carnegie worthies were fools parted from their money in this act of philanthropy. They were gulled, like so many before and after who put their faith in Australia's finer aspirations. It was a joke, a message of absurdity that made its point when the books were locked up in the felon's cell and left to be inexorably eaten.

Yet there lay the library's redemption. It nurtured Bill Harney, and Roger Jose, and the other no-hopers who held their intellectual debates on the shores of the McArthur River. It became a symbol of the power of learning in detention. Years later a Darwin prison administrator gave a lecture in which, not paying much regard to the facts, he cited Roger Jose as a man who had been enlightened by his time with books in the Borroloola jail.[5] Harney's formulation, 'It was no prison to me; within its narrow walls I travelled far', resonates with an ancestry in English-language prison literature, from Shakespeare's Lear, to John Bunyan and Oscar Wilde. 'Stone Walls do not a Prison make, / Nor Iron bars a Cage.' Nor corrugated iron either, it seems.

A massive gold-embossed *Webster's Dictionary* sits in solitary splendour in a glass case in the Old Police Station at Borroloola, now the museum, as a reminder. It's one of few survivors. The preoccupation with preserving relics of book culture stands in fetishistic contrast to the destruction of the oral, non-book culture of Aboriginal people that was running on apace. Artefacts inscribed with knowledge were freely pillaged, elders were dying without passing on stories, languages themselves were becoming extinct. But the library's books vanished too, transformed into something else. It is said that termites use what they eat to line the walls of their immense creations. Pieces of newspaper have been found inside the comb of corridors in a termite mound. Why not books? One of the books in the Borroloola library was a collection of stories by Henry James called *Terminations.* I see termites turning *Terminations* into a termitary, once the readers were through with it. That termitary looks to me like the Tower of Babel in Brueghel's famous painting, a great earth-coloured mound of many modules that mocks the disharmony humans have wrought with their divergent languages, and the gulf between one mind and another that words, and books, are supposed to span.

The library made Borroloola into a kind of open university, its pages freely available to those who wanted education. Part of the legend is of books reaching hungry minds far beyond the confines of academic walls, far from the alienating city with its harshly imposed pedagogic systems. That is how the poet Les Murray invokes the Borroloola library in his essay 'The Australian Republic' when he calls for a different kind of education that will

> not estrange people from their own culture and injure their rapport with their own people ... You must either give

> yourself one, or be taught by your elders in a more or less informal way outside the institutional system. This is the way all the vernacular cultures of Australia – Aboriginal, immigrant, and mainstream – *are* in fact transmitted, though the mainstream one does also get disseminated to a limited extent through books and other media. The most comfortable way to educate oneself is to do it at a university; the library there tends to be better stocked than that famous and perhaps mythical one in the cells of Borroloola lock-up, which is said to have educated a generation of Queensland and Territory wanderers.[6]

Again it's a classical and Renaissance vision put to new use, of untrammelled roaming through the fields of learning, of words passing in and out of books, as in a symposium of free and equal minds, of ideas flowing into active life. It's a far-fetched comparison for Borroloola, I know, but it helps to explain the appeal of that collection of 3,000 volumes.

Ted Egan, who was welfare officer there in the late 1950s, remembers the Sunday morning debates:

> there they were, the Borroloola Hermits. About ten white blokes, middle-aged to old, sitting around on a ring of army stretcher beds.
>
> 'Sit down son,' said one of them. 'Like a drink?' He passed me a bottle of metho … 'It's all we've got unfortunately. We usually have Bollinger.' Before I could leave they launched into the Great Debate …

> They had some fairly erudite debates and arguments whose titles I do recall. 'Karl Marx: right or wrong' was a fiery turnout ... More esoteric, and yet still lively, was 'Should Henry James be taken seriously?' and a reflective, serene sort of show revolved around the topic 'Is there a future in Buddhism?' The highlight for me was the day they debated 'Gray versus Browning' and Roger led the Gray team. He felt that Gray had no superior as a poet, and he held us enthralled ...[7]

They had absorbed the contents of books that were no more and were able to carry on discourse with the printed page left behind. It was their version of the 'sermons in stones, books in the running brooks' that the retreating gentlefolk sought in Shakespeare's *As You Like It*. They found their own reflection there. The disintegrating library stands for the resilience of the oral, or its revenge.

How the famous library really came about is not as romantic as the legend. Its history has been pieced together by one of the most venerable Territorians, Vernon O'Brien, a retired surveyor who is a genealogist, place-name etymologist and historical sleuth.[8] A library was under discussion from almost as soon as the McArthur River Jockey Club, the first priority, was founded in 1886. Books were the accoutrements of a new town's ambitions. When Corporal Power was posted to Borroloola in 1891, donations for books were already coming in from the government in South Australia. Power became librarian and presided over the purchase of many books, building up a collection that was unique in the Territory. Most of them came from Mudie's Select Library in London. Founded in Bloomsbury in 1842, Mudie's was a circulating library, like its rival W. H. Smith. Readers paid fees. The overseas section supplied libraries in the colonies with modish fare for the general reader. Some isolated donations from Carnegie Institutes in Pittsburgh and Washington reached Australia, but it is unlikely there was a special bequest to Borroloola. Andrew Carnegie supported the bricks and mortar of libraries, endowing some hundreds around the world, but he did not endow books. No doubt he preferred his philanthropy to take a monumental form. Much later, in 1936, the Carnegie Institute made an arrangement with Australia's national library to assist with books for remote areas in a programme known as the 'Carnegie Library Service to Outlying Commonwealth Territories'. Some of those books reached Borroloola and 'Carnegie Library Service' appeared on their bookplates. The story grew that Andrew Carnegie had endowed the library himself. In 1937 a cyclone damaged the courthouse where the library was housed. Restoration work was done, by Roger Jose among others, but at the end of the Second World War when the police station was closed most of the books were packed up and sent to Darwin. There was nowhere to store them and they just disappeared in the confusion of those days.

Of course the locals souvenired some. In Darwin I saw a copy of *Sand and Sea in Arabia* by Norman Lewis (published in London in 1938), a book of sumptuous photographs and text about another faraway place that must have struck a chord with the old-timers in Borroloola. It had the Carnegie Library stamp and inside the cover was shakily written, 'Given to me in 1953 at Borroloola by resident of old hotel Jack Mulholland as part of large number of decayed books in the remains of a Carnegie funded library.'

Funds had been found for new purchases over the years, partly through subscriptions, but it was hard to keep track of books. The catalogue was kept in triplicate and shared with the neighbouring police jurisdictions of Anthony Lagoon and Rankine River. The minutes of a library meeting at the end of 1934 note that 'all stations etc have been written to requesting a return of all library books in their respective possessions and quite a number were returned'.

In the Northern Territory archives I found an original minute-book for the McArthur River Jockey Club that had later been reused for the library catalogue, when a valiant attempt was made to take stock. Four hundred titles were listed, and another 1,500 numbered lines left blank, as if for overdue returns. Those listed were the typical titles of an Edwardian library. The rest had gone the way of all paper. There were novels of manly adventure by Rudyard Kipling and Robert Louis Stevenson and the plays of Strindberg and Wilde. Jane Austen and Thomas Hardy were there, and Charles Darwin on the fertilisation of orchids, and some lowbrow stuff by Zane Grey and Ethel M. Dell. Australian titles included Ernest Favenc's novel *Marooned on Australia*. *The Red Badge of Courage* was still on the shelf and a novel called *Disenchanted* by Pierre Loti, the orientalist Frenchman. I began to suspect that books were ordered for those 'marooned' and 'disenchanted' in Borroloola by their titles, if not their covers.

Another borer-eaten folio ledger from a later date still had a catalogue that included new purchases, 2,051 titles that went right up to Anita Loos's *Gentlemen Prefer Blondes*, published in 1925. There were not many blondes in Borroloola then. It's a wonderful list. If I was stranded there during the Wet, I could have sunk happily into reading through that comprehensive and diverting library. It was literature to be read for pleasure as well as self-improvement. Some of the names I recognised from my grandfathers' shelves, writers like Dornford Yates, whose books must have been standards two generations ago and are now forgotten. Maybe half the list has passed into limbo, but as many have survived, including classics like the Brontës, most of Dickens, Boswell's *Life of Johnson*, Goethe's *Faust*, lots of Emerson, and the *Arabian Nights*. I found Henry Lawson and *Howard's End*, Tolstoy and Mrs Beeton, Olive Schreiner, Zola, Stephen Leacock and Joseph Conrad's *Tales of Unrest*. And there was John Buchan's *The Thirty-Nine Steps*, the book that Bob had picked up for the flight from New York and would leave accidentally on purpose in the Borroloola pub.

The literature ranged the New World as well as the Old. It struck me as a bold and questioning list, designed to feed thought and imagination. Each title was supposed to be issued and returned within two weeks. As I fancied the cast of old-time Borroloola reading those books, the policemen and their wives, the publicans and the cattlemen, the eccentrics and wanderers and kids, the titles took on an added significance. *The Pilgrim's Progress* was there, and *Gulliver's Travels*, and *Three Men in a Boat*. They could have identified with any of those three. And especially with their favourite, the best-represented of all, Mark Twain. Like Huck, whoever was in Borroloola had lighted out for the territory.

The library encapsulates both a time and a place. It demonstrates the ties that bound the British Empire and the English-speaking world together. A good many of those books were to find their places in English literature courses around the world for a generation or two. What F. R. Leavis called 'the great tradition', a canon to be studied by students like me half a century later, was firmly in place in Borroloola a long while before. I thought of the books as physical objects, and the journey of those productions of ink, paper, stitching and glue across the seas to a fate of tropical humidity and desiccating sun and vermiculation, where they surely appeared both familiar and strange, as message sticks to be deciphered, deconstructed, digested and dissolved. They embodied that almost religious faith in the written word's immortal life expressed by Thomas Carlyle in a dictum I see every day, carved in the granite of the Mitchell Library's foyer: 'In books lies the soul of the whole past time, the articulate audible voice of the past when the body and material substance of it has altogether vanished like a dream.' But in Borroloola there was no stone for such sentiment when the books had vanished, only the impermanence of human minds.

I wondered what the books looked like. I checked a copy of *Terminations* by Henry James, published in London in 1895. It was part of Heinemann's Colonial Library of Popular Fiction, published for sale in the British colonies and India only, volume XLI of the Empire Library of Standard Works. Such grand product placement for what turned out to be a small collection of James's tales, and a most beautiful book, with its fine durable paper and lilac-coloured boards impressed with gold tulips. The volume sells for hundreds of dollars today. One copy's fate was to find its way to Borroloola to be devoured. What can they have thought of it? Perhaps they understood James's rarefied sensibility, his ordeal of consciousness, his complex fate better than I do. Perhaps, in all his obfuscations and omissions, they saw themselves reflected. Or perhaps they hated it, scoffed and felt they'd been had, which was how they came to debate whether the master should be taken seriously. I looked at the stories in the collection. One was 'The Altar of the Dead'. As I read over the first paragraph, I pretended to be one of the eccentrics of Borroloola, perhaps even Roger Jose, as I felt myself inside the words. Across that great gulf they made sense. James was writing, oddly enough, of the exaltation that might come with 'an immense escape from the actual'. That was something he longed for and yet disapproved of. It's what Borroloola allowed.

The lilac volume is just one unlikely example that graced

those shelves in the hot, narrow iron hut. The writings were alchemically changed there, finding their value not as rare collectibles, preserved in mint condition, but, quite the contrary, as words and images lifting off disappearing pages. A professional librarian who has studied its records concludes that 'the story of the Borroloola Library is not a tragicomedy of misplaced philanthropy and literature for termites, but a more stirring tale of people in difficult and isolated conditions finding the resources to provide the books they needed'.[9]

Still, I wonder how Henry James tasted to the termites.

VI

THE FEWNESS OF HIS NEEDS

Roy Hammer showed me the way to the grave. At a certain point we veered off the road and headed across country. He said there used to be a track. There wasn't one now. A ditch and a bank ran along the roadside, overgrown with stiff grass. We bumped down over it, scraping bottom despite our high clearance, the Toyota bucking in low four-wheel drive. The ground was black and corrugated after burning, with tussocks of stubble like turrets of fired clay. The grass that remained was as scratchy as copper wire. The dust smelled of ash. Roy gave directions this way and that. The only landmarks were a few spindly trees and two distant hills.

For years the grave lay unmarked in the wild grass beyond the end of the airstrip. It has been renovated recently, made into a memorial. Bones in the bush are history here. Covered with red gravel, bordered with concrete and protected by a chain fence, the grave has a crude cross made from a fence dropper and a rusty iron bar. Roger Jose is buried with his two wives, Maggie and Biddy, sisters. Three little plaques give names and dates. Roger Jose born 1896, died 1963. Maggie

The author with Roy Hammer at the grave of Roger, Maggie and Biddy Jose

Jose died 1957. Biddy Jose … Buried together, as they wanted, not in the town cemetery but in a place of their own choosing, beyond where Roger had worked felling trees and compacting earth for the extension of the airstrip at the start of the war with Japan.

Roy points out the trees around the grave. One is the sandpaper tree, its abrasive leaves used to smooth sticks. Roy Hammer is the Northern Territory's champion firelighter. Drilling a sharpened stick into bark he can make fire anywhere in record time. He never needs a match.

'That old man was my friend,' Roy says. 'He was a fair man. He was strong. He made you laugh. He looked after those two women and they looked after him. He was a good man.'

In this wide, seemingly indeterminate stretch of country the grave is a tether for the memory of Roger and Maggie and Biddy. Lives that left behind the most ephemeral of remains are cemented into history. Jose Street in town has been named in their honour. It's curious to stand at the spot and feel their legend.

I had spent the morning in the Old Police Station. It's a fine example of vernacular architecture, iron and timber, with an airy gabled roof and wide enclosed verandas, built by a Frenchman in 1886 with Chinese labour. The old pub is gone, commemorated by a stone under a tamarind tree, and the tank house is gone. Of Borroloola's scanty old buildings, only the police station survives, a museum now, grandly alone in an expanse of grass. Roger Jose is enshrined in a display there with photographs, testimonials and a hazy biographical account, as if – the most marginal of men – he were some local patriarch. Aboriginal weapons, Chinese ornaments, cattle brands, police journals, tall stories of unorthodox whites – the layers of objects in these venerable rooms are almost a parody of museology. Beneath a bark painting of a Macassan prau is a text that expresses Borroloola's present-day pride: 'It is indeed remarkable that with over one hundred years of contact with Europeans and white Australians, the Aboriginal people of Borroloola have kept a cultural distinctiveness but at the same time are quite perfectly able to function within the realms of white Australian culture.' And there is Roger Jose on the cover of the heritage brochure, as if he's looking towards that vision, white mane swept back from a bare brow, broad white beard, eyes sunk into the crags of his face, head angled upwards with inspiring strength.

He was a casual labourer at the police station back in the 1930s, a relief worker paid a subsistence wage by the police a day at a time. He cut posts and rails for the veranda, the fence and the horse yards. Using old iron he re-roofed the police kitchen. He fixed the fireplace and repaired the cell where the library books were kept, putting up new shelves. Then in February 1939 he announced that 'he wanted to have a spell and intended going to the coast for a week or two and would not be working'.[1] He did not return for a long time.

Roger looks like Moses or Lear in the photograph. How ironic, how unexpected, that an unregarded handyman should end up as the icon of the place. How apt that this capable, opinionated individual turned out to be a guide who showed the way. Roger Jose is remembered for goodness and justice, and for following his own path.

As I walk around the town 40 years after his death, everyone has a story about Roger Jose, including many who never met him. One woman told me that he was out walking on the red rock ridge at the back of the town and found a giant opal, the only one ever found in Borroloola. Another woman told me that when her kids wear cargo pants she laughingly tells them they look like Roger Jose, 'that old fella' who went round bare-foot with his pants cut off below the knee. 'Never heard a bad word about Roger,' says the historian who has talked to everyone in the district. When I asked another local resident how much of what was said about Roger was true, he replied, 'How long is a piece of string?'

Roger Jose walked to Borroloola in 1916. He walked in from Cunnamulla, more than 2,000 kilometres away in southern Queensland, on an overland journey that may have taken him three years. If the year of his birth is correctly given as 1896, then he was 17 years old when he set out. He may have come in with the packhorse mail for the stretch from Camooweal. All his life Roger preferred to travel on foot, what in Aboriginal English is called 'footwalking'. When he travelled with his wife Maggie, she would sit on the horse and he would walk alongside. He carried a yoke across his shoulders with buckets hanging from each end, coolie-style, that he used for his tools or for fetching water. Otherwise he pushed a wheelbarrow used for moving earth out bush on road-mending journeys that lasted eight months at a time. He would push his wife along in the wheelbarrow if she had trouble walking. He liked to put things to different uses from those they were meant for.

Roger Jose did not stay in Borroloola when he arrived in 1916. He was more than a footwalker, he was a wanderer. For the next 30 years, as I trace him through the old records, he appears in and out of the town, away for long stretches, living at other camps over a huge area of territory, including on islands in the Gulf. When not travelling by foot, he travels by boat. In November 1918, for example, the same month that peace was declared after the First World War, Roger arrived in Borroloola from the inland cattle station where he had been working and went off again by boat for rations, returning a month later. In March 1919 he was on a boat to Darwin.

He worked hard but intermittently, doing the most arduous jobs. Cutting timber for posts and rails for cattle yards was back-breaking work. Making and maintaining roads was not much better. The pay was never good. In 1950 he asked for an increase which was granted, with the Darwin superior adding a note to the internal file: 'Personally speaking I should say that it was worth 280 pounds for anyone to live in Borroloola, apart from doing any work.'

Roger had a big frame and powerful physique. Even his detractors acknowledged that he was an extremely good bushman, meaning he knew the ways of the bush. He had skill and stamina, and knew how to hunt and fish. He was good on water too, able to paddle a canoe long distances. Sometimes he worked on the wharf at Borroloola when the supply boats came in. He was an itinerant labourer who was equally capable of surviving outside the economic order. He didn't identify himself as working class or any other class. He was not a belonger. Beer he rejected as the drink of wage slaves. He drank rum if he could get it, or metho – pirates' liquor, or the drink of tramps.

It may have been while working on the railway from Pine Creek to Darwin that Roger met Maggie, a woman who belonged to the Brinkin people at nearby Daly River. They were married in the Darwin registry office in 1926. Maggie, whose age is given as 26 at the time, marks her name with a cross. Roger, describing himself as a labourer, signs 'R. Jose'. No surname or parents' names are given for Maggie and Roger gives only a father's name: T. A. E. Jose. Both bride and groom were outcasts.

While it was illegal for a white man and a black woman to cohabit, it was also unusual for them to be given permission to marry. It may be that Maggie and her sister Biddy were opium addicts in the dens run by Chinese on the goldfields around Pine Creek, in Adelaide River and Darwin. For a time in his wanderings Roger frequented the gambling dens where opium was peddled. Aboriginal people were given the left-over opium ash and became addicted. The Chief Protector's report for 1926–27 lists more convictions of Aboriginal people for opium-related offences than for drinking, adding that 'the supply of opium and liquor to Aboriginals … continues … Every effort is being made to suppress the evil.' Perhaps Roger smoked opium himself, as later in life he experimented with other substances. As a gambler he must have seen money come and go.

Was Roger's marriage to Maggie approved as a rescue attempt that would also include her sister Biddy, whether by

Roger and Maggie Jose, Borroloola, 1945

kinship or attachment? Roy Hammer referred to them as 'empty old women' when they came to Borroloola with Roger. They were far from their own country and their own people. They were not known to have had children before Roger married them, and they are not known to have had family with Roger. Venereal disease may be an explanation for infertility, or they may have had children who died in infancy or were taken away, as happened with the paler-skinned children of mixed parentage who were known as yellafellas. Or maybe the problem lay with Roger. He and Maggie are remembered for being kind to children, who liked coming to their house. Roger once told a boy, whose father had an aviary, to open the cage and let the birds go: 'You wouldn't like to be locked up.'[2]

The couple travelled light, apparently without even a dog.

Neither Maggie nor Biddy had blood relations in the Borroloola area, but they were accepted by the local people as 'countrymen', a loose de facto kin relationship. After Maggie's death in 1957, the law would require Roger to marry Biddy if she stayed on living with him in the tank house.

Roger and Maggie had a faithful loving relationship that lasted for 30 years. They went everywhere together and sustained each other in their unconventional, borderline life. The combo relationship was the stuff of jokes. The euphemism 'black boy' for a young Aboriginal woman who worked with a white man indicated a convenient transience. The depth of affection and loyalty between Roger and Maggie was exceptional. Part of Roger's activities were for the sake of providing for her and her sister. The bounty he got from dingo scalps might be spent on rolls of dress-making cloth, or rum for all three of them and their friends, black and white. He did a stint in jail for supplying it. After Maggie's death, Roger mourned, tending her grave lovingly and looking to the day when he would be buried beside her. Her absence might have contributed to the depression that was a likely factor in his death, allegedly from an overdose of the pills prescribed for his heart condition.

The mutuality of Roger's relationship with Maggie helped Aboriginal people to accept him. He demanded justice when they were mistreated and harassed the police when such matters went unpursued. He was also able to stand up for himself when he felt he had been wronged. Earlier in his life, at a fan-tan table in a gambling den in

Darwin, the Chinese proprietors had withheld his winnings. In front of the bouncer, Roger smashed the hurricane lamp that hung over the gaming table, stopping the play until he was paid.

Roger's relationships with the passing parade of police officers in the Borroloola district were not always comfortable. The police saw him as a ratbag and a disgrace to his kind. When Japanese bombing raids hit northern Australia during the Pacific war, the Borroloola police officer recommended evacuation for eight old white men, including Roger Jose, described as 'about 48, married to a lubra. Does occasional (only) work at yard building … and in between times lives "blackfellow" … None of these men are essential residents of the district; in fact, I believe they would all be better off for being evacuated, and those physically fit being obliged to work.'[3] But headquarters did not think it worth bothering. Roger and Maggie went bush for most of the war and, according to the story, lived in a cave out of harm's way.

Like other independent-minded individuals in the Top End, Roger Jose was not much interested in the war against Japan. He had his own analysis of geopolitics and dismissed the immature way Australia was drawn into other people's fights. That made the authorities suspicious of him, as if he might be a traitor or a spy, a question-mark that hung over other European loners in camps on the northern coastline who had regular dealings with Japanese fishing and pearling boats. Aboriginal people were suspected of being less than reliable in the war effort too. Their working and trading relationship with Japanese visitors by sea was outside politics. It was sometimes violent, but sometimes better than with white Australians. Roger's attitudes might be guessed by a comparison with novelist Xavier Herbert, who resembles him psychologically in some ways. Born in 1901 in southern Australia and uncertain who his father was, Herbert became a wanderer north of Capricorn where he reinvented himself in self-aggrandising stories. He adopted Aboriginal people and values as an alternative to the repressive money-grubbing conformity of a society that gave no place to him and his yearnings. He led a quarrelsome, erotically fitful life, with an uneducated Jewish woman from London's East End as his one anchor. He wanted to awaken his countrymen's vision, writing thousands of vibrant, caricatured, hectoring pages to do so. In a confused mix of militant nationalism and Nietzschean supranationalism, Herbert dallied with fascism, communism and even Zionism.

'During the critical period of the Pacific war,' writes novelist Randolph Stow of his cranky compatriot, '[Herbert] goes bush and stays neutral, flying his own flag, prepared to fight the Japanese on his own soil, but not otherwise.'[4] His own territory, cherished and lamented, he called by an Aboriginal English phrase picked up from Bill Harney that became the title of his massive last novel, *Poor Fellow My Country*. Weighing in at four and a quarter pounds, the book was dubbed 'Poor Fellow My Reader', of whom there are fewer and fewer.

When Roger and Maggie returned to Borroloola after the war, they lived in the tank house, Roger Jose's 'mansion', as it came to be called. Earlier Roger had lived at the back of the old hotel. After the hotel was damaged by a cyclone, he rolled a water tank to a place of high ground away from the town in the direction of the Aboriginal camp and created his own house. Not as eccentric as it sounds, the dwelling was a pioneer of environmentally sensitive design. The inner tank was encased in a skin of movable iron sheeting that provided insulation and shade as required. If struck by a cyclone, the central tank would roll away, to be rolled back easily later. It survived Cyclone Kathy in 1984. The tank house was a gathering place when Roger, Maggie and Biddy lived there, where Aboriginal kids would hang out and be given rice and stew. It became an obligatory call for visitors to the town. After Roger's death in 1963, Biddy sold it to a legendary Latvian crocodile shooter called Harry Blumenthals for £21 16s and 1½d, one of each denomination of Australian money as it was then. Blumenthals put a smaller tank on top as a second storey in which to accommodate a distinguished Latvian professor who arrived with two suitcases and a plan to transcribe the croc hunter's autobiography. The professor was fed on baked beans in a room lined with chicken wire that was stuffed with rum corks until he could take it no more. The autobiography never appeared. People were sorry when, after Blumenthals moved on, the abandoned tank house was demolished to make way for the caravan park. Today it would be a tourist attraction, a grass-roots precursor to the new ecological architecture of Australia advocated by Glenn Murcutt and his followers, all light durable materials and air-flow, zinc alume and louvred glass, such as displayed in the Marika house built at Yirrkala up the Arnhem Land coast in 1991–94, a Sarawak-style 'long house' which takes 'to new limits the idea of a changeable shelter in symbiosis with … natural elements', making the inside outside.[5]

Roger marked his outsider status especially in his dress. Sometimes he wore next to nothing. In one photograph he squats down outside the pub with his friend Jack Mulholland in cut-off trousers and a bandana tied round his head, showing his mighty tanned shoulders. Others of the hermits went naked when there were no ladies around, or wore a lap-lap, as in the case of Harry Blumenthals: a form of identification with the Aboriginal men, who traditionally wore only a hair belt and pubic sheath. Other times Roger advocated a full cover of clothes to keep out the heat. 'Most days you'd see him coming down for water at our tap, wearing several layers of clothing topped off with a filthy old dressing gown,' recalls one patrol officer.[6] 'Keeps me cool,' explained Roger. He felt comfortable in a home-made tunic and sash, Grecian-style, and a fez or turban.

He had a thing about hats, a taste he shared with many Aboriginal people. Observers mention a tea-cosy and an old ticking pillow case with one corner pushed in. David Attenborough describes 'a strange peaked hat, in shape like a French legionnaire's kepi but made to his own design from pandanus fibres', apparently made by Biddy on Vanderlin Island. Roger would wear this military-style hat to greet incoming planes, as if he were a resident official. He had a predilection for antic impersonation. To Attenborough he looked like someone from a production of *Treasure Island* in which the costume designer had gone over the top. In most of the photographs Roger does look like something vaguely theatrical – a pirate, a guru, an Aboriginal elder or Spike Milligan. Some locals derisively called him 'Chid', after Sydney's pioneering Victorian sex and dress reformer William Chidley, who roamed the streets in a tunic denouncing aggression when he was not in the asylum or the jail. In one photograph, pensive with pandanus hat, Roger becomes a Renaissance artist's Saint Jerome. For a man who had turned his back on society, Roger enjoyed playing with its masks and accoutrements, behaving at times like a lapsed dandy. A friend recalled a first sight of him stepping out of a coach at a country race meeting in patent leather shoes with an exaggerated sense of occasion as he came to try his luck on the horses.

The image he adopted sheds light on the role he lived out as a hermit. The comparison with Saint Jerome is not entirely fanciful. Of course there were people around, including his wife, but it sometimes must have seemed like a wilderness, where birds and beasts provided much of the company. Being a hermit was, in any case, an inward vocation, a spiritual calling. In stripping life to its bare essentials the hermit comes closer to God or wisdom. In Buddhism the archetype is Bodhidharma, who sat facing a wall for nine years, literally turning his back on the world but also on his own incarnation as a moving, acting body. The classic Christian example is Saint Jerome, who sought the desert, living naked in a cave with a lion lying down beside him, but always with pen and ink. He is typically shown contemplating a skull, the baldness of which matches his own, an old man facing death with emaciated virility. Roger looks old in his photographs, weathered by his life out of doors, his features doughy, his drinker's eyes lost in their pouches, turned to inner space. The photographs date from his later life, but Roger seems always to have been old, walking away from a childhood and youth of suffering.

Then there are the books. Both Roger and Saint Jerome were men of letters, their minds taut with words. In paintings of Jerome his stripped skin, like a blank parchment, suggests mental labour. He worked on the transition from classical philosophy to Christian belief, a cross-cultural project for which this angry, restless man centuries later became a patron saint of the Renaissance, a harbinger of the secular humanism that could be released from within religiosity. As a hermit, Saint Jerome was free to contemplate universal truths that could be carried from one language to another – as he did in reworking the Latin Old Testament – or converted from one place and system of thought to another without changing their essence. That was something that Roger Jose would have understood, because it was something he lived out in his own humble way.

A rhetorical flourish, rippling with irony, is found in the

large clear cursive of Roger's correspondence with his superiors. When he repaired the road to Anthony Lagoon, he wrote: 'While the Roman engineers who built so well for Julius Caesar would perhaps not regard it as a first-class highway, I feel confident that, were they able to make an inspection, I would be allowed to keep my head.' He was sent a cheque for £300 and returned it, asking that it be reduced to £102 so that he would fall below the income tax threshold.

Borroloola was supposed to be a place where money didn't matter. It was a kind of commune, operating, like some rural communities today, on a barter system. 'It was almost completely reduced to tribal level,' writes George Farwell. 'Since there were no wages, no floating money, men had to exchange what goods they had … The blacks, too, were adept at this kind of trading. There were plenty of fish in the river; huge barramundi, cod, and bream. They sold them for sticks of tobacco, flour, or tea.'[7] Roger Jose was a middleman for Aboriginal people in this trade, exchanging such items as tobacco, fishing line, hair oil and combs for dugong meat and Aboriginal artefacts.[8] In other ways, bush products came to substitute for things there was not always opportunity to buy: ant honey for sugar, *munja* (cycad palm nuts) for flour, lemongrass for tea. It was a two-way process of adaptation. Today car bodies are cut up for spears, and tappet rods from wrecked Toyotas for harpoon lines.

Politics was a topic of conversation for the local whitefellas, who tended towards radical views, conscious that their community was an experiment. One man, who had three sons with his Aboriginal spouse, named them Lenin, Trotsky and Stalin. Bill Harney writes in a slight malapropism that in Borroloola 'we had a totalitarian spot before we had ever heard of the word. No banks here, only the banks of the river.'[9] Roger Jose was as radical as any of them, a symbol of the anti-materialism on which Borroloola prided itself. His views are summed up in the aphorism he made his own, still pinned up on walls in the town: 'Man's greatness is the fewness of his needs.'

The hermits of Borroloola were existentialists, hippies, anti-racists and anti-consumerists before their time. That's what young journalists such as David Attenborough travelled to see in the 1950s and 1960s. Richard Baker notes that 'while European observers tended to be critical of Borroloola's "no-hopers" for "going Aboriginal", the [Aboriginal people] were appreciative of the way these men fitted in with their society'. Ted Egan insists that 'something should be said about the types of white people that were in the [Borroloola] region, because it's sort of dead-beat no-hoper stuff and the dead-beat no-hoper people were prepared to roll along with the punches and blend into the Aboriginal thing ... it wasn't rich station owner-managers, it was dead-beats and deros and fortunately a lot of them were benign dead-beats and deros who had read [...] books ...'[10] Those eccentric characters achieved a degree of harmonious, experimental co-existence that was impossible elsewhere. Roger Jose stands for that achievement.

The most striking example of how Roger Jose crossed over is the story of Sister Ruth Heathcock's journey to help a dying man on a cattle station along the coast. Ruth was the policeman's wife. Her husband was away when a message was brought by an Aboriginal man who had footwalked 60 kilometres in 36 hours to say that Horace Foster had shot himself in the leg. It was the Wet of 1941 and the Flying Doctor was called, but the plane couldn't land at Foster's camp in the bad weather. The only way the nursing sister could reach him was to go by canoe, down the McArthur River, threading through mangrove swamps and coastal channels along the shore and then up the Wearyan River to Manangoora station, over 100 kilometres in stormy weather. Roger Jose told her it could be done – he had done the journey in better conditions – but it would not be easy. Encouraged by this she set off, with Roger and his wife Maggie and two Aboriginal assistants. The voyage took three days and nights of high drama. They arrived in time to comfort Horace Foster but he was beyond saving.

Tony Roberts is an amateur historian who has devoted half his life to the study of Borroloola. He has pieced together every detail of this remarkable story and its consequences. Roberts found Borroloola 25 years ago through an interest in Australia's wild frontier. When he researched the town he discovered to his astonishment that Charlie Havey, who was the storekeeper and a decent Justice of the Peace there for many years, happened to be his great-grandfather's brother.

Roberts grew up in Adelaide like me and his family remember a smartly dressed relative from somewhere up north making rare appearances. Uncle Charlie was another black sheep, one of the more distinguished hermits. This piece of kismet drew Roberts deeper and deeper into oral history and the archives. He has retired to a mountaintop on the south coast of New South Wales to prepare his comprehensive store of information for publication – the area's first major history, to be entitled *Rough Justice: Old Days in Borroloola.* In that cool steep environment, about as different as can be from the Gulf, the historian has adopted another form of the hermit's life. He has generously shared many of his stories with me, his Borroloola cousin several times removed, including all about Roger Jose's presence in the attempt to rescue Horace Foster (whose sister, incidentally, was a literary critic in Adelaide).

When Ernestine Hill first tells the story in *Walkabout* in 1945, she describes Ruth Heathcock as accompanied by 'two white men and three blacks', but does not name them. When Ruth's own account was compiled in a book called *Sister Ruth* it was even more vividly fictionalised. Its worthy message is that 'in the whole of this vast territory, the Aborigine was in every sense of the word the key person, irrespective of sex ... such glory as exists shall go to [those] humble, unwept and unsung helpers'.[11] In a chapter called 'The Samaritans' Ruth sets off by canoe with Bessie, her house girl, and the tracker, Jupiter, with Maggie and her husband, Roger – all of whom are presented as Aboriginal people. She is confident that 'if her natives said it could be done – it could be done!' The trip was a marathon, with Roger guiding them through treacherous waters. 'Wielded with what seemed magical skill, Roger fended off submerged logs, masses of tenacious debris and uprooted trees … Hour after hour, the bronze, whipcord muscled figure deftly grappled with those obstacles …' Thoughts fly to Horace Foster, lying in his agony but still alive. 'They knew this, too – these black mystics!' The first night passes uncomfortably and the day begins with an encounter with a crocodile that lifts the canoe out of the water, a 'monster … carrying in its jaws the carcass of a goat, whose twisted horns [were] poised above the great jaws …' For the next night's camp they wade ashore through barking crocodiles and sea snakes, 'all coming up the estuary for mating and … deadliest and most aggressive … at this particular time'. The young nurse's imagination becomes feverish, but she holds the pole, the 'big fella waddy' that Jupiter extends to her as a lifeline. She does not disgrace herself. She is revived by hot tea and grilled fish, and a cigarette. '"Heavens! She was a primitive! Who cared?" she thought', looking gratefully at the four people who were 'using their marvellous knowledge … to help her'.

They set off again and the next problem is the eddying currents in a stretch of water called Crooked River, but Roger steers them through. Then, reaching the estuary, they are at risk of shark attack. In sheer exhaustion they think of giving up.

Philosophically, Roger lit his pipe and his dark eyes regarded Ruth with unmistakable pity.

He was a well-educated man, as natives go, having lived with white pioneers as a trusted servant for many years. Notwithstanding this, however, he had roamed this Gulf area from childhood and was as familiar with the great rivers and swamps as a civilised child knows his suburb in a great city. He was a Christian, and legally married. Legally from the point of view of the whites, that was, of course. His wife was his correct consort from a tribal standpoint also. He was a fine, compassionate and chivalrous man by anybody's standards – black or white – and innately a gentleman … Without hesitation, unpaid and the journey not really their concern, they, desiring no recompense, had placed their lives at her disposal … Much of a mystic herself, Sister Ruth realised the sublimity and sacrificial quality of their act.

'My Missus, I go with you,' says Roger, echoing the Biblical Ruth's words of devotion to Naomi, across race and culture: 'Whither you go, I will go.'

Ruth comes to trust unconditionally in the skill of Roger and the others, even as the canoe presses close to the waterline through infested swamps. 'These folk had twenty thousand years or so of experience behind them,' she thinks. 'If the white races lasted as long, they might be able to manage their affairs as competently.' She never lets on that her character Roger is based on a white man. As the canoe drifts through an infernal underwater world of writhing monster snakes, Ruth sees an apparition, a visitant's golden hands and smiling face, a bizarre childhood memory of a naval officer's 'pale gold hands' coming to sort out her troubles. She knows they will make it. More storms, more sharks, and the vision appears again, this time shared with her Aboriginal companions, of a protective Christ-like helmsman: 'What wonderful proof, she thought, of the gift of second sight the Australian Aboriginal had, a gift so rare in white folk.' Ruth acknowledges both her supernatural help and her Aboriginal help. She 'impulsively grasped Roger's hand in gratitude … and his fine face melted in unmistakable tenderness' as he replied in 'his own tongue' with the words: 'the Mother Goddess keeps her'.

Ruth enters into a final reverie: 'What a poor opinion the white people of the cities had of the Aboriginal … These people of hers were black without but white within. With what justice might the opposite be said of the white races … Hope awoke afresh as she heard the steady chanting of her crew as they drove the canoe past the last high point of land and edged into the quiet channel. At last!' They had made it, and Horace Foster was still alive.

Purple prose and mystical fantasy infuse this account of a journey that was probably not quite as hair-raising as it is made to seem. Roger, a skilled bushman, a speaker of Aboriginal language, a hero of superhuman capacities, is the saviour. He is an Aboriginal man, because that suited Ruth Heathcock's proselytising purposes, and perhaps also because there was something problematic about going into the wilds for three days and nights with a white no-hoper like Roger Jose. For Roger's virtues to be evoked, he had to be Aboriginal. In government correspondence about the Member of the British Empire award that Ruth Heathcock alone was given in 1946, for her dedication and courage in undertaking this voyage, mention is made of a 'half-caste' who had assisted – code for Roger Jose.

One of Roger's more remarkable performances was his consumption of strychnine, demonstrating the Aztec principle that a little of what can kill you will stimulate you to greater health. Ted Egan, who was a young welfare officer in the late 1950s, remembered Borroloola as 'a real sitdown place', in Aboriginal idiom, where people laughed a lot. He was taken with Roger and his stories, and he preferred the telegrams that Roger sent out through his office to those of the missionaries: 'This sort of thing: "PLEASE SEND SPUDS ONIONS TOBACCO SIX OLD SOLDIER", being the preferred brand of rum, as opposed to this sort of thing: "HAPPY BIRTHDAY CORINTHIANS 1:4 HOPE MOTHER WELL SEE YOU SOON EPHESIANS 6"'. One day Egan asked Roger if the strychnine story was true. 'You're welcome to watch,' said Roger and they proceeded to the airstrip. '"You can't run the risk of hitting your head on a tree when you take this stuff … stand back."' … He opened the bottle, poured and swallowed a teaspoonful of strychnine, shook his head a couple of times, hung on to the backs of his legs in a squat for a moment, and then came over to me. He took my hand, and put it on his heart. *Ptoom. Ptoom. Ptoom.* "Get a load of that, son.'"[12]

Egan was impressed. Whatever was in that bottle was potent, or it was a good act. Ted Egan, later in life a wonderful performer himself, added to the legend of Roger Jose with a song:

Roger Jose lived terrible close
To a place called Borroloola
Folks called Roger an old Death Adder
But don't let that fact foolya ...

He went to gaol a couple of times
But you'd hardly call the reasons crimes
Shared with a black man a bottle of drink
And did six months in the local clink.

On another occasion he got in strife
Just for living with his Aboriginal wife.
Didn't worry Roger, happy was he
Came back to Borroloola when he was free ...

In another place, another age
Roger would have been treated like a sage
Plato and Socrates, out at the Loo
Would probably be called Death Adders too ...

He had a long grey beard and a glittering eye
But Roger never, ever worked for a boss
A long grey beard and a glittering eye
But he wouldn't have shot the albatross.

And Roger liked to drink a little metho with his dinner
A spoonful of strychnine was certainly a winner
A rum and a johnny cake served for his tea
And he said Borroloola is the place for me.[13]

Roger Jose was the last custodian of the Borroloola library. He is said to have read all of its books in the spirit of a voracious autodidact, 'from top right to bottom left'. The library was extant when Roger Jose arrived in Borroloola in 1916 and may have been one of the things that attracted him there. The quality of the books Roger read was not always as exalted as those attributed to him in reminiscences after he died: Homer, Marcus Aurelius, Shakespeare and English poets of the eighteenth and nineteenth centuries. But those were the ones from which he absorbed words and sentiments into his own conversation. In fact they were the stuff of an Edwardian young man's education, along with the Bible, which was a central book for Roger. A little Latin went a long way too.

Roger enjoyed words on his tongue, often with subversive mimicry, his register ranging from North Australian Kriol to Shakespearean pastiche. Explaining a diet of bush tucker when killing cattle was a crime, he would speak like a stage poacher, 'I would fain crave my master's oxen, but I can't get 'em. Thus I am compelled to pursue the elusive marsupial.' His conversation was a mélange of literary quotation, often mangled, with names mispronounced, which made him and the other hermits an easy butt of humour for visiting journalists.

'You hear them arguing out "Thuky-dides" and "Themistockles" by the billabong,' wrote Ernestine Hill. 'Bunyan preaches and Shelley sings under a milkwood tree.' A patrol officer recalls that Roger pronounced Descartes as 'Dezcartays'. When there was no one else to talk to, Roger talked to himself. 'I find it's nice to talk to somebody intelligent every now and again,' he explained.[14]

Many of these comments come from the last years of Roger's life when his mood was low and his mind fading. The knowledge that he had absorbed appears as fragments shored against his ruin. He is like Winnie in Samuel Beckett's play *Happy Days* nudging a lapsed mind for literary quotations: 'What is that unforgettable line?' The language was starting to break down. Roger may have beaten the white ants to those books, ingesting them into his mind rather than his stomach, but now his mind was an image of that decomposing library, turned into oral form and conveyed to passers-by. In his head was a word-world that shrank in the last years to utterances of bald wisdom. He became a sage.

There are differing views of his spiritual persuasion. He was not a Christian and he was dismissive of missionary efforts to convert Aboriginal people from their own traditions to Christian belief. 'Rice Christians' he called such converts, adopting the term used in China for those who accepted

Christianity in exchange for a bowl of rice. Yet he donated iron to help build a mission school in Borroloola because he believed in education. He questioned the Bible, knowing it well enough to twist missionaries into knots in debate. He was incensed when modernisers interfered with the language of the old King James version. Sometimes he referred to himself as a Jew. His life had been an attempt to rid himself of the trappings of civilisation, the 'garbage that no nomad needs', which included unwarranted intellectual ideas. Yet he held on to an abstract belief in a supreme power. Some visitors made the inevitable comparison with Diogenes, the ancient Greek Cynic philosopher who lived in a tub. But Roger Jose was anti-materialistic in a different way, with an emphasis on quietism, appreciating the value of the passing moment and the simple life. He was 'content with his abundance of nothing, as long as it included freedom, peace, and the solitude necessary for meditation,' wrote Douglas Lockwood, who was sincerely impressed by his wisdom. When David Attenborough asked him what was the most important thing in life, Roger replied, 'Peace.'

His favourite poet was Thomas Gray. The cadences in which the famous elegy celebrates quiet, timeless lives no doubt resonated for him:

> Far from the madding Crowd's ignoble Strife,
> Their sober Wishes never learn'd to stray;
> Along the cool sequester'd Vale of Life
> They kept the noiseless Tenor of their Way.

Gray, gay and melancholic, was a scholar of tender sensibility and rarefied mind. Perhaps Roger felt a kinship.

He also loved *The Rubaiyat of Omar Khayyam*, Edward Fitzgerald's transmogrification of Sufi wisdom into high Victorian verse, first published in 1859. In plangent rhythms Old Omar sang the evanescence of life, the transience of the physical world, the powerlessness of humanity in the face of implacable, impersonal destiny. The poem celebrates the plenitude of the moment, the immediate emotional connection, the pleasure of simple needs satisfied, as in the familiar stanza with which Roger surely identified:

Here with a Loaf of Bread beneath the Bough,
A Flask of Wine, a Book of verse – and Thou
  Beside me singing in the Wilderness –
And Wilderness is Paradise enow.

Those were words that Beckett's Winnie could only grope for. Roger liked to quote Old Omar to his visitors from memory. Almost any stanza carried the message of a man who had managed to turn round a world he did not find conducive, to find his own purer, more contented life, close to earth, sky and water, closer to a freed humanity.

Old Omar was a mask for Roger Jose, as it was for Edward Fitzgerald, another kind of hermit who preferred to stay at home in Suffolk with his parrot. Roger was an angry man, prone to occasional outbursts, cunning or blunt in self-defence. How much did he struggle to find the peace he valued? He covered his tracks. Who was Roger Jose and where did he come from? To track him I need to look inside his head, interpreting affinities and contexts along with the biographical record and the sometimes fanciful witness that others bring. Why was he in Borroloola? *Why am I here?* He must have asked these questions of himself before he floated away on rum and Old Omar's riddling words:

> Into this Universe, and *why* not knowing,
> Nor *whence*, like Water willy-nilly flowing:
>   And out of it, as Wind along the Waste,
> I know not *whither*, willy-nilly blowing.
>
> What, without asking, hither hurried *whence?*
> And, without asking, *whither* hurried hence!
>   Another and another Cup to drown
> The Memory of this Impertinence!

Roger Jose seldom spoke of his family or the painful circumstances that had sent him out on the road at 17. The puzzle is that there is no record of his birth or of anything about him before he reached Borroloola in 1916. On both his first and second marriage certificates his place of birth is given as Picton, New South Wales, a small town outside Sydney. From the age he gave he was born in 1895 or 1896. But on his death certificate Goodna, Queensland, appears tentatively as his birthplace, which, along with nearby Boonah, is where some people remember him as coming from, closer to Cunnamulla, where he is supposed to have been before Borroloola. On the 1926 marriage certificate T. A. E. Jose appears as the groom's father, with no mother's name given. On the second marriage certificate in 1957 Thirza Jose appears as the groom's mother. Roger told a friend in Borroloola that his mother was a single woman. It may be that some fudging went on when T. A. E. Jose (Thirza?) was placed in the paternal column. But the genealogical records produce no Thirza Jose, and no Thirza who is a mother to anyone called Roger. In Picton there was an unmarried Thirza Morris who had a daughter in 1892. The birth was assisted by a nurse called Charlotte Catt. Of Thirza we know nothing more except that she could write, unlike many people in that rural area, and she lived to a good age. Her family probably came from Ireland. The birth of an unnamed male Morris was registered in 1894, perhaps by another member of Thirza's family. The boy might have been hers. That same year Thirza married John Catt, the nurse's kinsman, in a double wedding in which another Catt woman married another man called John. They were all neighbours along the Wollondilly River beyond Camden. In 1896 Thirza had her next child, a boy registered as Ashwin Clive Catt. Could that boy have turned into Roger Jose? It's possible if a Jose rather than John Catt was his biological father, or if, most likely through his mother, he had some other close association with a Jose, perhaps as an adoptive father. Thirza's husband John died in 1905, predeceasing her by more than 30 years. Of their boy under his registered name there is no further record, suggesting that at least the child did not die in infancy.

Roger claimed to be connected to the historian Arthur Jose. The story has stuck. Roger's relationship with Arthur varies according to different reports and sometimes the connection is made through Arthur's younger brother, Herbert Jose, who was my great-grandfather and a missionary in China from 1891 to 1899. If Roger was born in 1896, it requires a degree of ingenuity to postulate that his father was Herbert Jose in China. Surely Picton was not misheard for Peking? By the 1950s my great-grandfather was Anglican Dean of Adelaide, prominent in public life and something of an institution. If they came from South Australia, travellers through Borroloola are likely to have known of him. When they talked to Roger, the connection must have tickled their fancy, a study in the contrasting paths that family members can follow. It would probably have appealed to Roger too, who did not have much time for missionaries or the church. He let the story run.

There's an outside possibility, if Roger was Arthur's nephew, that his father was the third Jose brother, Aubrey. He was a wanderer too. Did Aubrey turn up in Australia a few years in advance of 1901, when he took the job of tutor to the governor's children, first in Western Australia, then in South Australia where the governor was Hallam Tennyson, son of Alfred, Lord Tennyson? That Jose is remembered for his laziness and his sporting talent. 'I have been dreadfully overworked & overstrained, Lady Tennyson,' the young man complained to his employer, who said he was 'very tall & not good-looking, but a very bright happy dear face'. When he did teach, he taught his charges well. As a child, Stella Bowen – the artist, and lover of Ford Madox Ford – played at Government House and had a different perspective when she recalled 'the perpetual click of bat on ball as Mr Jose, the handsome and muscular tutor in holy orders, bowled endlessly to Lionel Tennyson, already destined to become a star cricketer'.[15]

The three Jose brothers, all educated at Clifton College, Bristol and at Oxford, sought their fortunes in Australia because their father, William Wilberforce Jose, had lost out in a family struggle over money back home. The spoils had gone to another branch of the family, money that came originally from the Virginia tobacco trade. The Joses had shipped tobacco, harvested by black slaves, to Bristol where it was sold to firms such as W. D. & H. O. Wills. But William Wilberforce Jose's father, a mayor of Bristol, was a committed abolitionist, as suggested by the name he gave his first son, and sought to remove the taint of that evil trade through good works. He diversified into bricks. In the next generation, however, any proceeds were diverted from the offspring of his first marriage in favour of his second wife's children. Then the family firm collapsed.

Arthur Wilberforce Jose (1863–1934) left Oxford for Australia after a breakdown in 1882. When the family fortunes failed, he did not go back. At first he lived in the bush, working as a casual labourer, a teacher and a lawyer, before he established himself as a man of letters. He taught in Bathurst in rural New South Wales from 1885 to 1887 and was in Sydney after that. From 1894 to 1899 he ran the University of Sydney Extension Scheme, providing advanced education to country men and women. He was a travelling lecturer, a single man.

In *The Romantic Nineties*, his most influential book, he fondly remembers that wandering decade:

> 'You aren't going to bed yet,' some man would say. 'Come along and have a drink . . .' And one went, and for the next two hours (bar discipline wasn't strict in the country, and quite probably the local policeman was one of the company) the lecture was thrashed out and argued over and contradicted and confronted with every man's personal experience and beliefs until the lecturer felt that whatever had survived such a winnowing must be irrefutable truth ... 'I just had to meet you, Mr Jose! You were just wonderful, and I enjoyed your lecture so much! All the time you were talking I was sitting there saying to myself, "Why, the man's a GENIUS! Everything he says is just what I've been thinking for the last four years."'[16]

In 1895 Arthur Jose lectured in Camden on the topic 'Leaders of Modern Thought'. Around that time was the boy born, most likely in nearby Picton, who would become Roger Jose? Arthur visited Camden regularly until 1899 to lecture on such topics as 'Shakespeare', 'Darwin and His Work' and 'The Building of Australia'. In *Two Awheel and Some Others Afoot in Australia*, a book of sketches he

George Lambert, Arthur Wilberforce Jose, *1895*

published in 1903, Arthur waxes lyrical about Picton, Camden and the Wollondilly vales. He knew them in an impecunious, itinerant time of his life, he notes, when he had only 'an old Irishman' to help him.[17]

Is it possible that he had an interest in Thirza and her son? In an avuncular way he may have helped with the boy's education, especially after the death of Thirza's husband. *Two Awheel* was illustrated by Arthur's friend, the artist George Lambert. In 1905, at the age of 42, Arthur married Lambert's wife's sister. It was a marriage up and Arthur's father-in-law was wary of him. The situation may have been such that Arthur turned his back on Thirza, who was widowed in the same year, and on her son. But the boy was prepared for life with an educated accent and a taste for reading and writing.

Arthur Jose left Sydney for South Africa, India and London in 1899, before returning in 1904 with the plum job of Australia correspondent for the world's most powerful newspaper, the London *Times*. From then until 1915 he sent back long reports, advocating an emergent Australian nationhood within the embrace of the British Empire, often taking controversial positions in relation to local politics and received views back in Britain. He was not always popular or comfortable in such an influential posting. As his *Times* colleague in China is remembered as 'Morrison of Peking', Arthur might be known as 'Jose of Sydney', since Sydney rather than Melbourne, then Australia's capital, was his beat. He received a gracious tribute in the first *Dictionary of Australian Biography* as 'one of the best Australians ever … educated in England', a phrase subsequently construed to question the roots of his Australian nationalism.[18] He often backed the wrong horse.

Arthur Jose was independent-minded even to his own detriment. He didn't care about money. He sometimes comes across as arrogant, a queer fish with quick wits and a good memory. In a backhanded compliment one friend called him 'universally informative'.[19] He sounds like Roger in so many ways, or Roger sounds like him. But Arthur Jose was never a big enough fish for Roger to have claimed him merely in a wishful identification with no basis in fact. If Arthur Jose was a presence in the life of Thirza and her child and let them down, it would explain Roger's rejection of the world Arthur represented.

Arthur advocated character in the service of building the nation and the English-speaking people. He had been educated in the Arnoldian traditions of Clifton College, Bristol. When he first came to Australia, he taught at All Saints' Bathurst, where Edwin Bean, a friend from Clifton, was headmaster. Bean's son Charles, Arthur's pupil, became the esteemed military historian C. E. W. Bean. The young Bean saw the call of Australian troops to war in 1915 as an opportunity for the forging of Australian manhood in blood. Arthur, too old to fight, worked as an intelligence officer during that war, and later, commissioned by his former student, wrote the history of the Royal Australian Navy. Roger turned his back on all that.

What happened to his mother? There's another Thirza, or Thurza, initials T. A., surname New, who lived near the town of Inverell, halfway between Picton, New South Wales, and Cunnamulla, Queensland. Thurza was an unusual Hebrew name. Her mother was Thurza too, her father Emanuel, a farmer originally from Dorset. She was born in 1878 and seems not to have married until 1929. She could have met Arthur Jose when he lectured in the Inverell area in the 1890s. If she fell pregnant, she may have gone to New relatives at Picton for the birth. If she was Roger's mother, she would have been about 18 when she bore him. The baby may have stayed in Picton to be raised. It's a speculation, I admit, to fit the trail of information Roger left behind. Whoever his mother was and whoever brought him up, the time came when he set out on his own, a young man and a bastard, at least in his own mind, carrying troubling memories in the name he used.

Ernestine Hill, to whom Roger confided his story, refrains from identifying him by name in her account of the Borroloola eccentrics. As a woman alone and a professional writer she may have been betraying a discreet sympathy for Arthur, a fellow hack. Hill understood the stigma of falling from grace. A distant press baron was rumoured to be the father of her son.[20]

In 1916, the year Roger walked to Borroloola, many other young men were enlisting to fight the Germans and the Turks. There was intense pressure to do so on those who saw themselves as the heirs to Empire, the sons of property owners and the aspiring middle classes, mostly of British descent and Protestant convictions. Irish Catholic working-class young men were more likely to resist, as were those of other creeds or who fitted nowhere, even if it meant enduring opprobrium and going it alone. Later in life Roger Jose showed a contempt for war and the economic system that sustains it, whether in relation to black–white conflict or militarism in Europe and Asia. He was a pacifist. As a young man he would have had the clarity of intellect to think his own way through what was happening and to make his own decision. He headed for a place that was as far away from it all as he could go.

There he found the library Borroloola was famous for, and an environment where he could live by his own hands, free, without ties, at a distance from the crowded places of the world and as close to Aboriginal people as he wanted to be. Later he would find the woman, Maggie, who could provide a lasting attachment, a love that would not abandon, and with her he would make hearth and home in his own wandering way.

VII

THE FEWNESS OF THEIR WANTS

The road from Borroloola heads east across rising rivers and the many lesser channels that skitter from the Tableland into the Gulf. It's less a road than a gravel scrape. In the Wet an hour of tropical rain lathers the dust into a sticky chowder. Water hides potholes the size of bathtubs. People make new tracks on the edges to avoid the slop in the middle and the road spreads. The route passes by Wollogorang station on the Northern Territory side of the border and Westmoreland station on the Queensland side before reaching Hell's Gate. Abandon hope, all ye who enter! I'm approaching from the other side.

The world of Roger Jose is long gone. I'm looking for its legacy. He lived through situations that have given rise to today's angry struggles in this part of the world. The past slouches into the present, spreading out along the coast. Roger must have seen what was happening. That larger story moves me on.

My friend Bob is back home working on his novel. The season has changed. No one is flying long distance from New

York just at the moment. My travelling companion now is a Garawa man. He's too young to have known Roger Jose but he has heard the stories and is happy to regard me as some sort of nephew. He knows his own culture's law too, and disapproves of those who speak of it too easily. He's an expert on country, particularly on how to burn to keep it healthy and full of life. He tells me that it will be time to burn as soon as this Wet ends.

Roger's aphorism about the 'fewness of man's needs' works with a terrible irony as a motto for how settler Australia has treated the original inhabitants of the Great South Land: the fewness of their wants, rights and deserts. From the moment Britain possessed the country as *terra nullius*, on the assumption that there was no one with whom to settle things legally, as little as possible was given. Aboriginal populations were rendered invisible, made to disappear, driven off their lands as if they could live on air, rounded up, put on rations, under protection, in camps, given alcohol, made servants, targeted for 'breeding out', assimilated, denied. 'Pay the rent,' demand contemporary activists, but the rent has been kept low, replaced by welfare that, however well-intentioned, has too often betrayed a tragic incomprehension of who Aboriginal people are and what they want.

'Evidently settlement must be delayed until the work of extermination is complete – a consummation of which there is no present prospect – or until some more rational and humane method of dealing with the blacks is adopted,' editorialised *The Queenslander* over a century ago.[1] One method after another has been tried, with no shortage of passionate indignation as successive 'remedies' failed. But settlement was never delayed.

In the late 1960s the courts awarded equal wages to Aboriginal workers in the cattle industry. An unintended consequence was that many stockmen and their families were moved off the cattle stations, often their traditional country, where they had lived, working seasonally in return for rations. The stations preferred white workers if they had to pay them a living wage. Aboriginal people were moved into meagre settlements or the fringes of towns, were put on welfare and allowed to buy grog. Little consideration was given to the effect of unearned money on people's long-term self-respect, especially for men in their prime, nor on where the money went. People scrambled by one system were dumped into another. Between 1967 and 1974 the population of Borroloola swelled from 200 to 1,200 and alcohol became a problem. The situation was the same all across the north.

I got into trouble once for writing that Aboriginal issues were therapy issues for non-indigenous Australians.[2] I was thought to be trivialising matters when, on the contrary, I meant to imply that the issues live inside all of us, inseparable from us. That is why we bristle when we are told to shut up and listen for a change.

The worst thing is that Aboriginal Australia is so often thought of as a problem to be solved. Hidden in this thinking is an unstated desire for a final solution, an aversion to the complicated, dynamic continuance of living peoples. Xavier

Herbert put it with provocative simplicity: 'There is NO Solution to the Aborigines' Problem.' Get used to it, he meant. Contemporary Aboriginal communities complain about the unending efforts of policy-makers and assorted do-gooders on their behalf. 'We live in a goldfish bowl,' says one woman. During the 1990s Decade of Reconciliation, non-Aboriginal Australians were encouraged to make friends with indigenous people, who comprise about two and a half per cent of the overall population. Reconciliation would mean that each Aboriginal person has to make 40 new non-Aboriginal friends. No wonder someone reacts by protesting, 'Why can't they leave us alone?'

My other travelling companion is an old book. Before I left home a copy of Alejo Carpentier's *The Lost Steps* surfaced from the back of my bookshelf, packed and unpacked for 25 years. Unbelievably the Cuban novelist is almost entirely out of print. I was glad to see the burgundy hardback again. It bounces around on the seat. Carpentier presses against exclusion in that novel as his narrator presses up the Orinoco River into deepest jungle, speaking for atavistic people who have kept the outside world out at all costs. They face 'the worst of all tyrannies,' he says, 'that exercised by those who love over the person who does not want to be loved …'[3] I mark the passage in my foxed old edition.

Hell's Gate marked the outer limit of police protection for travellers moving across from south-eastern Australia in the last decades of the nineteenth century. Protection was offered by the Native Police, a notorious force of co-opted Aboriginal men, sent from elsewhere to safeguard settlers in this remote country, clearing the way for cattle. They were black mercenaries under white command, protecting white people against other blacks. In aggressively 'dispersing' and 'quietening' the local Aboriginal people, the Native Police carried out some of the bloodiest acts of frontier violence.

In her harrowing account of the conquest of pastoral lands in Queensland – in part the story of her own family – the poet Judith Wright explains that the Native Police's 'discreet reports of "dispersals" really meant that men and women had been shot and tomahawked, all the children killed, and the lot left to be eaten by native dogs. The black troopers were mere slaves and automata of murder, unable to leave the service, shot without mercy if they deserted … Public opinion in Queensland encouraged these horrors and called for blood and more blood.'[4] Wright describes the 1860s and 1870s when the 'Queensland government could count on silence, if not on outright support, for the policy of expulsion [of Aboriginals] on which it had embarked', including from the government back in Britain, since 'the livestock which went out to occupy the new runs was bought largely with British loans'.

A gap in the escarpment made Hell's Gate a natural ambush site. Interlopers found themselves on their own in an unpoliced shadowland between jurisdictions. Conquest was provisional there – perhaps still is. The country's wildness, its unvisited islands, inaccessible cliffs and caves and extremes of climate, protected traditional culture from outsiders and gave scope to continuing Aboriginal resistance. Violent conflict between indigenous people and invaders in the border zone occurred within the span of handed-down memory.

More than 200 kilometres east on the Queensland side of Hell's Gate is Burketown. It was a busy little port with four hotels and a customs house when Bill Harney shipped off to war there in 1915. Like Borroloola on the Territory side, Burketown marked the outer limit of civilisation, in that tattered euphemism. Between the two towns was a fiercely contested land, populated, in imperialist eyes, by the wrong people. Is that what Banjo Paterson meant in his dreary 1897 poem 'By the Grey Gulf-Water'? He was writing to promote the area, but I read his lines as a grimace of disgust:

> A great grey chaos – a land half made,
>   Where endless space is and no life stirreth;
> There the soul of man will recoil afraid
>   From the sphinx-like visage that Nature weareth.

Oral accounts speak of 'atrocities by native police' that 'include smashing children against trees and rocks "so their brains came out" and, after shootings, cutting up bodies, burning bodies, and hanging up parts of corpses in trees where other Aborigines would later find them. People were often shot at daybreak in camp.'[5] At Westmoreland station black–white revenge killings took place in 1884, bequeathing the name Massacre Inlet where a creek flows into the sea and people were hunted down and shot. At Wollogorang in 1897, a party of white men from the station attacked a group of Aboriginal people holding a ceremony, firing on many of them. The last shooting of an Aboriginal by a European in armed conflict in the region happened in 1943. Some would say that such coercive violence persists covertly into the present.

It was at Wollogorang nearly a hundred years later, in 1991, that a young station hand first started reading the Koran. He was a teenage kid escaping the oppressive boredom of Adelaide suburbia, and an ace rider in the Borroloola rodeo. David Hicks became a mercenary and converted to Islam while fighting with the Kosovo Liberation Army. He went on to fight in Afghanistan, where he was caught and handed over to the United States with the prospect of being tried for treason. At the time of writing he sits in Camp X-Ray at Guantanamo Bay, Cuba.

'[Hicksy] was no drama,' remembers his boss at Wollogorang station, 'just another young fella looking for a job, a roof over his head and a feed. Them sort of blokes just drift in and out of this country, the Gulf Country.'[6] Like many a wandering soul before him, many a traitor to convention, Hicks was attracted to wild country and wild time. For this particular militant wanderer for hire, Australia's Gulf was not far enough. He dressed up the romance of violence with the mystique of alternative religion and set off to find a war. He read Buddhist writings and the Dead Sea Scrolls, and sought instruction in Aboriginal spirituality from his rodeo-riding mates. As a child he had been possessed by bad dreams and his parents had him exorcised by an Anglican priest. That turned him off Christianity for life. Once he had found Islam Hicks travelled on to the more famous Gulf of Arabia to fight for the Taliban against the infidel, who came to include his own countrymen.

How much did this semi-literate pumped-up army reject from South Australia understand? His loyal dad described him as Indiana Jones without an adventure. He retraced the path from the city of churches to the farthest shore, as legions of young men from Adelaide and everywhere else in Australia had done long before when they sailed for Gallipoli – for the sake of adventure as often as not, from which not all returned. Men like Bill Harney. Australians are prone to fighting other people's wars in foreign places, seldom discouraged by the cost. A couple of hundred Australian special troops have performed well in Afghanistan with the United States and her allies in the coalition against terrorism and al-Qaeda. Presumably those crack soldiers do understand what's going on. Unlike the hundreds of Australian mercenaries fighting around the world, Hicks did not manage to disappear. He has only become more visible, hunted by media cameras for a glimpse of the blue eyes that betrayed him as not a true Afghan fighter. The Australian government would like to wash its hands of him. The Foreign Minister, also from Adelaide as it happens, denounces Hicks as a 'complete foo', swallowing the final 'l' in the Adelaidean way.

Our conflicts at home have generally been more sugar-coated, seldom characterised in public as war. When I returned from the Gulf of Carpentaria I stumbled into a conference at the National Museum of Australia on how massacres of Aboriginal people should be presented in the media and to schoolchildren so as not to diminish pride in Australian achievements. Massacre discounting, if not outright denial, was in full swing among the academics and political advisers that day. The controversial suggestion that the National War Memorial in Canberra should commemorate those – black, white or brindle – who died on both sides of Australia's own frontier wars got pretty short shrift. It remains unfinished business.

David Hicks is a naïve militarist to Roger Jose's simple pacifist. Perhaps the choice depends on the times. The mavericks along the northern coasts were prepared to sit out the Japanese invasion, but there are crazies in their camps today armed to the hilt for when the Indonesians come down. War came close to this coast in December 1942 when an American B-24 Liberator called *Little Eva*, returning to base from a bombing mission in the south-west Pacific, lost its way in a storm and crash landed near Moonlight Creek between Borroloola and Burketown. Grady Gaston and three other airmen bailed out together and watched their plane burn in the distance. It was hot and wet and they had only four bars of chocolate between them. They managed to walk downstream to the Gulf where they mistakenly headed west. They covered 400 kilometres, swimming wild rivers, and found only an abandoned paperbark hut where they prayed and sang carols on Christmas Eve. His three comrades died but Grady Gaston, from Frisco City, Alabama, survived alone in the wild living on bush melons and cockles from the mud flats of the Gulf. He hung trees with shells inscribed 'I am alive' and still no one found him. Then after 141 days an Aboriginal man called Strike-a-light was riding along the beach on horseback and saw the desperate figure. 'My heart almost jumped out of me with joy at seeing a human being,' said Gaston. 'Poor bugger you,' said Strike-a-light. Gaston was fed on goat meat, milk and young bullock and an Australian army patrol hacked through from Borroloola to bring him in for recuperation. 'There wasn't a damn thing wrong with him other than loss of weight,' said his captain.[7]

The Yanyuwa people made a song out of the event, as they had of other milestones in their lives, associating it with the advent of military aircraft into their world:

> High up they are fighting
> In the east and the west …
> Here at Moonlight Creek
> The pilot fell from the sky …[8]

To perform the song men paint up with white stripes, laughing as they scissor off each other's nipple hair. The dancers make hats out of painted beer cartons and use the fluffy insides of disposable nappies as substitute for featherdown adornment. A plane is made on a timber frame covered with

Leonard Norman, Johnson Timothy and Horace Joe perform the Aeroplane Dance at Borroloola in 1993

leaves. At the end of the dance it burns, leaving only blackened sticks behind.

Roy Hammer performed the Aeroplane Dance in Darwin as part of the celebration of Australia's Federation in 2001. Proudly painted up, he marched with the Australian armed forces to commemorate the victory of the Allies in the Pacific. His people had obliged when white Australia asked.

In 1606, two centuries before Flinders, a Dutch captain called Willem Jansz visited the eastern side of the Gulf of Carpentaria in the *Duyfken* ('Little Dove') and became the first European to record details of any part of the Australian coast.

Just to get our bearings in time as well as space, let's recall that Shakespeare's *Macbeth* was first performed the same year, with its indelible warning that 'blood will have blood'. I went aboard a replica of the *Duyfken* when she visited Sydney Harbour as part of the millennium celebrations. She was round like a walnut shell, half the size of Captain Cook's *Endeavour*, no larger than a bus, with no standing room below deck and no designated sleeping quarters. The novices who volunteered to crew her must have come to know each other quite intimately as they traversed the waters between Australia and Indonesia in retracing the *Duyfken*'s original journey. I thought of the owl and the pussycat going to sea in a beautiful pea-green boat. The replica of the little ship was a carved, painted work of art.

The original *Duyfken* reached Cape Keerweer (meaning 'turn around') halfway down the coast of Cape York and turned back. An English trader who watched the battered ship return to the port of Banda in the Dutch East Indies noted that 'in sending their men on shore to entreat of trade, there were nine of them killed by the heathens'. The *Duyfken* had pulled into a river to replenish water and a fight ensued with the local Aboriginal people over women. Silas Wolmby, a Wik elder and descendant of those people, recalls the story as it has been handed down. 'This beautiful girl was standing near one of the Dutchmen. Her hair came all the way down her back. That Dutchman grabbed the girl. Right there, with the white hand on the black arm, there was trouble.' Wolmby's ancestor 'hit the Dutchman … the Dutchmen began firing their guns' and Wolmby's ancestor 'speared one man, then another … [and] burnt the rowboat'. The Dutch went on a retaliatory rampage, 'killing scores of unwitting people from a different clan'.[9]

So 'the first mob' of Europeans left their mark on the history of the continent. Other accounts suggest that perhaps the Wik ancestors loaned two wives to the Dutch sailors who kept them for too long. In the recreation of the Cape Keerweer encounter four centuries later, the forgiving Wik elder mentions that the girl at the heart of the conflict must have been very good-looking and perhaps stood too close to the Dutchman. 'Maybe she liked that fella?' he wickedly suggests.

The Dutch were looking for a route from their East Indies territories direct to the South Seas and America. In 1623 they sent Jan Carstensz from Ambon, or Amboyna, to follow up. It was the year after the infamous episode in which the Dutch governor of the island, van Speult, suspecting a conspiracy against his rule, tortured and put to death 10 Englishmen, half the English population who were trading there, along with nine Japanese and one Portuguese. The Dutch Governor-General in Batavia (Jakarta), the formidable Jan Pieterszoon Coen, who had supported his deputy's hostility towards the English, was recalled to Amsterdam by way of punishment for what had happened. The massacre at Amboyna outraged Stuart Britain and was remembered for the next half-century. In the train of compensation that followed the British turned their attention away from the East Indies, eventually wresting Manhattan from the Dutch in 1667. John Dryden wrote a crude propagandist tragedy about the massacre, *Amboyna, or the Cruelties of the Dutch to the English Merchants* (1673), in which Gabriel Towerson, the English leader, dies cursing Dutch inhumanity. His words might apply to the hostilities being repeated today between Muslims and Christians on islands in the Indonesian archipelago, including Ambon, where the trading Dutch introduced Protestant Christianity:

> But you, as if not made of the same mould,
> See with dry eyes, the miseries of men,
> As they were creatures of another kind,
> Not Christians, nor allies, nor partners with you,
> But as if beasts, transfixed on theatres,
> To make you cruel sport.

The Dutch regarded what they knew of the coasts beyond the East Indies as theirs. Coen's replacement, the milder Pieter de Carpentier, supported further exploration of what was called New Holland – the western and northern part of Australia. Captaining the *Arnheim* and *Pera*, Carstensz returned to the same river on the Gulf shore that the *Duyfken* had reached 17 years earlier. He and his crew became 'the second mob' in the Wik version of history. The captain named the river Carpentier. It was later changed to Batavia, when the governor-general had the whole Gulf of Carpentaria named after him. As ordered by his masters, Carstensz kidnapped an Aboriginal man for questioning about spices and minerals.

After seeing what happened to their countryman, other Aboriginal groups fought the Dutch ships off. Anyway, Carstensz was unimpressed: 'In our judgement this is the most arid and barren region that could be found anywhere on the earth ...'

The traditional owners today would beg to differ. 'There are lots of wild fruits here,' says Silas Wolmby. 'Also crabs, fish, birds, dugong, goannas, sea turtle. I was born here, and I will die here.' The Dutch captain was asking the wrong questions, recording of Wolmby's forebears that 'the natives are in general utter barbarians, all resembling each other in shape and features, coal-black, and with twisted nets wound round their heads and necks for keeping their food in; so far as we could make out, they chiefly live on certain ill-smelling roots which they dig out of the earth ... they are quite unacquainted with gold, silver, tin, iron, lead, and copper; nor do they know anything about nutmegs, cloves, and pepper, all of which spices we repeatedly showed them without their evincing any signs of recognising or valuing the same'.

Arthur Jose calls those comments 'the first considered judgment of an Australian land area by a thoughtful European'. In his book *Builders and Pioneers of Australia*, he commemorates Carstensz for turning back at Cape Keerweer as the first mob had done. 'Why elaborate this futile departure from a land they had found so uninviting?' Jose asks, flying a characteristic kite of informed speculation. 'Within [Carstensz's] reach – but for one obstacle – was the long-coveted gate to the South Seas, to the fertile lands of Eastern Australia, to a new Dutch colonial empire. But ...'[10]

A way was signalled on the map made by Carstensz's pilot, but the contrary trade winds kept them back, like other mariners before and since. After Carstensz it was Abel Tasman's turn. He failed in 1644. That left the way clear for James Cook to navigate the strait between the Gulf and New Guinea through to the more amenable eastern coast of Australia, claiming the Great South Land for Britain in 1770. The Dutch had merely visited the 'selvedge of a vast landmass', in the words of a later Pacific historian.[11]

Those like me who have not done much curtain-making may not know that 'selvedge' is the end of a piece of cloth that is finished to prevent fraying. To a butcher or a cook it's the fatty edge on a cut of meat. It's a good description for the Gulf.

I asked one of the shipbuilders of the *Duyfken* replica how he explained what they were doing to those who take a less positive view of colonial history. He told me of the time they ran into pirates in the Arafura Sea. He used the Indonesian word *kembang*, which means 'flowering', as a metaphor for their enterprise. The word also means 'expansion' or 'development', suggesting the profit that can come when an old example is honoured, as when a ship built with the same materials and methods used in the past sails into the present. It's a recognition that inherited know-how underlies what we do today. That was enough, apparently, for the Indonesian pirates to escort the modern *Duyfken* safely to an island harbour for a hospitable banquet. In a similar vein the Wik elder incorporates the replica's visit into tradition, laying his hand on the skipper's shoulder: 'We've been telling the *Duyfken* story for a long time. Now you've made the old story new again ...'

Today in the Gulf of Carpentaria a massive commercial vessel ploughs past out to sea, taking zinc ore to a smelter in Rotterdam. In the hinterland of Hell's Gate the world's biggest lead and zinc mine, Century, is up and running after much controversy. The ore slurry is pumped by pipeline 300 kilometres to the coast and then shipped to Holland. There turned out to be valuable minerals on those shores after all, billions of dollars' worth, which twentieth-century technology brought to the surface. What the Dutch East India Company imagined four centuries ago has come to pass, yet with little more comprehension of Aboriginal values than Carstensz showed in his early interrogation of that kidnapped blackfella.

The Dutchman who put his hand on the girl was cheeky. There was a lot of that sort of behaviour, and it only got worse. The word 'cheeky' has survived in Aboriginal English, in an insouciant linguistic inversion, to mean 'violent'. 'Them white man now cheeky one where they been killim 'bout people – most they been killim now,' remembers one senior woman from a coastal community. 'Old people they been killim, some of them young people they been killim ... some what sit down with them, they take'em, quieten'em, make'em work ... some woman too.'[12] But if they are descendants of violence, Aboriginal people in the Gulf region are also proving to be heirs to a remarkable capacity for coming to terms with what has happened and turning it around in the fight for recognition and justice.

In 1901 Walter Edmund Roth, the northern Queensland protector, joined those who were lobbying for a system of reserves as a way of safeguarding land for Aboriginal people. He understood that state borders and property divisions cut arbitrarily across Aboriginal domains and that the reserves would fail if adjacent pastoralists blocked off or used up the crucial waterholes, driving Aboriginal people into exodus across country. 'Aboriginal trade-routes have … been adopted from times immemorial on account of the suitability of certain water-holes, grass, native-foods &c, and so in great measure have come to be utilised as stock-routes [that] in turn now come to serve as avenues of escape for horse-thieves, and cattle-duffers into Northern Territory and for the surreptitious immigration of Chinese into Queensland,' Roth reported. They also provided escape routes for Aboriginal people.

Roth wanted laws made uniform and policing to be coordinated between different administrations. He asked for a policeman to be posted to Wollogorang, 'a very important Aboriginal centre' where blacks, specifically women, were cruelly treated by whites, and were driven to flee over the border to Queensland. Roth asked for protective police patrols to be sent into the area, adding 'that only men of proven worth, humanity, commonsense and tact be appointed to carry out such duties … the whole success of these reserves' would depend on that.[13] But it didn't work out as Roth hoped. A good man is hard to find.

By the 1930s, with the wild time mostly over and many Aboriginal people 'quietened down' into a largely unpaid labour force for the cattle industry, 'the domination of Aboriginal society [in the Gulf Country] had … been achieved,' writes anthropologist David Trigger in *Whitefella Comin'*. Aboriginal people became dependent on the state in a way that established the material basis for 'a prolonged process of pauperisation'.[14] They were ripe for the missionaries.

The road reaches the weir of a river and a rusty old sign with an Aboriginal flag on it announces Doomadgee Aboriginal Council. The settlement started life in 1936 as the permanent site of a Christian mission that went there to be as far as possible from the scorn of ungodly whites. Doomadgee did not exist at all when Roger Jose first walked up the road from Camooweal in 1916. Today it's the only town in the 500 kilometres from Borroloola to Burketown. It's an Aboriginal-run community with a population of 1,200 and permission is needed to go in. Officially no alcohol is sold there. Such rules are loosely observed. The nickname of the place is Doom City.

David Trigger arrived on a field trip in 1978 with an image of Doomadgee as a 'closed authoritarian mission settlement'. No doubt he carried with him 1970s liberal misgivings about the apartheid-like segregation and paternalism implied. It was an Exclusive Brethren mission that had been run on strict lines for 40 years. Decorum was demanded, violence condemned, extramarital sex a sin, alcohol and other drugs banned. Aboriginal traditions were discouraged and the outside world largely despised. Trigger gives a vivid image of his welcome to Doomadgee:

> As I finally slowed the vehicle to a stop at the crossing of the Nicholson River just east of the settlement, a very inebriated middle-aged man climbed up on to the running board and tried to hold a disjointed conversation, while attempting to focus his gaze on my face by peering in the open side window. After a short time, aware that I was trying to drive off, one of the women with him (also very drunk) sought to persuade him to get down, using vigorous verbal abuse. When words failed she punched him, and I drove off leaving the pair struggling by the side of the road.

The anthropologist dryly adds, 'The approving reports several individuals had given me about Doomadgee being something of a Christian haven away from the damage caused by over-consumption of alcohol had apparently portrayed only part of the reality.'

But Trigger didn't take this sight as confirming a cliché about drunken blacks. He analysed it. 'As I experienced settlement life, I became aware of a complex interplay between different aspects of social action among Aboriginal residents, which appeared variously to constitute both accommodation and resistance to the wider society within which they were encapsulated. In one sense, their situation was clear.

Aborigines' material circumstances were much poorer than all but the most destitute of non-Aboriginal Australians.' In another sense, however, inspired by the Italian philosopher Antonio Gramsci, the anthropologist finds glimpses here, 'of society as an arena of incessant conflict whereby a consensus is imposed but also resisted ...'[15]

By the time I reach Doomadgee more than 20 years later such anthropological generosity is under attack as a version of political correctness. It is claimed that well-wishing policy-makers conveniently ignore the sociopathic dysfunction of Aboriginal communities. Doomadgee, moving into Borroloola's old slot, is often cited as the worst of problem places. Massacre denial is irrelevant, say critics, compared to denial of terrible realities on the ground. The sons of murdered South African freedom fighter Steve Biko paid a call on Doomadgee in 1998 and said they had 'never ever seen people live in such atrocious conditions ... Here [by contrast with South Africa] there is no kind of progress.' Overcrowded housing, limited education, disease, domestic violence, substance abuse and youth suicide make up the new image of the town. I was warned about the humbug and told not to walk around after dark. A state government minister blamed the situation on 'a jumble of historical factors' and 'did not pretend to have a quick fix'. Their minds blown by gunja or petrol sniffing, young men commit crime so they can be sent away to jail, which they call the 'fattening paddock', as a rite of passage. When a journalist visited on a personal journey of reconciliation in 2000, nine young people had attempted suicide that week. He called his account 'The Hangman's Shadow'.[16]

The town was closed for the funeral of an old woman on the afternoon I arrived. The next day families were flying offshore in charter planes for the funeral of a senior lawman and dancer on Mornington Island. One of those families had just returned from Darwin from yet another funeral, of a local young man. Wakes are ceremonies as well as gatherings: life revolves closely around death.

On such occasions disputes can flare up. Booze is bought at the Burketown pub, ferried down the road to Doomadgee and sold at inflated prices – beer, port and sly bottles of rum. When things get bad, white health workers and teachers are evacuated, sometimes in a knee-jerk reaction that brings bad press and only makes things worse. When Mount Isa's *North West Star* sensationalised one of these incidents, the kids from Doomadgee School replied with a media release: 'We think Doomadgee is a beautiful and peaceful place.'

The township sits on one bank of the Nicholson River, called Ganalanja by the Waanyi people and Ganalanda by the Gangalidda people, whose domains meet around here. Ganalanja means 'long river': its source lies ultimately in the deserts of central Australia. The name indicates a unitary conception of the continent across vast distances and radical contrasts of terrain. After the rain kids stand waist-deep in the river's bottle-green water, joined by horses cooling off from the heat. The only crocodiles up this far are the benign freshwater kind, I'm told.

Revealing its original mission layout, the town is contained, unlike Borroloola which straggles off into the bush on both sides of the river, giving space for people to get away from each other. Here the grid is neat, a pressure when feuding breaks out. The hospital is neat. The school with its award-winning garden and dazzling swimming pool is neat. A bakery sells flash cakes and pies, and displays a sign that warns against bootleg liquor, telling people that if they're paying 100 dollars for a carton of beer or 50 dollars for a cask of wine they're paying the sly-grog traders too much.

Yards overhang with shady trees, poinciana, golden rain trees, trumpet trees, profusely in flower, making a domestic contrast to the smoky greens of the bush. Gardens are watered at dusk, kids playing in the spray in the heavy heat, guarded by lazy dogs. A little girl with golden hair sits on the verge sucking the last orange fibres of a mango seed, big sister to the smaller kids who line up beside her. Every yard has a mango tree drooping with fruit.

Works are in progress, new houses built to the latest specifications, with upper storeys for air flow and car spaces underneath, security grilles on the windows and solar hot-water heating on the roof. A women's refuge has just opened, all shiny tin and ramps for disabled access. But many dwellings are derelict and abandoned, vandalised or burnt out. The older houses of fibro and cement brick spill out into the grass where people sleep on old mattresses under the trees. Power is off, water goes off, no maintenance done, too many people crowding in, no decent personal space. It's a shanty town with a twenty-first-century frontier. At night horses wander into the yard of the house where I'm staying to graze on the grass. If a car hits a horse in the street, the driver can sue the cash-strapped council for failure in its duty of care. The council building lost its roof in a tornado months ago and is still waiting for the resolution of an insurance claim.

'Not their fault they were put in the pound,' says my Aboriginal companion, referring bluntly to the way people were herded together into missions like Doomadgee. One consequence is the perpetual contest for authority between different clan groups, often in the form of family divisions and aggravated by evident inequalities. Mangoes turn into weapons, hurled from one side to the other in a brawl until there's a king hit. If you talk to one group, the other group stays away. I got a warm welcome to one household and the cold shoulder from another.

When I say warm, I mean burning hot. One of the veterans of the biggest fight ever to engulf the town shakes my hand like a brother, a man my own age who has burnt himself out in a 10-year war with his own people and with white miners and Australian governments and one of the largest mining companies in the world. The anger of this wiry black man in a baseball cap is undiminished, fuelled by a clear, strong sense of right. The Waanyi people, whose land the mine is on, said no. Their no was not heard. Instead they were paid off with an agreement that promised benefits. Five years on, in the view of this Doomadgee community leader, those people have got nothing. Despair has not reduced his passion, but he's totally stressed out and smoking way too much. 'I hate them,' he says of the mining company, flicking his lighter. He would like to see the mine go up in flames.

On this particular Wet day the ground is like glue. I'm wearing my thongs and the soles stick in the clay after a downpour. Flip-flops is another name for these things, but there's no flip to my flop. They are pink and white rubber, worn wafer-thin by use. I bought them years ago for a dollar in Port Mathurin on the island of Rodrigues, made in China, my only souvenir of that trip. I was attached to my thongs but they were no longer attaching to me, sticking in the mud like road kill. If I stepped in the wrong place, I'd have to dig in the slurry to retrieve the thong – and find somewhere else to put my other foot. An onlooker called out with a laugh that I'd be better off barefoot. Next time I peeled the thong free I didn't put it back on. I waded through the puddles carrying the thongs, rinsing my feet clean, and went on this way down the road. Going barefoot was the proper thing to do.

Murrandoo Yanner, the young Aboriginal and Torres Strait Islander Commissioner for north-west Queensland, told me how he did not wear shoes until he and his brother went away to boarding school. On his first trip back home, his father met him at the airport and told him to take off his shoes so he could feel his earth beneath his feet once again. A couple of years ago Murrandoo tried that in a fishing resort on Mornington Island, offshore Gulf Country with which he has traditional links. He approached barefoot, and his way was blocked. After a noisy altercation with management he compromised by putting on his thongs. But once he was inside he was jumped by three men and knocked unconscious. He was in the police van on his way to the lock-up before he realised what was happening. Seeing the situation, an old white fisherman, a New Zealander, provoked the police to get himself arrested and put in the van too so that he could watch over Murrandoo. He knew how deaths could occur in police custody, how young Aboriginal men were shot while allegedly trying to escape or bashed when police were the only witnesses. The old Kiwi was a war veteran. He told the police he didn't fight the Nazis so people could be treated like that. Murrandoo told me he owes his life to that whitefella.

The fight goes on at Doomadgee and at the former Presbyterian mission on Mornington Island, places where the nexus of church and state control reached extremes in an earlier generation. In 1953, at the high point of the missions, the Exclusive Brethren superintendent was able to report progress at Doomadgee: 'What a change the Lord Jesus Christ has made in the lives of so many of these dear dark-skinned people. Long … captive to the power of darkness, bound by superstitious fears, enslaved to vice, to uncleanness, to dishonour.'[17]

But the story did not end there. While older people may remember the discipline of the mission days with some approval, younger people have grown up having to make their own way through a zone of strained, shattered value systems. Wadjularbinna, a Gangalidda woman who works for the people at Doomadgee, interprets the message of youth suicide as a plea for the recognition of underlying spiritual beliefs as 'the things that make us live'.[18]

Doomadgee is a sticky place. My hand sticks to the page as I write. Through the louvres of the window the land disappears in waist-high black-tipped grass and red antbeds to a line of trees. Crows caw in the silence. On the noticeboard outside is a thank you for support to the family that has lost its grandmother. 'Doomadgee is home to us', it states categorically. Last night while I was making notes a baby owl flew out from behind the bathroom door and narrowly missed the ceiling fan on its way through the light to the open front door and the darkness. Full-throated shouts carried across the night from the centre of town where the funeral party was being held. But where I was on the edge of the grid lights were out by eleven o'clock and all was quiet but for the owl's soft call.

VIII

EXCLUSION ZONE

In November 1930 a missionary couple and a single young man arrived by boat in Burketown and set up camp. The town's brief heyday was over and the difficulties the missionaries faced with its remnant population and scant support must have tested them sorely. 'All the ground is black soil and open plain country, across which the wind blows at a terrific pace … There is no doubt about the devil being against us, for everybody meets us with strange coolness, almost resentment,' wrote Leonard Akehurst as the rain started to fall. 'It came through the night. We are camping at the racecourse and sleeping in the grandstand. When the rain came we went into the jockeys' dressing-room, but being flooring boards above, the water pours through … and two or three inches of water runs at our feet, so we have to perch on benzine tins.'[1]

The trio was undaunted. 'Oh, what a privilege is ours. Whatever the burden, whatever the trial … give me my Aborigine, that I can tell him of Jesus and His love,' professed Will Sharpe, an idealistic 21-year-old, in a keen letter home. But finding their Aborigine was not as simple as that. Their first catch was 'a half-caste Chinese young man' called Bruce Chung who could read and write English. (Chong, a variant of Chung, is a common Aboriginal surname in the area, originally generic for Chinese.) The message proved 'too pointed' for the white community, who soon 'ceased to attend'.

I had experienced the severity of that message from a family of Exclusive Brethren who lived in the Adelaide suburb where I grew up. The problem, for me and for them, was their Exclusiveness. We became friends but whatever their impulses towards fellowship, a counter-mechanism of exclusion was also at work. They were, after all, the elect, those granted direct intimacy with God, a gift they guarded closely. Their unshakeable conviction – most strident when actually closest to being shaken – meant drawing a line in the sand between themselves and the rest of us, the sheep and the goats. That tight discipline made them paradoxical missionaries, because for every soul they might gather, they would turn away dozens more. And the gathered were exposed to such scrutiny that they might well slip back in humiliation. You were in or out.

The daughter of the family struggled. She had genius. She loved to laugh and dance and flirt, wanting to experience everything the world offered, select even among the select. Like a witch, she constructed false selves with which to entrance people. Then she would turn and curse whatever she had been and done, her romances and intrigues, the poetry she wrote, as tricks of the evil one. She met a boy from our circle in those druggy days, a wild confused youth who was the wholly innocent, infinitely suffering creature she needed, a Christ to redeem her guilt. I saw him after his conversion, in hand-me-down jacket and baggy flannels, railing on a street corner against the sins of the world. It was what nutters did. Yet they married and went bush, trained for missionary work and raised a model family.

I see their faces in those Burketown missionaries and I am wary of their conviction. The woman's writings, in bold, careful script, explained her religious commitment as a vigilant warding-off of deception in order to preserve the Truth and Grace of intimacy with God. She felt the pain of being a Chosen Person, judging harshly and harshly judged. It was not enough to be perceptive, sensitive, intelligent and detached if you had not found your truth, she wrote. What good would a person's books be when they were dead? Confetti on the grave! The phrase cut to the quick. Spiritual pride plays a mean game of exclusion. It can dismiss language, with which the world might be understood, as the agent of a con job. But the life of language lies precisely in its questioning, its rubbing against the world and the flesh where dirt and bodily fluids stick. It can be the very devil. Yet our capacity clumsily to articulate, and the reciprocal capacity to listen, may also save us.

Alejo Carpentier comes along with me. Deep in the jungle the narrator of *The Lost Steps* encounters a new world that is 'without … the preparation of the written word'. In a rhapsodic moment he dreams of a language beyond language, asking himself whether the highest form of expression does not 'consist merely in a supreme understanding of creation. A day will come when men will discover an alphabet in the eyes of chalcedonies, in the markings of the moth, and will learn in astonishment that every spotted snail has always been a poem.' But as he presses further, freeing himself of the mental trappings of the old world, he loops back in one essential respect, as Saint Jerome and Roger Jose had done: 'I had managed to dispense with everything I had been accustomed to in other days; I had discarded objects, tastes, clothing, pleasures, like unnecessary ballast, arriving at the supreme simplicity of the hammock, of cleansing my body with ashes, and the pleasure to be found in gnawing ears of corn roasted in the embers. But I could not do without paper and ink, without things expressed or to be expressed by these mediums.'[2]

How strange that faith drove the Brethren as far as possible from their own condemned world to the line of confrontation with another. Not hiding their trials, they solicited donations from affluent Brethren living in comfortable suburbia when they wrote home from the Gulf, in the same way their colleagues reported back from other heathen lands, China and Japan and places in darkest Africa. For all their efforts the harvest of souls was pathetically small.

My great-grandfather, Dean Jose, was a missionary too, in China for the Church of England. I remember him as a white-haired patriarch in a dim study that glowed with intriguing objects. There were two black wooden panels on which lines from the Lord's Prayer were painted in gold Chinese calligraphy. There was a Chinese Bible, an opium pipe with the smell of opium still in the bowl and a local passport in a leather pouch on which his surname appeared as Zhou, the same Chinese name I would use when, nearly a hundred years later, I went to see what I could find in the little town on the coast south-east of Shanghai, where he and his family had lived.

The region is one of the most prosperous in China, a heartland of milk and honey, but politically riven where today, despite every attempt to extirpate it, Christianity flourishes.

The missionaries on the Gulf of Carpentaria inhabited a more elemental landscape. The Brethren and their charges might have been reliving the book of Genesis, the remnant saved after the Flood. Their Calvinist vision of life rested on a literal interpretation of the Bible's verities. A favourite text was Christ's teaching of the last judgement: 'For then shall be great tribulation, such as was not since the beginning of the world … but for the elect's sake those days shall be shortened.' In that remote world the Brethren were preparing for the end of history: 'When the Son of man shall come in his glory … before him shall be gathered all nations: and he shall separate them one from another, as a shepherd divideth his sheep from the goats.'[3] In an atmosphere of unanswerable urgency, the Brethren asserted the supremacy of one value system over another.

What they bequeathed at Doomadgee was an exclusion zone, a literal and moral separation between the missionaries and Aboriginal people. The settlement was physically divided into the downstream village where Aboriginal people lived and the upstream mission where the school, hospital and church were and where non-Aboriginal people lived. The division of 'up' and 'down' structured life. Working within their own language-rich realm, which the Brethren were unable to penetrate, the assembled Aboriginal groups responded with an exclusion zone of their own, a survival mechanism that in the end outlasted the mission.

The Brethren hold meetings in which people volunteer to speak confessionally about themselves and accusingly about others. There's a raw group politics at work without the structures of power being made explicit. The system meshed fiendishly with the politics of their Aboriginal charges, as the two exclusion zones pursued the stratagems of co-existence. They needed each other, they shaped each other's lives, with both affection and friction between individuals, and with great gulfs of power and communication. Aboriginal people spoke of living 'under the Act', meaning the Queensland government's Aboriginal Protection Act that allowed the mission to regulate their lives. They knew the Act was a yoke, a marker of the same enslavement of spirit that the Brethren denounced in the Babylonian world from which they were escaping.

One Aboriginal woman offered herself as a language teacher to Dorothy Akehurst, but numbers in Burketown in the early days were thin. The missionaries had an almost comic determination to achieve speedy results. One Sunday they interrupted a corroboree and got permission from King Peter Dow Dow, the Aboriginal elder who acted as broker, to sing hymns to 20 men seated in a semi-circle. 'To our amusement and amazement they clapped us after each hymn. Still they will learn not to do this. Many of them could not understand a word we sang, but we trust by the grace of God they soon will.' The missionaries struggled against a double devil, trying to overcome traditional Aboriginal culture on one hand ('witchcraft and superstition') and, on the other, the hostility of non-Aboriginals towards their work. 'Who were we that we should tell them they needed to be saved! What good had we done coming into the place … and what did we think we were going to do with the blacks …,' complained people in the town. The missionaries quoted scripture to bolster themselves: 'we wrestle … against principalities and against powers, against the rulers of darkness of this world'.

Among their enemies was the same Australian state that supported their missionary endeavour through its Department of Native Affairs. In such a remote area the Queensland government was prepared to leave the welfare of Aboriginal people to those with a vested interest in saving souls. Out of sight, out of mind. Yet the missionaries chafed at the state's limited control of their activities and sometimes had trouble getting local officials on side.

When they decided to move out of Burketown, the Akehursts sought permission to build on reserve land along the coast where they would be in 'more intimate touch with the people'. They moved first to Old Doomadgee, as it is now called, then upriver to a new Doomadgee. The local government officer reported confidentially that he did not consider the missionaries to be 'suitable persons to control and train natives. They have been here for 9 or 10 months and … have done practically nothing. They inform me that they have no backing, but live on faith …' – and donations they prayed for from Down South.[4] For young missionary Will Sharpe the plight of the Aborigines was an indictment of secular Australia: 'Sad, sad is the story of our native race. Once they were the proud rulers of this sunny domain, but now a weak remnant, despised, down-trodden, and cursed by the white. Their land has been taken from them, and in return they have been given sin and vice and abuse, and even denied the right to live. The treatment of the Aborigine is a sad blot on the page of Australia's history.' It was also an indictment of the churches, including his own. Sharpe saw the missionary message as 'water falling upon a dry parched land … Oh, how long they have waited!'

Like the missionaries themselves, the dispossessed Aboriginal people might have welcomed a 'better country' somewhere, a 'good home' prepared by Jesus. But the government's representative was sceptical that it would materialise on earth. 'I am very doubtful if any of the natives, apart from a few that always live on the Reserve, could be induced to settle there permanently. The old natives have what they term their own country, and would rather die there in poverty … than leave it for any Promised Land.' The missionaries allowed for instant conversion and believed in total change, as they must have experienced in their own lives, but they also acknowledged the need for 'thinking black' to get their teaching across.

'Sing along my country way,' King Jimmy Dow Dow said, requesting hymns to be sung in his language. Sharpe describes the kids he teaches as 'full of life, bush children, and not used to class … They will want to talk … about wallabies, etc., and someone wants to know if there are any snakes in Heaven … Little Cecil, age about three, wants to continually shake hands with me … I would not part with my children, and I claim each one for the Lord.'

Dorothy Akehurst sent a before and after photo for publication in *Australian Missionary Tidings*: 'Nina, an Aboriginal girl. CHANGED … in less than three months … in a Christian home.' Nina goes from staring to smiling, from a drab smock to a radiant white tunic.

The mission grew as people in need were drawn to it across a familiar range of country and culture – including folk from Borroloola. Sustenance and shelter were provided by those who abided by the mission's administrative and evangelical regime. Was there good faith or bad faith? The toll on the founding missionaries was considerable. They retired broken in health after five years, handing the reins to the next Brethren couple. The new man remained as superintendent and protector from 1936 to 1951, when there were around 300 residents of whom about 85 were

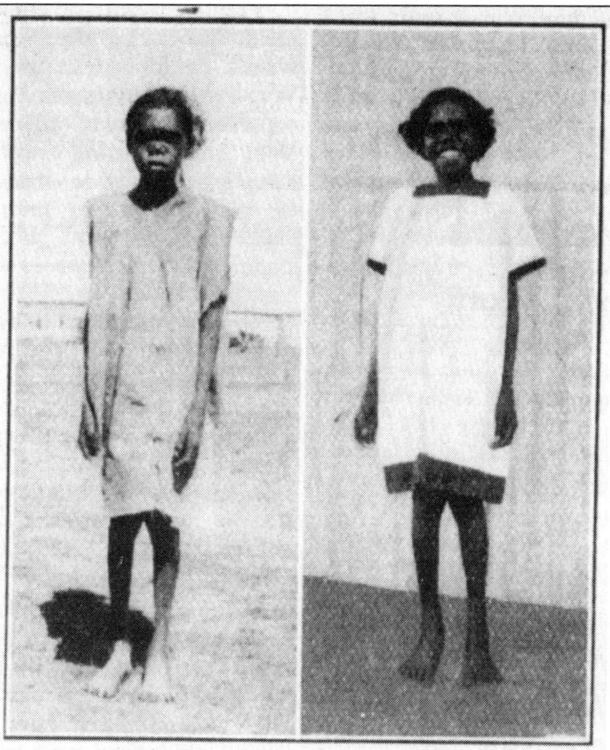

Nina, an aboriginal girl.

CHANGED.

Wherever it is received, the Gospel of Christ is responsible for great changes in the lives and prospects of believers, fitly expressed in Scripture as—"From death unto life," "from darkness to light," "from the power of Satan unto God." The above photo. illustrates this change in Nina, after three months under Christian influences in the home of Mr. and Mrs. Akehurst, at Burketown.

Reproduced from Australian Missionary Tidings, *1 September 1931* 'in fellowship'. Roger Jose would have found such conversions dubious.

Doomadgee mission was run on authoritarian lines. From on high, representing God and the state, the superintendent and his colleagues intervened in the residents' birth, education, beliefs, marriage and death. The mission handled people's housing and finances, including government benefits, and acted as an agency to provide stockmen and domestics to stations across a large area, especially during the labour shortage of the Second World War. These powers, underwritten by the state, were the linchpin of the Doomadgee economy and the superintendent guarded them jealously.

When the Director of Tuberculosis inspected Doomadgee in 1950 he found some things to commend, including 'abundant vegetables and an excellent variety of crops due to energetic gardening and an excellent irrigation system', but the core of his report was damning. 'The Doomadgee natives were the cleanest, best fed and the best housed seen. They were also the most severely restricted … I wish to record the strongest criticism … of continuing the dormitory as a prison in which adolescent girls and single young women are confined because of their sex.' It was 'indistinguishable from slavery,' he said. With males away at work, all the work of the mission, including building and farming, was done by girls 'up to 24 years of age' who were forbidden to leave the mission compound unaccompanied during the day and locked up overnight where they slept on the floor and the sanitation was poor. No amusements other than hymn singing were permitted and their heads were shaven for any sexual waywardness.[5]

The superintendent countered that the 'prison' was for the protection of women who had been 'brought to the lowest moral level through civilisation so-called'. 'It takes time,' he insisted, 'to overcome the influence of past years filled more completely with evil contacts than with good dinners. Our aim has been to lift the natives up morally and socially … and to slacken off necessary restrictive control as it is found the folk can rightly use and not abuse freedom …' That's why it was called the pound.

Doomadgee is an extreme case of protection offered for people's own good. How did it affect those who lived under it? David Trigger concludes that some residents were truly colonised by Christian thinking, believing that through missionary education they were able to 'climb up' from a lowly or cursed state, eventually ascending to heaven.[6] A white supremacist interpretation of the Bible was current that saw Noah's white son Shem placed above his black and yellow sons, the dark son Ham being lowest for seeing his father naked and drunk. In this vein one Aboriginal elder considered that Aboriginal self-government was against God's way. Sermons were broadcast through village streets in the evening and people who had already known great tribulation could be scared into seeking salvation in a hurry.

Traditional culture survived in secret. Knowledge, whether of healing skills, bush craft or sorcery, was highly valued. Power structures, invisible to outsiders, reflected family and kin relationships and standing within clans. People had changing beliefs about matters of life and death but seldom abandoned old practices completely. The extreme isolation and containment of Doomadgee may even have intensified people's sense of who they were. And not too far away, out of missionary reach, Borroloola continued as a powerful regional centre and source of traditional ceremony and law.

After the superintendent's retirement – he and his wife broken in health like their predecessors – the mission was increasingly at odds with new thinking in the wider community that opposed its authoritarianism and disliked its fundamentalist message. By the 1960s and 1970s its discipline was considered a form of apartheid enforced by fear and humiliation. 'The achievement of equality [entails] the disappearance of isolated and protected communities maintained ... by distinct agencies of government,' concluded one report.[7] By then the population of Doomadgee had doubled and more Aboriginal people had been absorbed into the administrative apparatus. One researcher who visited at the time felt that the mission 'stepped on the people very hard and [beat] out a lot of their spirit and self-respect'. David Trigger caught the last years of the mission when 'things were far from completely serene, stable or cooperative. Public drunkenness ... with its loud verbal abuse, violence and intervention ... was one of the obvious indicators of a lack of social harmony ... And this was just one aspect of a broadly contested, complex series of views ... about how people should behave and what they should think … On most days I would hear people saying "we buggered for smoke", as they commented on their lack of tobacco' (which the missionaries forbade).[8] Finally in 1983 the Queensland government took over the running of the community from the missionary managers. Divisions quickly resurfaced among the different Aboriginal groups left there. As Andrew McMillan puts it in relation to comparable communities in Arnhem Land: 'the memories and warnings of interclan distrust and skulduggery annex centuries in seconds'.[9] The Christian haven proved to be a place of unextinguished conflict all along.

To imagine life on the mission from the inside there is no better place to go than the extraordinary novel *Plains of Promise* by Alexis Wright, a Waanyi woman whose traditional country is not far from Doomadgee. Unlike most writing about this region that, like my own, starts from colonial outposts on the coast, *Plains of Promise* begins with the interior, the heart of a vast territory mapped by myth or 'songlines' for generations back. The book retraces the journeys of displaced people. Remembering where they have come from, they are able to recover a sense of wholeness from tragedy and despair.

Alexis Wright's maternal great-grandmother, Opal Marinmarm, was taken from her traditional country in 1881. Frank Hann, the first owner of Lawn Hill station, was crossing Waanyi country along the Queensland–Northern

Author Alexis Wright with a rock cod she caught on Mornington Island

Territory border when, in his own words, he 'caught the gin' Opal and another little girl sitting up a tree. Hann had a reputation for brutality. Three to four hundred Aboriginal people are estimated to have been shot on Lawn Hill in the years he was there. Recalling her grandmother's version of the story, Wright can only speculate 'about why two frightened little Waanyi girls were found up a tree, alone in the bush. Where were their families? Why were they hiding in the tree? Were they survivors of one of Hann's murderous attacks on their people? Did he take pity on them?'

Hann gave Opal to his cook, Sam Ah Bow, a Chinese man trained in traditional medicine. The eldest three of the couple's surviving children were sent back to China to avoid being removed as 'yellafellas' or 'half-castes' by Australian officialdom. A daughter, Dolly Quinsen, was allowed to stay. She grew up on her father's sublease at Louie Creek and married Johnny Ah Kup, another man of Chinese ancestry, when she was 15. Travelling Waanyi land, she learned traditional law. But the sublease was not passed on to the family when her father died. By the 1930s they were under the surveillance of the local Protector of Aborigines who talked of taking the children to Doomadgee or Mornington Island mission. The family moved south out of the way, where Opal died in a local hospital in 1941. Her daughter Dolly, Wright's grandmother, died in 1999.[10]

Dolly Quinsen was locked out of Lawn Hill until it became a national park in the 1980s, when she was in her eighties and could make a return journey. 'This was her dream and she spoke about Louie Creek often,' says Wright. 'Grandma's way of transmitting knowledge was to tell the stories about the country … She knew how to explain the natural world in terms of traditional knowledge that she learned at Lawn Hill', bringing 'the remote Dreamtime into the present …'

Alexis Wright draws on the inheritance of this visionary attachment to country in her fiction. Through the story of four generations of Aboriginal women, *Plains of Promise* paints a huge, harrowing picture of people suffering the consequences of having their world torn apart. Despite their apparent powerlessness, they find ways to heal the wounds. The novel begins with an Aboriginal mother, seduced by a white man's false promises of love, arriving at the mission with her young daughter. The mission superintendent takes the child away. In the mother's despair spirits in the form of pecking crows come for her in the night. She finds kerosene and immolates herself.

That first violation symbolises a wider pattern. Like the crows, the woman comes from 'sickness country'. Her death initiates a string of violence and suicide in the mission. Blame for the curse passes to her daughter, Ivy, who falls victim to sexual abuse by the mission superintendent, Errol Jipp. 'He would, by God, push the evil out of the "she-devil" who was possessing him,' he imagines as he rapes her. When Ivy falls pregnant, Jipp marries her off to a young man called Elliot. Elliot wants Gloria, but Jipp grants Gloria as a token to Delainy, an Aboriginal lay-preacher, who chains his young wife to the door post to break her desire for the other man. When Ivy bears Jipp's child, the pale-skinned infant girl is immediately taken away and sent Down South for adoption into a white family. A tornado whirls through the mission. After the evacuation, only Elliot returns. Unknown to him, his wife Ivy is institutionalised in a distant city in trauma from the loss of her child. She is tormented by electric-shock therapy and by the spirit-crows she has inherited from her own lost mother.

It's a tough piece of telling that does not flinch from the squalor and emotional chaos of the characters' lives. The novel tracks explanations back to their origins, historically and psychologically, listening intently for the terrors, intuitions and fantasies of people who are bound to their land by relationships and memories. Country is rendered with a turbulent physical reality but is also spirit country, a dreaming of mythic potency. The narrative exists in two domains: one temporal, epic and European, the other magical, poetic and linked to Aboriginal lore.

Healing begins when Elliot is chosen to go into Ivy's mother's country 'to find out the reason for the big mob of sorry business affecting them all'. He finds as his guides an old Chinese medicine man and two Aboriginal women. They reveal that the dying across the country is caused by 'big trouble in the ancestral world'. The interior lake where life breeds is drying up. The problem is embodied in the fate of Ivy, removed from kin and homeland and abused by authority of the white man's God.

Elliot 'saw his footprints left upon the cracked, sun-baked clay … He walked inwards on the large expanse of the dry clay until his feet sank in sticky mud and eventually reached the water's edge. There he sat in the water amongst the floating black swans, pelicans, ibis and wild ducks … [until at night] the crows … sent up the first noisy alarm … A roaring body created by thousands and thousands of winged creatures lifting off in unison hid the light of the moon … It was the Great Spirit troubled into action.'[11]

Part two of the novel traces Ivy's return, when the psychiatric hospital to which she is confined collapses in scandal and she is sent back to the country as a welfare case. She is fearful of what people might do to her and haunted by her communion with a world beyond the visible. In an apocalyptic scene the house where she stays is struck by lightning and burns to the ground and Ivy disappears again, to live with goats on the edge of town. 'The kids thought she was a ghost. "Long white hair like a goat's, down to the ground" – "White skin, like she got no blood." '

Part three takes us to Mary, Ivy's child, adopted in infancy, who is now a young woman in search of her identity. She becomes the lover of an Aboriginal activist in far away Melbourne. 'It was a fight all the way,' he teaches her, 'a struggle to be Aboriginal. There were no free rides …' He would laugh, explaining how in the early days 'the black man had sung the Whites, to make them greedy and miserable in the blackman's land'. He insists that it is 'a war of the mind … The mind must be in harmony with the land.' He urges Mary to find out who she is. Before he leaves her with his child, the activist discovers that Mary was born on the mission and introduces her to Delainy as the beginning of a way back. The old preacher has 'a reputation for recognising family members … anywhere in the Gulf country'. He invites Mary to come and work on the former mission.

'You know, the poor buggers don't even have matchbox Land Rights,' Mary's boss at the Aboriginal organisation tells her. 'Not even room to swing a cat. Not even room to bury themselves – the government even makes them pay for that. It's time to count the beans, Mary. It's time the beans paid dividends.' Encouraged by the organisation in its wish to break the hold of church and state influence over Aboriginal communities in the region, Mary makes the journey:

> Any twisty road in the northern Gulf country will take you through kilometres of gravel winding through plains of papery grasses ... This is scary country at night ... an old rust-bucket of a truck passes by, travelling slowly, like an animal on the lookout for its prey. Over the tray dozens of dead kangaroos, looking like a pile of dead grey wood, weigh the vehicle down. But then the eyes of the dead creatures catch the light and shine like distant stars, and you can see tails and legs hanging over the side, almost to the ground ... If you tell the locals what you have seen along the road, they look around as though there must be invisible people watching them.

At first people keep their secrets from her in a land that suggests mysteries behind the appearances of things. Mary meets Elliot, unaware he is the first husband of the mother she never knew. He takes Mary and her daughter to a lonely outstation where they shelter from a tropical storm. Someone else is there with them in the iron shed: 'At first Mary thought it was an animal. A wild animal cowering in one corner. A 'roo or emu, with long, matted fur or feathers.' It is Ivy. When Mary holds up her daughter, she is 'rewarded by a gentler look from the old woman', who has been living in the bush all these years waiting for her daughter to come back. Elliot's task is now complete. His song has been sung. The secret of water, returning to the interior lake, renewing the country's and the people's inner life, has shown its power.

'You needed to have been through it all in order to understand,' Mary realises. *Plains of Promise* takes us through it all – history, belief, passion, endurance, politics, connection – to achieve a full, subtle rendering of a people's exodus and return. The book has the sweep of a Gulf cyclone. It does not shirk the raw, mixed-up nobility of its material. Its plot is intricate. Its writing, homely and surreal in turn, flickers with the subversive energy and humour of Aboriginal speech. As a literary form the novel is inscribed with the same nineteenth-century conventions as the colonising, Christianising enterprise of Australia. Here its means are pushed to the limit, challenged to carry other truths. Alexis Wright's subject is the violent misconception in which Australia was conceived. In determining that the novel can go this far – in the great tradition – she exposes the comfortable evasions of so much other writing about Australia to achieve what one critic has called 'an authentically Australian magic realism'.[12] The truest fiction can be a way of going where factual investigation can't go. *Plains of Promise* is a guide.

IX

GULF WARRIORS

It occurs to me that my loose-wired mind has linked Carpentier the writer with Carpentaria the place, as if that would explain something. My genealogical ability quakes at finding a family tree that will ramify between Carpentier, seventeenth-century Dutch governor-general, after whom the Gulf was named, and Carpentier, Cuban novelist. Alejo Carpentier's father was French. His parents emigrated to Cuba in 1902, where two years later their son was born. The father abandoned the family when Alejo was a teenager, never to be heard from again. That's as far as my search takes me. When Bob in New York hears about his replacement in the passenger seat, he reveals that years ago as a boy editor he published *The Lost Steps* in paperback. That's when I first read Carpentier's great work. Aged 20, I read it in a funk of desire under a tree in the Barossa Valley, north of Adelaide, in a hot summer, surrounded by thoroughbred horses, with a bottle of wine beside me – 'and Thou'. It seemed like good preparation for what was to be my own wandering life, my lost steps to come. Carpentier invented 'magic realism'. He gave the phrase currency in a passage published in Caracas in 1948. He saw it as a modern version of baroque literature, identifying its characteristic as outlandishness rather than formal perfection, not a straight line or a circle but an elliptical curve. Here in the Gulf Country his book whispers in my ear. I am no longer on a fixed journey around one centre, my end in my beginning. I am pulled by another centre, away from Roger Jose and into the present, my trajectory an ellipse. I mark the margins. 'I asked myself whether, in bygone days, men had longed for bygone days as I, this summer morning, longed for certain ways of life that man had lost forever.' But the answer is no. The unreachable past is something we have invented quite recently, fearing that we are out of hearing range of our own long-accrued wisdom.

In earlier days people longed for a future that would be better than the world they knew. Alexis Wright's *Plains of Promise* takes its ironic title from one such vision of the black-soil plains of north-west Queensland, as described by Captain John Lort Stokes from HMS *Beagle* in 1841, the same ship that had taken Charles Darwin around the world, from Plymouth to Patagonia, and to Sydney in 1836. Stokes named Port Darwin, today's city, after his shipboard friend, with whom he shared a tiny cabin and a table at a time of intense shared intellectual activity. Stokes was retracing Flinders' route when he pressed on up the Albert River and, according to his journal, 'breathed a prayer that ere long the now-level horizon would be broken by a succession of tapering spires rising from the many Christian hamlets that must ultimately stud this country'. Stokes succinctly coupled pastoral industry with Christian conversion in an image from picturesque tradition when he coined the phrase 'Plains of Promise' – in the best of advertising traditions, since Stokes wanted to 'sell this vast country to his English superiors and to generations of future settlers'.[1] The country has proved hostile to aesthetic transformation, although after the Wet, flushed emerald with fragrant, fattening grassheads, the wetlands that extend into salt along the Albert River can look like Constable's Suffolk, if you imagine the air temperature dropped by half. It's the setting for Burketown, the oldest port in the Gulf.

Burketown is named after one half of the doomed duo Burke and Wills, who died returning from their trek through to the Gulf from Melbourne in 1861 in the classic Australian story of defeated promise. They never even saw the coast, despite triumphal depictions of their hailing the azure ocean from seaside dunes. There was no coast to see on these ragged shores, only an extended selvedge, an 'edge' where 'self' lost its definition – to take up the old Dutch etymology of this word – for the explorers and for Australia's sense of herself too. Pity those entrusted to the leadership of the inept and delusional Robert O'Hara Burke: 'he burked that expegition [*sic*], right enough,' wrote novelist Joseph Furphy.[2]

The grim tale made the Gulf of Carpentaria a destination for a time. In the Wet of 1882–83 the 21-year-old George Ernest Morrison, years before he became Morrison of Peking, adviser to republican China, showed what he could do by walking Burke and Wills's route back to Melbourne from the Gulf alone with just a swag, covering 2,043 miles in 123 days. He commented dryly that another person might have done it 'more quickly and … more easily'. *The Times* of London declared it 'the most remarkable of pedestrian achievements'.[3]

Nevil Shute disguised Burketown as Willstown in his popular novel *A Town Like Alice*. The happy ending envisages a future of supermarket, cinema, swimming pool and 'proper tarmac road' for the town. It hasn't quite happened like that. 'Prince Albert Land, as [the Plains of Promise] came to be called, is still waiting for those village greens and spires,' George Farwell commented in *Ghost Towns of Australia*, visiting in the early 1960s. But he was premature in diagnosing Burketown's demise.[4]

The forward-looking vision has passed into the hands of the Aboriginal community of the town, the Gangalidda people, Murrandoo Yanner's mob. They make up the majority of the town's population of around 150. In the last 25 years Burketown has become the unlikely powerhouse of a new energy that is not only transforming the locality but sending a charge far beyond. It's anything but a ghost town.

Instead of spires there's a telecommunications tower and a water tower with a red beacon light on top for incoming planes. Council workers in orange safety clothing drive earthmoving equipment up and down, slashing grass and mending washaways. Lawns are watered, tennis courts tended, yards neatly fenced. Kids in yellow school uniforms ride bikes or play cricket till dusk under the watchful gaze of extended family who sit on the high verandas of their houses drinking pots of tea. The original customs house remains from 1865, now the town's only pub, decorated with old guns and a barramundi made from green cans of Victoria Bitter. The corner bar is reminiscent of a sailors' pub on the Thames estuary, or in Ipswich or Harwich, a place for battening the hatches and yarning out your days – except, that is, for the security cameras. An Irish barmaid and a German barmaid merge in my mind as Isolde. The whole town wanders through.

Burketown's other tourist attraction is a 700-metre well sunk into a saltwater aquifer a century ago, maybe by Chinese, that spews up scalding-hot water rich in mineral content. The water is used to de-feather poultry. Its deposits have formed a gnarled, slimy, sulphurous mound that suggests a view from inside a diseased body part. It's called the Burketown Bore. There are a few of them around.

It's refreshing to blow history away and go fishing with Murrandoo Yanner. At 29 he's a big, good-looking man with sleek cropped hair and the trimmed beard of a Venetian corsair. His face ignites with emotion as he talks of his love of the freedom of life out on the water. Then, as he gazes into the distance, his expression takes on the sage-like calm of inner commitment. He speaks all ways – fast, dirty, political, poetical – jumping through registers. Broad-shouldered, barrel-chested, Murrandoo is a married man with four small sons and a baby daughter. He is the charismatic spokesman and acknowledged leader of his clan. Out on the river he lets rip. 'Hold on, me hearties,' he grins. He has made talk an art form. 'If you can't dazzle them with brilliance, baffle them with bullshit,' is how a mate sums up his style.

Murrandoo powers the boat from the Burketown wharf downriver to the Gulf, 30 kilometres as the crow flies, twice as long as the serpentine river doubles back on itself through the mangroves, a great wild river, fed by other incoming flows in king tide, widening as we reach the mouth. Our lines are overboard, baited up with mullet netted upstream. The sun sets over the vast estuarine wetland of mudflats, saltpans, lagoons and mangrove. A white-bellied sea eagle lifts. Our lines jag with blue-nose salmon, sweeter eating than the famous barramundi. A bright moon rises. Murrandoo stands at the helm of the only boat in sight, a prince in his domain. The swelling river is Goomboommounda to him, a name from long before the *Investigator* or the *Beagle*.

He throttles up the boat, slaloming the wake in the moonlight as we head up the channel. The land and water here are as pristine as anything on earth, virtually unchanged since the *Beagle*'s brief visit over 150 years ago or any time before that. It teems with life and diversity. Murrandoo is on a journey as epic as the *Beagle*'s to keep it that way. He wants a marine park around the islands in the Gulf, like the Great Barrier Reef marine park, under the custodianship of his people. In time he will probably get it.

'Don't sign anything away,' he warns. At present the Carpentaria Land Council, the Aboriginal representative body for north-west Queensland, based in Burketown, is running a sea claim on the waters around the South Wellesley Islands that Flinders mapped in 1803, an hour or two by boat from the mouth of the Albert River. A thousand years of common law provide no precedent for lawfully closing off right of passage at sea, so rather than seek to exclude passage, the traditional island people have decided to claim a right to prohibit passing ships from leaving or taking anything. They want to prevent pollution of their waters and exploitation of their fisheries and natural resources.

That is only one of many battles for Murrandoo Yanner. In Gangalidda his name means 'whirlwind', those waterspouts that mysteriously appear in the Gulf and can suck up a boat or pull down a plane. Re-invention is part of the strategy, being two places at once. As I drove to Burketown to meet him, he was flying between Brisbane, Mount Isa and Mornington Island. Like the Scarlet Pimpernel, you seek him here, you seek him there, without necessarily pinning him down. As a boy, he was taught by his father to look after himself. His charm and well-directed temper serve him nicely.

Murrandoo Yanner's great-grandmother saw her husband beheaded in a massacre of Aboriginal people by Europeans along the coast a hundred years ago. Murrandoo identifies that legendary great-grandfather as a powerful example in a line of warriors and freedom fighters. The widow came into Burketown with two small daughters, seeking sustenance after her people were decimated. One girl married a Chinese man called Kum Sing. The other married Jack Yanner, son of a European emigrant who had joined the rush to the Victorian goldfields in the 1860s. Jack Yanner disowned his family Down South, their origins perhaps Spanish-Moroccan within the Austro-Hungarian Empire (according to Murrandoo), and joined the black sheep in the Gulf. He fathered his youngest son, Phillip Yanner, when he was in his seventies. His Aboriginal wife was half his age, but both parents were lost while Phillip was a child, leaving him to be raised by his aunt with a brood of siblings and cousins and foster kids. From that aunt, his adoptive mother, Phillip Yanner learned about his people and became an advocate for their rights in the face of dispossession. He was a tough, smart man, a boxer and a politician. In 1981 Phillip Yanner became the first representative from the Gulf region to be elected to the National Aboriginal Conference. He was a witness for the Nicholson River (Waanyi/Garawa) Land Claim in the Northern Territory, a claim granted in 1985 in a powerful regional precedent. He is credited with getting the Bentinck Islanders' land back for them, the largest island in the South Wellesley group.

Up to that time Aboriginal people were living in camps, in humpies in the bush outside Burketown, including the old woman and her kids. Phillip Yanner established the Moungibi Housing Corporation and helped people move into proper accommodation in town. That marked Burketown's turnaround. Moungibi has since grown into a general service provider and focus for Aboriginal enterprise. It runs a fuel depot and store that sells milk, bread, fruit and vegetables. The town is expanding. Many in the community look to the day that Burketown will reclaim its traditional name – Moungibi.

I'm introduced as Book Brother. For dinner Bull Yanner, Murrandoo's elder brother, cooks up a fresh catch of sea turtle from Mornington Island. The pieces are tossed in flour and fried with garlic and ginger, then accompanied by chilli pickle and fresh, fluffy damper. It's delicious. I missed the previous night's crocodile curry, with coconut milk and honey, made with flesh from a black crocodile, its skin stained with tannin from the ti-tree swamp where it was caught. Then, once the football game on television is over – North Queensland Cowboys versus Brisbane Broncos – lights are out and by ten o'clock the only sound in this quiet hamlet is the hum of the generators on which it relies for power. Without the generators there'd be no air-conditioning and the Carpentaria Land Council would not be able to go on-line to lawyers in Sydney and bureaucrats in Brisbane and Canberra to continue its fight.

Like all small towns, the feuding here can be intense, along family or political lines. Although people are civil and usually don't bear grudges, there's no escaping from conflict. Racial issues divide people, although less along racial lines than between racists and anti-racists in the community as a whole, or between Aboriginal people and 'black cunts' (a categorisation identified for me by an Aboriginal man who has been in the thick of it). The main line of confrontation is between the majority Aboriginal community, supported by the Carpentaria Land Council, the Moungibi Housing Corporation and the large Yanner and Kum Sing clans, and the Shire Council, the official local governing body, the arm of the state, on which the Aboriginal population is inadequately represented. That makes for suspicion. Arson is one of Burketown's ways of sorting things out. The town has an Australian record for arson incidents, without one prosecution. On New Years' Day 1996 the Shire Council Library was half burned down. Suspecting Yanner's mob, the police came to drink with them, hoping that tongues would loosen and spill the beans. While the police were at the party with the Yanners, the other half of the library went up in flames across town.

Phillip Yanner died suddenly in 1992 at the age of 44, seemingly exhausted by political struggle and his efforts on behalf of his broad family. His son Murrandoo was away being educated – church boarding schools, university, a cadetship in radio broadcasting. On his father's death, Murrandoo, aged 19, came back to Burketown to 'take up his father's spear,' as he puts it. He was elected co-ordinator of the Carpentaria Land Council and subsequently regional commissioner for the national Aboriginal and Torres Strait Islander Commission. He is supported by his elegant mother Irene, who wryly implies that her son could have done anything but has chosen, thanklessly, to 'work for blackfellas'. He is supported by his wife Rachel, a woman who came from Mornington Island, the daughter of a revered Papuan preacher. He is supported by his sisters Shirlene and Justine and brothers Bull, Phillip Junior, Jagama and TJ, all of whom have key and complementary roles in community organisations, all young and smart and blessed with the gift of the gab in this oral world where talk is currency, whether in the Burketown pub or in a grab for television.

Their father lies buried in the little cemetery out of town across the saltflats. A few thin trees shade old graves lost in the long grass, some with marble headstones that record early deaths, often of women – quite a few in 1916, as if they succumbed to tropical disease on top of bad news from the front. It is moving to contemplate Phillip Yanner's legacy as I stand beside his grave. At its head is a boomerang, incised with turtles and crossed with a spear on which the word 'Peace' is just legible. Bailer shells and plastic flowers mark its border. He lies near the old Aboriginal woman, born around 1900, who was brought into town as a little girl after the killings and passed on what she knew to so many children that, unlike the old woman in the shoe, she did know what to do. Her grave is freshly painted a brilliant white.

Genealogy is all-important here, where you come from and where you belong. The anthropologist in the Carpentaria Land Council office uses the latest family-tree software to produce records of all the Waanyi people in the area and their attachments to specific places, preparing for a large, complex land claim. She builds on the journal entries of Norman Tindale, who assembled genealogical material in a 10-day fieldwork stay at Doomadgee in 1963. His handwritten lineages, deposited in the South Australian Museum, provide rare records of dispersed, sometimes anonymous lives. But memory is strong, reinforced in the telling. What Tindale jotted down 40 years ago comes back to life in corroborating oral testimony today.

To become who you are for an Aboriginal man like Murrandoo Yanner, however, you must go beyond genealogical knowledge and be initiated into the law of your people. Most religions have a coming-of-age ceremony. In many Aboriginal groups the tradition was broken by the disappearance of lawmen qualified to pass it on, partly as a result of the prohibition of practices that were regarded by missionaries and others as dangerous, primitive or evil. That was the case for Gangalidda people, who had missions established in their heartlands where they were 'put in the pound'. To learn the law, Murrandoo had to go further afield across the border into the Northern Territory. He had to make the journey to Borroloola. There the initiation ground was still in use after decades. Young men would come from across the Gulf to be painted by women's hands and led, heads covered in blankets like cowled monks, with loud joyous singing to the ceremony, which was carried out under the guidance of one of the most revered lawmen of northern Australia, a Garawa man called Blue Bob.[5] He passed away not so long ago at a mighty age, white-haired and unlined.

Why Borroloola, and how Blue Bob survived, absorbing knowledge from elsewhere as it disappeared across a wide band of country, are mysteries. I like to think it has something to do with Borroloola's almost mythic reputation as a crossing-place, a backwater sanctuary. It may also be a case of the times, no matter how discordant, and the place, no matter how destroyed, giving rise to the person who is needed to carry people forward, a hero of the spirit, a leader. 'So much one man can do, That does both act and know,' as the poet Andrew Marvell said succinctly of Oliver Cromwell, England's revolutionary Protector, in 1650.

On the basis of traditional affinities, alliances and linguistic similarities between Garawa, Waanyi and Gangalidda people from Borroloola through Mornington Island and Doomadgee to Burketown, a regional cultural force has developed, centred in Borroloola. Senior Borroloola lawmen had learned the Gangalidda songs as well as their own Garawa songs. Not only did they welcome young Gangalidda men to be put through initiation in Borroloola, they saw it as part of an exchange by which they were carrying out their mission to reinstate traditional law in those Queensland communities where it had been stamped out or had otherwise fallen away.

For Murrandoo Yanner initiation was transforming. He wears the scarification marks on his back with pride. But it's less the cutting that marked him, including of the foreskin, numbed and anointed with milky sap from a particular tree, than the depth of cosmology and tribal knowledge he was taught by the lawmen in the weeks of preparation. Murrandoo says it cleaned out all the rubbish that Christian boarding schools had left in him. He would willingly have let his arm be chopped off for what he gained.

His brothers and male cousins have since gone on that same journey to Borroloola and more will follow. It is a process of generational and geographical transfer in which 'culture' is both recuperated and reconstructed as a political commodity for a postmodern world.[6] In time the centre may shift to a new area. It may move back to Gangalidda country. A young warrior may, if he survives, become an old lawman. It would be premature for Murrandoo Yanner to say so, but Blue Bob may already have identified him as a chosen one.

X

MINE OF THE CENTURY

Burketown, Doomadgee and Lawn Hill form a triangle. From Burketown to Lawn Hill the last part of the road, past the Century mine turn-off, is burnt out. The hogback ridge line of the Constance Range bristles in steamy light. A fire has flayed the country, exposing its musculature and bones. Giant blocks compact in crenellations above blackened slopes. I stop to sketch the jutting crest of those lode-bearing hills but, failing to fit it on the page, I press on to the fossil site at Riversleigh.

Fossils are a stretch at the best of times. 'Looking backwards, we could only be looking for ourselves,' writes Gustav Sobin, reflecting on the 'vertical typology' that fossils suggest, as they allow us to exult 'in an intensely reciprocal, if not fusional, state with our very origins'.[1] In responding to these sought-after things we elaborate systems in which we have a place too, a connection with the archaeology of our own psyche, as individuals and as kinds. I examine a fragment of fossilised leaf, all skeletal membrane, and mortality fuses with a countermanding sense of larger-scale survival. Impossible not to wonder why these stones are delivering their messages here and now. Or did others before us just read them differently?

Twenty million years ago in the Early Miocene the rock under my feet was the slimy mud of a rainforest lake bed where ancient animals were buried. The sites here at Riversleigh have revealed dozens of unknown species of prehistoric fauna. Over 20,000 specimens have been found, representing 150 faunal assemblages, spanning 25 million years. 'Only in one or two places on the surface of our planet,' says Sir David Attenborough, drawn back to this remote region of Australia, 'have conditions been just right to preserve anything like a representative sample of the species living at any particular time. Those places are the rare treasure houses of palaeontology.'[2]

Fossils mark the winding trail, clear white markings, like X-rays, on deep grey ground, the vertebra of a macro crocodile, the thigh of thunderbird, the gentle arch of a turtle shell expressed in the few curving marks that a master painter might make. At the laboratory back in Mount Isa I had seen the fossil of another turtle shell, its scaly pattern like the latex skin of a movie monster. The more ephemeral the material, the more amazing its relic. Fossils are like photographic negatives. As the camera converts light into an image, fossilisation turns once-living matter into a sculpture of the original by the chemistry of molecular exchange. I saw the fossil of a marsupial lion emerging from rock in the acid bath, a 20-million-year-old dog-sized creature, its jaws and snout intact and yellowish as it came at me from remotest time. It surely would have frightened the children of the rainforest in the prehistoric dark.

Across the ravine rocks sit in grey piles. 'Cambrian pancakes anyone?' says a sign. Michael Archer, director of the Australian Museum, Sydney, and a Riversleigh expert, writes enthusiastically of time as the fourth dimension of the creation. 'LIFE – the whole colossal thing that is, was and will be – quite literally is one gigantic time-travelling creature, without a single physical or temporal break in its four-dimension being.' He calls it the 'Bioblob' and describes 'Riversleigh's fossil record [as] one of the world's great refuse piles! Here discarded fragments from the Bioblob, like dandruff, were cast off during the creature's travels through space and time. From study of these discarded fragments, we can obtain an, albeit imperfect, vision of [its] true shape . . .'[3]

The urge to think metaphorically is irresistible, with an anthropomorphic frame of reference, throwing up flotsam that's cute and cosmopolitan as part of the trade in images. Sites have names like Archie's Amphitheatre and Cleft of Ages, taking us jokingly to the origins of archaeology in classical cities and Biblical lands. The cave where a lot of bat skeletons were found is the Gotham City site. I look at the scorched hillsides. Fire, clearing out the grass and exposing fresh rock, is a boon to fossil researchers, who will be here on another expedition as soon as the Wet is over – and to vandals who have removed many fossils from this unguarded place. The only thing standing on the hills now are the termite mounds, grey, slender, two metres high, as if wrapped in fireproof cloaks. I think of Jacob Epstein's sculpture of Lazarus rising, miraculously alive in his winding-sheet after having been dead. I think of television images of refugees trekking across the desert slopes of Afghanistan, their robes blown round them head to toe. I think, viewing these unruined termite towers with a new sombreness, of the Twin Towers of New York, turned to smoke and rubble before our eyes.

Back at my desk I use a fossil as a paperweight. It is in the form of a coiled worm that spirals inward to vanishing point, black and shiny and comfortably cool when it sits in the palm of my hand. It was found by a palaeontologist in China's Great Northern Wilderness in the late 1950s when he was sent to a remote region to reform his thinking. He believed that palaeontology was politically innocent. His son gave it to me after he marched in the democracy demonstrations at Tiananmen in Beijing in 1989, fearing he would be arrested and his possessions seized. It reminds me of the tenuous and less tenuous, direct and less direct ligatures of history.

I was in China then, partly under the influence of ancestral curiosity, following my great-grandfather's steps. In this Australian fossil landscape of concertinaed time, of belonging and disruption, I can hardly help wondering where I belong. Am I a cosmopolitan of no belonging? I feel like that here, yet I *am* here, my feet on the hot, hard ground, acknowledging that someone else was here before me, as is the case everywhere on earth. When territorial claims become fanatically exclusive, perverting history in a one-dimensional argument, they become self-destroying.

For Aboriginal people, the place of conception is a primary site of belonging. I happened to be conceived in Spain, at Tossa del Mar on the Costa Brava, where my parents were holidaying. My father had a job in Sheffield, England, studying new approaches to management in post-war Britain. I was born into November snow in London and taken back to Australia when I was a few months old. On the last leg of the journey, crossing the Great Australian Bight, I fell ill with salmonella. As soon as the ship reached Adelaide I was rushed to hospital to be baptised by that same great-grandfather, the Dean. A nun at the hospital, Sister Mary Thomas, nursed me until I pulled through. I put on weight and within a year of that London snow found myself in the outback, at Broken Hill, where my father had gone to work for Australia's largest mining company. I think of that as my second birth. So where do I belong? The streets of Broken Hill are named after minerals. We lived in Iodide Street. On weekends my parents would drive out into the bush, to places like Mootwingee, an important area for Aboriginal rock art. They would spread the picnic rug and, desperate for a break from their pestering child, tell me to run away across the soft red dirt until I was out of sight. It was a game for a two-year-old. 'Run, run,' they would encourage me, and I ran. I sense that exultation again when I'm out on an endless road with no one else in sight.

I'm snapped from my reverie by the tell-tale rumble of a flat tyre. A poor specimen to begin with, it has been ripped apart by heat and gravel, and I can't find the wheel spanner. A car comes along – the only one I've seen on this road – an Aboriginal family heading for Doomadgee who understand the situation at once. Another crazy tourist … Everything's hot to the touch but in no time at all we have changed the tyre using their tools. They escort me to where I'm camping and I fill up their tank in gratitude. The woman gets drinks for the kids. The man gestures down the road in the direction of the Century mine.

'We've got the mine,' he says, as if that is the main fact a visitor needs to know. He tells me he worked at the mine for two years before he'd had enough and went home to his family. Now he drives earth-moving equipment in Doomadgee. He says the fire that came through was started over by the mine.

Later I walk up Spinifex Ridge where the fire was hottest. The rock underfoot is orange. Higher up the outcrops of boulders could be charred muffins. Patches of white powder mark fallen trees, like shadows. Some trunks are leopard-spotted, as if glazed in the heat. Others are the colours of old paint torched on a wall: red, yellow, caramel. Bark curls like bacon rind. Seed pods gape from grey twigs. Yet even here in what the ranger calls Napalm Valley trees are sprouting from the base in bright feathers of green. Tender shoots appear, lines of green fire along blackened limbs.

The fire came late in the season when there was an excess

of flammable material. It burned through neighbouring pastoral country at hotter than usual temperatures – no benign walking fire this one – and entered the national park, destroying trees that were set to become large old specimens. Kangaroos and turkeys could jump the fire line—the turkeys were the first back in – but smaller wildlife suffered, especially the nestlings. There was no vigilance, says the ranger. The fire allegedly started with sparks from a miner's drill. No one was ready for how quickly it spread. Each time the drivers went down into the mine's open-cut for a load and came up again, the fire had leaped to the next ridge. Six weeks later it was still burning, more than 250 million hectares, way over to the Northern Territory border, with no one acknowledging liability.

From level with the liver-coloured plateau that stretches into the distance, all burned bare, I look down. Below me is Lawn Hill Gorge with its long body of deep jade water flowing between blood-red rocks. A single white cockatoo flies in to land in the lush vegetation along its shores. There are river gums, palms and cluster figs. A Leichhardt pine reaches to the top of the cleft rock in one great pillar that sprouts lozenge-shaped leaves the size of kitchen plates. Called *Nauclea orientalis*, it's a tree shared and admired from New Guinea to Burma and Sri Lanka – another reminder of the zone of exchange in which the Gulf Country sits.

I don't know whether this magnificent, isolated gorge even knows that the fire has been through. On its banks grow pandanus with hard grenades of fruit. Under the rock overhang are middens of mussel shells and rock paintings. I look to distinguish art from the colours and patterns formed by water leaching through rock, making the same sort of chemical transformations that form fossils. Lowering myself into a shaded lagoon where water churns over a spongy red tufa wall and fish swarm, I bathe up to my neck, gazing at the blue lilies that float on the surface at the other end of the pond. I wish I was not alone. I wish my wife Claire was here. She's a curator. She's away in China, researching a certain brush-and-ink painter at the Fine Arts Academy in Hangzhou. I wish Bob could be here again from New York to enjoy this part.

A large turtle with a spiky knobbed head paws towards the verge. Is it a Gulf snapping turtle, *Elseya lavarackorum*, the identical one to the 50,000-year-old fossil found at Riversleigh and thought to be extinct – until they were found swimming here in the gorge at Indarri Falls? As I watch, drops of rain spear the surface, sending out ripples. The drops get heavier and faster. The heat is breaking. Soon tropical rain is pouring into the gorge. I can smell the rain on the sooty earth, smell the carbon.

For Waanyi people, like Alexis Wright, whose grandmother was born by this water, the place is Boodjamulla or Rainbow Serpent Country. The songline of the Rainbow Serpent, telling how he created the waterhole to keep his skin wet, runs through the area. It intersects here with a dingo songline that travels from the mining town of Mount Isa, 250 kilometres south-east, to Mornington Island out in the Gulf, making this a powerful as well as beautiful place. Like the dragon in Chinese mythology, Boodjamulla can be understood as a symbol of the good or ill that lies with water in a land prone to drought and flood, veined with unruly rivers. Twenty per cent of continental Australia's freshwater run-off flows through these channels to the Gulf. If the Rainbow Serpent is disturbed in his dwelling place, there'll be big trouble. That is what the Century mine has brought.

The place I'm camping in is called Adel's Grove, after Albert de Lestang, a French botanist who ran an experimental garden here back in the 1920s on a pocket of land downstream from the gorge. Alexis Wright's Waanyi great-grandmother and Chinese great-grandfather had their market garden on the nearby banks of Louie Creek. When the river dried up for the first time in living memory, they thought it must have been because the Frenchman was messing with the water-courses. Lestang's hermit dwelling and a trunk containing all his research were mysteriously destroyed by fire while he was away one time. A few exotic trees and some clumps of bamboo are his legacy.

The camping ground is in the care of a couple. At least they seem like a couple, but they turn out to be strangers to each other. They are helping out the owner, the woman's friend and the man's sister, while she's away. The woman is having time out from her miner husband in Mount Isa. The man is back from Spain for a while. I'm their only guest. The man's crucifix bounces on his sweaty belly as he and I lever a new tyre on to the old rim.

'Whore!' he swears, repeatedly. 'Whore!' He tells me Australia has become a police state because there are fines for serving drinks to drunks in pubs. After a couple of beers I retire to my tent. There's a phone here, but it isn't working. There's no light to read by so I put *The Lost Steps* away. I think of the phone boxes I've stood in on this journey, trying to get through to people. They're like vertical coffins of light in dark empty streets and the conversation I overhear in the next booth is always the same.

'It's me, babe. I love you. I want you with me tonight.' Human beings separated by vast distances. Agile wallabies scratching round outside my tent.

~

The Century zinc mine came into operation the year before my visit, following an agreement with Aboriginal communities that took years of acrimonious negotiation.

Those who opposed the mine were concerned, among other things, about its impact on the environment, so close to Boodjamulla, the name now given to Lawn Hill National Park and the Riversleigh world heritage site. Century has moved a mountain for its mine, literally, a 340-metre deep open pit. It makes a gap in the range that looks, from a distance, like a missing tooth.[4]

The first mining lease, known as Silver King, was pegged at Lawn Hill in 1887. A century later Conzinc Rio Tinto Australia Exploration Ltd was granted tenements for the working of what would be billed as the biggest zinc mine in the world.

They named it Century. Who deserves the credit for such discoveries? The deposit is located in a band of mineral-bearing rock that extends from the McArthur River in the north to Mount Isa in the south. The discovery of what became the Mount Isa mine, then the world's biggest silver and lead producer, is credited to a prospector called John Campbell Miles in 1923. But in 1980 David Trigger interviewed a Garawa man who swore that when he was young he was the one who showed that first mineral deposit to the white man. The Aboriginal man was known as Old Silver, but the name was all he got. It seems to be a law of mining that the one who cries 'Eureka!' is seldom the one who runs away with the spoils.

The Century mine is in two parts, the ore body at Lawn Hill and a pipeline to take the mineral slurry – 5 million tonnes of ore a year when fully operational – to port at Karumba on the Gulf. There it is transferred by barge to ore carriers moored at sea for shipping to the company's zinc smelter at Budel in the Netherlands. The zinc concentrate at Century, a form known as jarosite, became crucial to the company after the Dutch government outlawed other kinds of zinc concentrate because of the amount of toxic waste that was produced in smelting.

From the outset there were powerful expectations that the mine would go ahead as planned.

In 1992 the company acquired the Lawn Hill pastoral lease that included a 1907 camping and water reserve, a common for use by Aboriginal people. It also purchased Riversleigh and adjoining leases to a total of 15,000 hectares

Lawn Hill Gorge (Boodjamulla)

and sought a special lease of a corridor of land for the 300-kilometre pipeline. Early proposals included a route to the coast near Old Doomadgee through land and waters of particular sensitivity to Aboriginal people. That 'started a groundswell of absolute opposition'. The Waanyi considered themselves the traditional owners of the land round the mine. In buying up those leases, the company – CZL, a subsidiary of Conzinc Rio Tinto – had become the holder of most of the Waanyi estate in Queensland.

In a spirit of good neighbourliness CZL wrote to the Carpentaria Land Council, the representative Aboriginal body in the region, that 'it is our desire to ensure that the Waanyi benefit from the project, although we do not believe we have any statutory obligation in this regard'. The company offered

$100,000 compensation to those affected by a mine that would cost $1.135 billion to build and would generate profits worth nine times that amount in its 20-year life.* The offer was ignored. In the argument that ensued there were three main players: intransigent government; a pragmatic company willing to try anything to get its mine; and fractured Aboriginal groups with very little bargaining power.

In June 1992 the Australian High Court's *Mabo* decision recognised that Aboriginal people had rights to land they had occupied continuously since British sovereignty was imposed. The Native Title Act 1993 attempted to codify these rights. It was arguable that on pastoral leases in remote Australia Aboriginal people had indeed maintained their traditional connections with the land. But these were unexplored issues in June 1994 when some Waanyi people lodged a native title claim for the common at Lawn Hill. Murrandoo Yanner organised a sit-in of 400 people at the gorge to support the claim. The sit-in alarmed people with the scale of force that could be mustered seemingly from nowhere in that sparsely populated land and made Murrandoo a marked man.

The action brought Alexis Wright back to Lawn Hill to join the Louie Creek mob. She knew them from years earlier when she had lived on Mornington Island, taking part in the fight for local control of the community. An old Waanyi woman there, an old friend, had been delivered by Wright's great-grandmother. They were her people.

On appeal to the High Court the Waanyi were permitted

* All currency amounts in this chapter are in Australian dollars.

to register their native title claim, in the face of every effort by CZL and the government to 'extinguish' it – as if Aboriginal rights were like wildfire. The registration of the claim forced the company to negotiate within the framework of native title. The High Court's *Wik* decision of 1996 set a further precedent for native title rights to co-exist with other rights on pastoral leases. Advice back in 1848 from the Secretary of State in London, Earl Grey, to the colonial Governor of New South Wales was used to justify the finding: 'Leases are not intended to deprive the natives of their former right to hunt over these districts, or to wander over them in search for subsistence, in the manner to which they have been heretofore accustomed … except over land actually cultivated [or] fenced in for that purpose.' In other words, a pastoral lease had never guaranteed exclusive possession.

Behind this contentious decision lay a potential re-examination of the concept of property itself, with a renewed stress on what legal philosophers call the Lockean proviso. In his *Second Treatise of Government* (1690), John Locke argued that property can only be held lawfully with the proviso that 'there is enough, and as good left in common for others'.[5] That might also apply to different kinds of rights held simultaneously over the same property. It could come to apply to degrees of autonomy or even sovereignty that might co-exist in one territory, pointing the way to a more flexible concept of nationhood than operates at present. Such advances might be the ultimate, far-off legacy of small beginnings in this disputed, disputatious part of the world.

A local parliamentarian suggested that the newly recognised Aboriginal rights, if not extinguished, would create 'a Berlin Wall stretching a third of the way down the spine of Queensland'.[6] The federal government under Prime Minister John Howard set about dismantling the *Wik* judgement with a provocative ten-point plan, which lawyers warned would discriminate against Aboriginal people. At the height of the row, the mine at Century was in the spotlight.

In August 1995 CZL had upped its compensation offer to Aboriginal people to $60 million, to be matched by $30 million from the Queensland government – a considerable advance on the initial offer of $100,000. The list of benefits included education, employment and training of Aboriginal people, development assistance to Aboriginal businesses in the region, measures to protect the environment and nurture Aboriginal culture, and the transfer of pastoral properties acquired by the company to Aboriginal ownership. It was a significant package, agreed in consultations between the miner and Aboriginal communities. In November that year the Queensland government acted unilaterally and granted the company approval to go ahead. The state stood to gain $460 million in royalty payments.

But the company wanted a watertight agreement with local communities. The Carpentaria Land Council, led by its co-ordinator, Murrandoo Yanner, flatly opposed the mine and any agreement negotiated behind its back. The Land Council was prepared to insist on a power of veto. Yanner questioned the good faith of the company and the state government.

Murrandoo Yanner, watched by Clarence Walden, meets Queensland Premier Rob Borbidge, Karumba, April 1996

'We are on the warpath,' he is quoted as saying. Pressure was coming from all sides to accept the package – from the company, from national Aboriginal leaders interested in brokering an outcome, and from within local communities seeking benefits for themselves. 'North West Queensland has hit the billion dollar jackpot,' trumpeted the Mount Isa *North West Star* newspaper when the mine looked like going ahead. Against all this Murrandoo stood firm. 'We have a thousand warriors,' he swore. 'We aren't going to sell the environment or sell our souls.'

The government blustered. Queensland premier Rob Borbidge denounced 'meddlesome, self-seeking activists [who wanted to kill] off a golden goose that promised so much'. The company was more sanguine. They knew that hostility from local people could make life very difficult for them on the ground. By this stage a local Gulf Underground Resistance Movement had declared its readiness for guerrilla action. In that remote area it would be difficult to protect a mine against sabotage or to counter large numbers of militants. The spectre of Bougainville hovered.

In 1988 indigenous resentment towards the mighty Bougainville copper mine in Papua New Guinea had erupted. Mine installations were bombed and, in the escalating violence, the islanders demanded their independence from the PNG state. Mining has seldom been good for indigenous peoples. In Australia the concept of Aboriginal land rights was forged when the Yolngu of Arnhem Land took bauxite miner Nabalco to court in 1970–71. A rare positive example is the case of gold mining in central Australia where the Central Land Council worked with Warlpiri people in the 1980s to minimise 'the worst excesses of imposed mining' by seeking 'a commitment to empowerment rather than simply conflict management'.[7] Where there is a mine, there is likely to be a movement for greater autonomy and for more direct control of resources. That lesson has not been lost in the Gulf, where indigenous people who are fighting for their freedom by any means possible have strong traditional relationships across the water – with the Torres Strait Islands, where Eddie Mabo pioneered the recognition of native title; with newly independent East Timor; and with West Papua, where the politics of secession from Indonesia is fuelled by disputed benefits from the rich Freeport gold mine. Examples of indigenous militancy further afield have also inspired these present-day Gulf warriors, such as the armed stand-off by Canadian First Nations peoples to stop a stretch of trees being levelled for a golf course in Oka, Quebec, in 1990, and the deadly confrontation between members of the American Indian Movement and the FBI in the Black Hills of Dakota in 1975, described in Peter Matthiessen's book *In the Spirit of Crazy Horse.*

At the height of the hysteria about Century confidential memos were circulated in Canberra that Murrandoo Yanner had dumped three kangaroo carcasses at the gate of the mine site to intimidate the company. Murrandoo laughs at this fabrication, saying if he had killed anything it would have been three bullocks. Around the same time Black Hawk helicopters from the Australian army were sent to patrol the bush in the area, on the pretext that a stash of beer stolen from Burketown could be recovered by infra-red detection of the heat it gave out at night. The Land Council complained to the Australian government that the last time Black Hawks were sent in it was to support PNG government forces in quashing the revolutionaries on Bougainville. In Doomadgee I saw a faded fax message on the notice board from those same Bougainville revolutionaries, supporting the struggle to stop the mine.

The scenario that terrifies the mining company has inspired a scene in Alexis Wright's new novel *Carpentaria*, where she imagines the destruction of Gurfurritt, the biggest mine in the country: 'All it took was a simple flick. A flick,

flick, here and there with a dirt cheap cigarette lighter ... Like guyfork night. Booom! Booom! Over and over. But one hundred times more louder than that. Ripped the lot ...'[8]

Murrandoo Yanner earned his spurs in the fight over Century. It was another kind of initiation into rhetoric, theatre and the power of ambit claims. The envelope is there to be pushed, laws are for testing, rights to be won. With all the ancient issues at its heart, this is also a contemporary game of public relations at home and abroad, legal and political process without end, brawling and bravado.

Murrandoo's success can be judged by his enemies' efforts to defuse him. Of the many instances of harassment during the Century fight, the best known and most bizarre is the crocodile case, which ended up in the High Court. In 1994 Murrandoo was charged with spearing two young crocodiles in territory near Burketown. Apparently the police found the crocodiles in his freezer. Burketown is usually a place of live and let live. This was a set-up. The Queensland Fauna Conservation Act protects crocodiles as property of the Crown. Murrandoo argued that he had a native title right to hunt wildlife for food and skins according to tradition.

In a landmark ruling in 1999, to which the name Yanner is forever attached, the Court found in his favour, arguing that conservation measures may regulate the use of fauna but do not extinguish native title hunting rights. The court transcript takes us into the *Alice in Wonderland* world that lawyers must enter to consider property rights in these new contexts. The implications extend far beyond crocodiles to other attributes of land and traditional waters, including the valuable mineral resources that may lie beneath:

> QC FOR THE RESPONDENT (QUEENSLAND): Fundamental to our proposition, of course, is that the language of section 7 of the Fauna Conservation Act is effective to confer on the Crown what we have described as absolute property, or absolute ownership.
>
> JUDGE A: But first do you not have to catch a crocodile? It is all very nice to talk about it, absolute rights. Until you have caught it, you do not have any, in practice.
>
> QC FOR THE RESPONDENT: At common law, of course, the position was such that the Crown did not have title or ownership to wild animals save, perhaps, for the special case of the royal animals, swans, cygnets and the like. However, it was within the power of the Parliament to enact a provision such as this and, in our submission, the language which has been adopted is appropriate and effective to achieve the result for which we contend.
>
> JUDGE B: It is a strange notion of property, is it not? A cockatoo is your property until he flies over the border.
>
> QC FOR THE RESPONDENT: Your Honour is quite right, but if we take any example whatsoever, whilst the bird or the mammal, or other animal, is beyond the boundaries of the State it, necessarily, cannot be the property of whatever character, whatever meaning we achieve.

JUDGE C: Why is that? The Queensland Parliament has extraterritorial jurisdiction if it deems a cockatoo, even perhaps a crocodile in Queensland, to be Queensland property of the Crown, and it wanders into New South Wales and then wanders back or wanders into the Northern Territory and wanders back, why does it lose that property because it goes into another jurisdiction? … Does that not prove that you have to read down the word 'property'? It just does not mean property in the sense of full ownership, all the bundles of interests that go with ownership. It is a special kind of property for the purpose of the Act.

At the time of the crocodile case, the Prime Minister's office in Canberra, alerted by local fears of guerrilla militancy, took an interest in Murrandoo Yanner and the affairs of the Carpentaria Land Council. After one incident Murrandoo was charged with assault. Given a suspended sentence, he had to wait two years before taking up his elected position as an Aboriginal and Torres Strait Islander Commissioner. Sympathy for him wore thin in many quarters. In the *North West Star* his protest actions were denounced as 'treason'. He 'has the potential to become a great leader,' said one Aboriginal elder at Doomadgee, but 'he needs guidance from the right people'.

Murrandoo sought advice from the powerful Central Land Council in Alice Springs. Tracker Tilmouth, one of the most experienced of Aboriginal strategists, came across to help. Tilmouth is another member of the stolen generations.

He had grown up in a 'half-caste' mission home on Croker Island, off the coast of Arnhem Land, as had Irene Yanner, who knew him from those old days. With Clarence Walden from Doomadgee Council and Gangalidda activist Wadjularbinna involved too, the Carpentaria Land Council was prepared to put up a good fight.

Greenies were concerned about the mine too. They questioned the company's strategy of 'de-watering' the aquifer beneath the mine to prevent the pit flooding. 'It seems almost insane to take water out of a dry area,' said the co-ordinator of the North Queensland Conservation Council, unconvinced there would be no impact on the area's riverine ecosystem. People worried about spillage once the ore slurry reached Karumba and was transshipped. What would happen when the cyclones came? Both environmentalists and workers' unions would have preferred to see the zinc concentrate transported via Mount Isa on the existing rail track to the well-equipped, unionised wharf at Townsville. That would have protected the Gulf waters for Aboriginal people, fishing and tourism alike.

Older people at Doomadgee and other communities focused on opportunities the mine might bring their grandchildren, if not their children. Local schools, for example, stop short before the end of high school. If they are to complete their education, kids must go away to school, which costs money. Of the benefits package, $45 million was earmarked for training, employment and other job-creation activities. Century flies most of its workforce in and out from

Townsville, 1,000 kilometres away, however, which means that local Aboriginal people are rarely employed at the mine. Two hundred jobs were promised for local Aboriginal people by 2001. But of 1,200 staff at Century in November 2001, I'm told that only 40 were Aboriginal people, of whom a mere 10 had local connections.

The Carpentaria Land Council derided the benefits package as beads and trinkets. 'Aboriginal children [deserve] to grow in a free and pristine environment with a strong cultural bonding to the rest of their people,' insisted Murrandoo Yanner, underlining the grassroots connection between his indigenous politics and his environmentalist vision. 'We are not selfish people but we don't want our waters poisoned,' said one woman.

Wadjularbinna travelled from Doomadgee to Rio Tinto's annual general meeting in London in 1996. It was closed down before she could speak. Protesting against the smelter at Budel, she told the Dutch government that, cajoled by the company, 'Aboriginal people are agreeing to destroy themselves'. Behind the scenes some traditional owner groups were ready to accept the company's offers. In Doomadgee and Burketown discord was rife, often along family lines. The 'mine was generating some "anti-white" sentiment,' reported the chairman of Doomadgee Council.

Such divisions played into the fractured history of displacement and dispossession experienced by most people in the region, and especially at Doomadgee. It was near impossible for the community to speak with one voice as an equal partner with a transnational corporation in a complicated, speculative negotiation. The fight became as much about Aboriginal political issues as it was about indigenous versus non-indigenous interests, but 'neither company nor government people showed much understanding of the complexities of Aboriginal politicking over this sort of matter'. Any agreement under such conditions would 'likely be strung together under considerable tensions, as a delicate web of threads,' conclude Robert Blowes and David Trigger in their analysis of the negotiation process.[9]

On 28 June 1996 a decision of implicated communities approved the mining agreement by 12 votes to 11. The Land Council pronounced the vote invalid. The company had 'openly declared war on Australian soil in the Gulf of Carpentaria,' said Murrandoo Yanner. 'Blood will flow.' He meant that the company was prepared to take what it wanted, come what may, crashing through its legal obligations to negotiate with native title claimants. The Mayor of Burketown, speaking for those who saw the mine as an economic boon, lost patience: '[The Aboriginal groups] are travelling at Dreamtime pace when we are going into the 21st century,' he opined. A week later a second vote was taken which opposed the mine unanimously. At the request of the company the state and federal governments considered enacting special legislation 'in the national interest' that would allow the mine to go ahead without Aboriginal consent.

A similar approach had been taken by the Northern Territory and federal governments in 1993 to enable the

McArthur River lead-silver-zinc mine near Borroloola to proceed. Within a month of the company submitting its environmental impact statement, approval was given. Prospectors had staked claims in the area for over a century and Mount Isa Mines had been carrying out explorations since the 1950s, but the metallurgical know-how required for the rich deposit was not at hand until the 1990s. Delays had cost the company. For the sake of its long-suffering shareholders the mine was pushed through.

People from Doomadgee were brought by the Century negotiators to see the McArthur River mine. The ore is taken by road-train on a land corridor to Bing Bong where it is loaded on to a barge that chugs down a specially dug channel to a vessel waiting offshore. That required a deal with Mara, Garawa and Yanyuwa people for whom Bing Bong is an important ceremony site. It's not clear how satisfactory a deal they were able to strike. Bing Bong is off-limits to the public, an efficient-looking deep-water port where there is no deep water. Given the toxicity of lead-zinc extraction, the transfers need to be monitored properly. Mining companies are supposed to clean up after themselves, but, according to Northern Territory government minister John Ah Kit, fine-sounding environmental undertakings are not always enforced. McArthur River is a self-contained, fly-in, fly-out mine and leaves Borroloola alone. Maybe the people of Borroloola like it that way.

'This is the first test for the right to negotiate process [under native title] and it has failed,' said the *North West Star*.

Aboriginal groups were suspicious that the Century negotiations had not been in good faith from the start. There was talk of secret arrangements in which different Aboriginal parties were played off against each other. One Waanyi group withdrew when sweetheart deals came to light, feeling 'duped by one of the world's largest mining companies and betrayed by their own people'. Large loud meetings were staged in which opposing groups argued for contending versions of what their culture required of them. It looked like a newly politicised form of traditional Aboriginal ceremony.

At the height of the impasse senior elders from Borroloola stepped in to give their wisdom. They came with the authority of a regional stronghold of Aboriginal culture, a place where law has remained strong and important ceremonies are held which people attend from all over. The late Yanyuwa lawman, Mussolini Harvey, expressed it as a defining principle: 'We … have had to fight for country. We have had to stand up to keep our law safe … This law is the way we live, our rules. This law is our ceremonies, our songs, our stories; all of these things come from the Dreaming … Our law cannot change.'[10] Yet in a crisis that law found ways to adapt to unprecedented times. Those Borroloola elders spoke the law. Murrandoo Yanner's teacher, Blue Bob, was among them. They said that the hill the mining company wanted to move should not be regarded as a deal-breaking impediment. It may have been a place where many people had camped, but it was not a spiritually charged site. Those senior lawmen would not stand in the way.

'Mine saga ends' hailed the *North West Star* in May 1997, commenting philosophically on the lessons learned: 'There is an old saying that everything on this earth is either mined or grown. Therefore, respecting the needs of all parties, mining and farming are needed for the survival of all people.' The newspaper was harking back to an old gag about Australia being no more than a farm and a mine. The Century zinc deposit is undoubtedly a valuable asset. But is now the best time to sell it off? I thought about zinc, first produced by Indian metallurgists in the thirteenth century. It's used for brass and semi-conductors, television screens and photocopiers, cosmetics and antiviral agents, bleach and dental cement and for galvanizing and welding and in alloys of all kinds. Without zinc the body cannot survive nor the mind function. I thought of Zinc Street, Broken Hill.

The Carpentaria Land Council lost the fight. The compensation package may have been reasonable, but the process was ugly and wounding. In a genuine attempt to build relationships with Aboriginal people, CZL's management learned to be more flexible than their own legal advisers, paying more than they had to, if only as a means to an end. Some Aboriginal protagonists still feel they were rolled. The agreement, now under a five-year review, may not have been implemented fully, perhaps because it was inadequately negotiated in the first place. Century has proved to be an uncongenial environment for many who have worked there, especially those who did their 12 months' training and were not kept on. A disaffected workforce that knows how it works from the inside does not make the mine any more secure.

Tracker Tilmouth is clear about the problems. Mining on the Century model brings benefits far away but little to Aboriginal communities. He points out that the company's $60 million 'rent' amounts to 0.6 per cent of the value of the mine. He wants a new kind of resource economics to factor in such goods as the environment and social harmony. Base-level data are needed against which changes in community well-being can be measured. The impact assessment statement prepared by CZL included Aboriginal issues only as a supplement to the main report on which decisions about the mine were made. As accountants Andrew Chew and Susan Greer explain, no philosophical consideration was given to the underlying moral relations in the imbalance of power between proponents and opponents of development. The exploitation of land for economic gain depends on its severability. It's a piece of real estate. But for Aboriginal people the land asks to be looked after rather than exploited. The *yang* values in mainstream developmental accounting suppress the *yin* values of environmental and community nurturing. 'I will not sell that land – it is my blood,' is how one committed opponent of the project summed up her feelings.

No sooner was the Century mine up and running than its parent company, now Pasminco, went into voluntary administration thanks to some excessively *yang* currency hedging by its managers. In September 2001 trading in its shares was suspended and the mine was put on the market. Suitors sniffed around, but the offers were too low. The Waanyi, Mingginda, Gkuthaarn, Kukatj, Century Agreement of May 1997 gets sold with the mine. The last thing the company wants is any indication that the mine is encumbered with problems from indigenous people. But if the spirit of the agreement has been breached, there could be grounds to re-open the whole thing. 'We'll ratfuck them,' grins one sceptical participant in the review.

For the Carpentaria Land Council, though Murrandoo Yanner probably would not say so, Century was a strategic defeat. The fight was also about winning back dignity and self-respect for people who have lost almost everything. Strength comes with wearing the loss and being ready to fight another day. The strain on the Yanner family has been considerable; the solidarity too. Young leaders have flexed their muscles. The stakes have been raised. There won't be another mine in the Gulf in a hurry.

Whoever you talk to about Century has something different to say. It's not black and white. A textured account must bring in legitimately varying, even conflicting points of view. My sketch of what happened is no more than a mud map.

'The history of the last ten years is the history of one man – Murrandoo Yanner,' says a veteran of many Aboriginal legal struggles. But it's not only a story of David versus Goliath in the boardrooms and backrooms and courts of law. More importantly it's a story of complex relationships on the ground – family, clan and community – through which local action coalesces and stands up to power, changing the political equation for good. It's in part a story of the legacy of those old men of Borroloola.

What about the mighty fire, burning to the edges of the gorge? Has the Rainbow Serpent been disturbed? At the end of its 20-year life Century will be a grave. Maybe by then the children of the Gulf Country will have grown up healthy and confident about the next moves in making the dream of running their own lives in their own land a reality.

EPILOGUE

CRANKHANDLES

Cattle roam the roads, waiting round the bend for a car. They are the most common road kill. The baggy hide, lying there after birds have eaten the flesh, looks like the donkey costume I remember from children's parties, where one child would be the front and one the back. The warning sign shows a car smashing its nose up against an unmoved beast, making a genuflection: Obey the Cow God![1] These are Brahma cattle mostly, *Bos indicus*, that come from India. There's Hereford, Shorthorn and a cross with Angus called Brangus and an Indu Brazil improvement and a mix known simply as Brown Plains. There are wild ox brought long ago from Indonesia. But Brahma dominates across the Gulf Savannah. It's on every menu, OK if you know how to cook it.

They are complicated-looking animals with their humps and bumps, their ears like wet laundry, chopped for branding, and their Bette Davis eyes. When a steer gambols in the rain, throwing hooves high in the air, you can feel the temptation to chase it and wrestle it down in a real-life merry-go-round. But when a big old Brahma bull stands his ground in the middle of the road there's not much you can do. His chin folds all the way to his pizzle, an extended knob that bobs to the ground with an aureole of black hair. He knows his ancestors were adored. Their images were painted on cave walls by the earliest mark-making humans. He has been the fatted calf and the golden calf. His qualities explain months and years in a never-ending cycle, Taurus, the Year of the Ox. Humans covet him for his taste and his protein and her milk. Cattle are currency, revered under the golden arches of hamburger outlets around the world. Is this the real religion that the interlopers introduced? It was their desire to feed on bullock that brought so many Aboriginal tribes into fatal conflict with Europeans, even as it was Aboriginal people who sustained the cattle industry with their labour. Only now are people questioning whether beef is sustainable in this country. Cloven hoofs break up the environment, unlike the kangaroo paws that have padded here for centuries. The bull blocks me with his ancient dignity then, nostrils flaring, the great Brahma moves delicately out of the way.

You might think this is a wandering book, but I have followed my nose, bringing along the baggage of an overstocked mind with all its stray threads. I didn't ask at the outset what finding Roger Jose would mean. There have been many dead-ends and blocks along the way. Often I felt excluded from what I wanted to know. I have had to accept that nothing is definitive, and then make discoveries, learning that a complex past leaves a human map for the present, with tracks pointing to the future.

One of the maps that got me here goes back to Adelaide and the Writers' Week at its festival of arts. I was sprawled on the grassy bank at the back as a visiting speaker – Oliver Sacks or J. M. Coetzee? – performed the loaves-and-fishes miracle of language to the 5,000 or more people flowing up the hill from the hot tent. 'It's the real thing,' quipped a London publisher, tossing the hair out of his eyes. Alexis Wright was sitting with me on the shady mound when she turned and said: 'Why don't you write a book about what's happening in the Gulf?' That was in 1998. 'Go on,' she dared me with a husky laugh. Later, as I thought about her invitation, Borroloola floated into my mind with the image of Roger Jose as a starting point.

At the second Adelaide Festival, way back in 1962, a visiting David Attenborough gave public lectures on the wonders of nature in the Majestic Theatre. At Writers' Week he could have met Douglas Lockwood, who won first prize that year for his book *I, The Aboriginal*, or those old literary scrub bulls, Xavier Herbert and Bill Harney, all offering pointers north. Twenty years later at another Writers' Week it was introductions from Robyn Davidson, the author of *Tracks*, that pointed Salman Rushdie and Bruce Chatwin north from Adelaide to Alice Springs and the desert. In a few years' time Nicholas Shakespeare, also visiting for Writers' Week, would follow in Chatwin's footsteps on a biographical quest north.

In *The Songlines* Bruce Chatwin quotes Rimbaud, writing home from Ethiopia: 'What am I doing here?' The question became the title for Chatwin's posthumously published journalism and has come to be identified with him, as he identified with Rimbaud, symbolist poet and gay nomad, who dealt with a writing block by exchanging poetry for trade in Africa. Chatwin came to the deserts of Australia knowing precisely the answer to Rimbaud's question. He was there to write the book about nomads that he had been planning all his life. He wanted to bring Aboriginal understanding into it. Their songlines – a term created by the anthropologist T. E. H. Strehlow – were his prize exhibit. But in the end he had to make up a lot of it. *The Songlines* is an Englishman's love letter to Australia, a sharp romance and still one of the most influential books ever written about the country. Like Alexis de Tocqueville, a French aristocrat reporting on democracy in America, or D. H. Lawrence, who wrote *Kangaroo* in a six-week stint in Australia, Chatwin tried to see beneath the skin as he passed through. He already knew Australia through some of his lovers. Earlier, in Patagonia, he had filched a copy of *Kangaroo* from an Australian backpacker. *Kangaroo* is a love letter too, of the passionate insightful rejection that DHL specialised in. Lawrence felt denied by what he called the 'withheld self' of Australia.

Chatwin felt something similar in relation to Aboriginal society. He was angry that he couldn't just fly in and fly out with what he wanted. Those who blocked information or questioned the superficiality of his theories are caricatured in *The Songlines.* His friend Robyn Davidson, who sent him to people in Alice Springs who knew about Aboriginal life, suggests that Chatwin realised 'he was just scratching the surface and he *was* excluded. He found it very difficult as an idea that there were some things you couldn't know.'[2] Others describe the exclusion Chatwin experienced as a response to him as a predator, a coloniser, 'part of a uniquely English tradition of men in rumpled white shirts at the far-flung corners of the world'. [3] Nicholas Shakespeare explains that 'Aboriginal society is, by definition, a secret society. Even to gain a rudimentary knowledge you have to pay your dues in a profound way.'[4] An anthropologist who met Chatwin in an Aboriginal community in the desert called him the agent 'of a cult without secrets. There is something intolerable in the West about secret knowledge. Everything has to be transparent.'[5]

Nothing is transparent, except words well used, and then they only show us through to the opacity of life. Chatwin's solution was to create the character of Arkady, a cosmopolitan who has renounced the city for the desert, a wise man who can give him the good oil. In real life Arkady was Toly Sawenko. He is Alexis Wright's husband. Tourists trek to their door in Alice Springs clutching copies of *The Songlines.* At the time Sawenko didn't know that Chatwin was writing a book and after it came out he wasn't sent a copy. Chatwin died in 1989. Sawenko says generously that Chatwin 'missed a tremendous opportunity by not posing his conceptual questions directly to the people he was writing about'. Arkady was used instead as 'a convenient artifice': Chatwin 'hadn't sorted the protocols through'.[6] The way was left open for Alexis

Wright and others after her to write the true fiction of the songlines.

Some of the story is being told in visual art. One of the greatest of all contemporary painters is a Mara man called Ginger Riley Munduwalawala. He was born in 1937 and grew up in Borroloola. Roy Hammer, the elder who showed me Roger Jose's grave, is his younger brother. As a teenage stockman Riley travelled across country to central Australia where he met Albert Namatjira, the pioneering desert watercolourist. He always remembered how Namatjira had created his 'colour country' using whitefella materials. Riley started as what he calls a 'tip painter', working on whatever junk was to hand, using the vibrant colours of synthetic polymer paint to create his own mythically intense colour country, with perhaps a memory of the brilliant textiles the Macassans had brought or the sumptuously clad Chinese.[7] A younger artist, Judy Watson, takes the heritage of textiles and the water consciousness of the Gulf Country into more abstract work with canvas and other fabrics, some of which is inspired by journeys back into Waanyi country with her mother and grandmother. In *driftnet* she stretches stringybark across the cotton surface, woven 'with a dillybag stitch to represent a net held across a watery expanse, evoking notions of fluidity and visceral passages'.[8] Using more traditional means too, coastal people are using their art to assert their indigenous belonging to sea as well as land, with native title over traditional waters at issue in Australia's highest courts. 'Our designs, embassies and homelands' is how one

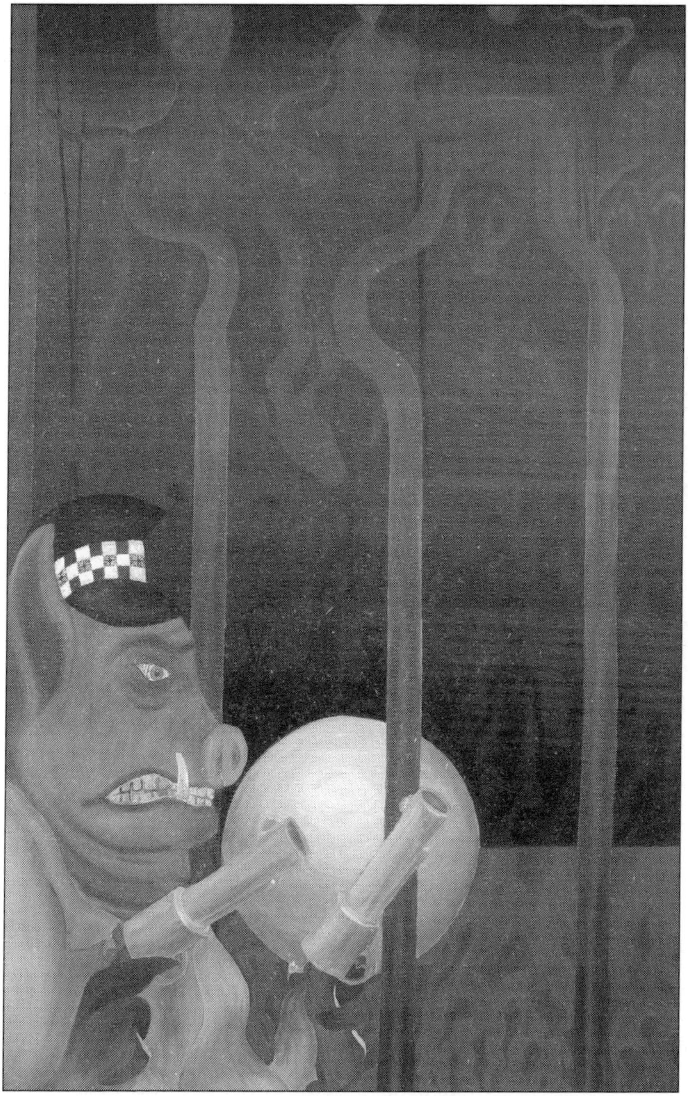

Gordon Hookey, Bully-min bin luck hup habrid-jinny plag, *1995*

senior Arnhem Land painter sums up their work.[9] Aboriginal curator Djon Mundine concludes that 'using only the materials of their own bush, the artists here trace a serene current through the raging waters of controversy'.[10]

Down South, far from his Waanyi land, a younger, more overtly political artist called Gordon Hookey lacerates the rapacity and prejudice of the Australian state through in-ya-face images inscribed with rap lyrics. (Hookey is another transliterated Chinese name.) The artist depicts a 'Redneck-ocracy' with the Minister for Immigration and Aboriginal Affairs as a redcoat Ku Klux Klan priest. 'Terra-ism', Hookey's painting of a kangaroo with a shotgun, fills a wall in Murrandoo Yanner's home in Burketown. The Yanners and the Hookeys feuded over the Century mine. Gordon Hookey's gift of a painting is his personal peace offering to the Carpentaria Land Council.

Aboriginal people have found new ways of staking their place in Australia since Roger Jose's day. It's Murrandoo Yanner's time now. But latter-day eccentrics exist alongside the new generation of leaders. The hermit headcount at Borroloola is still seven. There are dopeheads and misanthropes and refugees from the CIA, old white men living out bush who are seen in town maybe once a year. Everyone has a story. The Gulf is home to lunatics with shotguns and trucks and pitbulls ready to take on any invading hordes. It has changed and not changed in 100 years.

At times I have been frustrated that things were hidden from me because of my outsider status and that so much was regarded as flotsam and jetsam to be washed away by time in this land of willing oblivion. I had to be patient with the vast spaces I could never compass and the corners into which I could never go, understanding that it was often my own shadow – the direction I was coming from – that kept me in the dark. Had I been only a visitor that might not have bothered me. But unlike Bruce Chatwin I was not completely an interloper. I was a partial insider, seeking to find where the ground might be shared. Between Roger Jose and Murrandoo Yanner, across a chasm, there's a geographical and even a political continuity. Those old lawmen of the Borroloola region knew Roger when they were young. One world has given birth to the other. As a modern Australian I need to find that connection in myself.

Part of acknowledging a shared zone of responsibility is granting the infinite space for all the things that do not and cannot concern me. That's a way of respecting the freedom of other people with whom I find connection. Toni Morrison quotes Saul Bellow's *Henderson the Rain King* to suggest why Western writers went to Africa: 'The answer, forthrightly, is desire: "I want, I want, I want."'[11] She interprets the problems they identified as 'imponderables … riddles that defied solution; conflicts that not only did not need to be resolved, but needed to exist if the process of self-discovery was to have the widest range of play'. To get over that sense of exclusion without having to crash through or project fantasies outward is to accept a common humanity, a shared situation. Shiva Naipaul was never sourer than when the Northern Land

Council banned him from entering traditional Aboriginal land. The itinerant writer was in Darwin researching a book on Australia that sadly he didn't live to complete. He damned Aboriginal politics in his own exclusionary response: 'The flight into Aboriginality, into blackness, is a flight into despair; an escape from the challenges of history.' But who is resisting history here? Naipaul skewered white Australians in a one-liner too: 'Rob that man of his racism and you rob him of everything.'[12] Is there no way to step outside that uncharmed circle of identity and counter-identity? Misunderstanding of the protocols of exclusion and inclusion threatens to turn many Australians toxic towards the aspirations of indigenous and minority groups even now. Perhaps acknowledging the personal imperatives of history is a start. The clue is to step back from abstraction, the frame of reference that an outsider seizes on, and move closer to the way people improvise actual lives.

A story like this should end with a recognition scene, a moment of reconciliation between lost and found. I do not know if I can be Cordelia to Roger Jose's Lear. Is there a family resemblance? Of course I can see one. My friend Bob sends a message from New York to say I should go on the road as Roger Jose in a one-man show, put on the turban and wallaby slippers and recite garbled chunks of inspirational literature in a bardic voice, before snorting an abusive substance. But I don't have Roger's quads or pecs.

Besides, there are many other Joses who could be related to Roger. It's an uncommon surname in Australia but was less so in the nineteenth century when many Cornish Joses came out from Britain to work in tin and copper mines in South Australia. Across the border from Cornwall in Devon the name can be spelled Joce, as it is Joyce over the sea in Ireland. These and many other variants ultimately go back to the Hebrew name Joseph, adoptive father of Jesus. Our family goes back to Joses in St Ives, Cornwall, in the eighteenth century. There may be earlier Portuguese or Spanish connections around the Cornish coast, through pirates or the Armada or conversos and Huguenots fleeing the Spanish Inquisition. Charles Bean, the historian, saw his teacher and friend Arthur Jose as a throwback to a Spanish ancestor in the way his nostrils dilated when he played the piano. A fisherman of Spanish origins called Nicholas Jose proclaimed his dissenting convictions in Land's End, Cornwall, in 1663, so George Fox records in his journal, claiming him as an early Quaker. According to my great-grandfather, the earliest Jose is Sir Joce de Dinan of Ludlow Castle, a border enforcer for King Henry II against the Welsh in 1150. Then there's a Rabbi Jose at Bury St Edmunds in 1173. That Jose line may have disappeared in the expulsion of the Jews from England in 1290, or survived by transforming into Anglo-Norman respectability. By 1309 there was a Sir John Joce knighted for killing 18 Scots, possibly a remote Jose ancestor. The lines loop around voyaging people and traders, border police and people of challenged consciences, people of social movement, up and down. It's a wide net that also takes in Roger Jose.

At least I have discovered that he has not entirely disappeared as wind on water. There is now a plaque in his memory on the esplanade in Darwin: 'Roger Jose, Eccentric'. How do I ask forgiveness on behalf of a family that may have wronged him? Australians are starting to say sorry for how they and their predecessors have treated Aboriginal people. Is Roger Jose part of that, for me at any rate?

There's a striking phrase in *The Songlines* where nomads are called 'the crankhandles of history'. Aboriginal people were never really true nomads. They just have a bigger backyard than most other people. Traditionally they moved with ceremony and the season, retaining the strongest possible attachment to particular places. But in the larger, looser sense in which Chatwin thinks of nomads, the concept takes in everyone who is driven to wander, travelling light. Those wanderers include Roger Jose, born Picton, died Borroloola, or Arthur Jose, born Bristol, died Brisbane, or the people of the Gulf of Carpentaria, moving by volition or force across their country, or the Macassans in their annual migrations, or Murrandoo Yanner, here, there and everywhere. The mistake is to assume that the starting place is ever left completely behind.

A better metaphor might be bamboo, admired for its lightness and flexibility. It travels far where it grows, thanks to a tenacious, extensive root system, and further when it is harvested and put to light, durable use. From the movement

Roger Jose, eccentric

of individuals and groups comes the world. There are patterns in that movement, surprising baroque curves, I realise, as I follow a hermit who was neither celibate nor alone, a comic sage who lived in an upside-down water tank with Maggie and her sister Biddy – the good man of Borroloola.

That's how it looks from the air as the little plane lifts over the Gulf, taking me to Cairns on my journey south to Sydney and home. Inlets of the sea interlock with the mudflats of land like the fingers of two hands. Channels, salt or fresh, branch into green fringes and white crusts with the diminishing form of anatomised arteries or veins. Way out there's a line where the silt clears and the water becomes deep blue.

In the end it hardly matters if we are related. That's what I tell Bob when he asks how this story ends. I am proud to adopt Roger Jose, as he has adopted me.

NOTES

Prologue **Lost Steps**

1 W. A. Steel and J. M. Anthill, *The History of All Saints' College, Bathurst, 1873–1963* (Sydney, 1964), p. 214.

2 David Attenborough, *Quest Under Capricorn* (London, 1963), p. 122.

3 Douglas Lockwood, *Up the Track* (Adelaide, 1964), p. 147.

4 Tasman Festing, quoted in Lockwood, p. 148.

5 Sue Neales, *The Gulf Country* (Terrey Hills, NSW, 2000), p. 132.

6 Alejo Carpentier, *Los pasos perdidos* (Mexico City, 1953) translated as *The Lost Steps* by Harriet De Onis (London, 1956).

I **Booze and Blood**

1 D. Andrew and H. Finlay, *Lonely Planet: Northern Territory* (Melbourne, 1999), pp. 236, 240; Ernestine Hill, 'Wings to Borroloola', *Walkabout*, 1 October 1945, p. 8; Peter Riley, quoted in Richard Baker, *Land is Life: From Bush to Town: The Story of the Yanyuwa People* (Sydney, 1999), p. 43.

2 W. E. Harney, *Content to Lie in the Sun* (London, 1958), p. 72.

3 Ross Duncan, *The Northern Territory Pastoral Industry, 1863–1910* (Melbourne, 1967), p. 10.

4 This quote and the two following are from C. E. Gaunt, 'The Birth of Borroloola', *Northern Standard*, 13 October 1931, reprinted in J. A. Whitaker, *Borroloola: Isolated and Interesting, 1885–1985* (Darwin, 1985).

5 Duncan, p. 12.

6 Ibid., p. 122.

7 Baker, p. 54.

8 Andrew McMillan, *An Intruder's Guide to East Arnhem Land* (Sydney, 2001), p. 69.

9 Hill, pp. 7–10.

10 Quoted in Baker, p. 44.

11 Paul Toohey, 'You Should've Been Here Yesterday', *The Australian Magazine*, 2–3 June, 2001, pp. 18–22.

12 Cuthbertson report on Borroloola, 21 January 1886, p. 7, National Archives of Australia, Canberra, CRS A3 225/1886, quoted in Baker, p. 79.

13 National Archives of Australia, Darwin, CRS F1 1948/15.

14 J. C. Webb, 'Borroloola Ration Depot: An Appreciation', 28 February 1956, NAA, Darwin, CRS F1 1952/770 Part 1.

II **No Humbug**

1 John Moriarty with Evan McHugh, *Saltwater Fella* (Ringwood, Vic., 2000), pp. 155, 176.

2 Ibid., pp. 5–6.

3 C. C. Macknight, *The Farthest Coast: A Selection of Writings Relating to the History of the Northern Coast of Australia* (Melbourne, 1969), pp. 4–5, 8. See also C. C. Macknight, *The Voyage to Maregé: Macassan Trepangers in Northern Australia* (Melbourne, 1976).

4 Quoted in Macknight, *The Voyage to Maregé*, p. 25.

5 Ibid., pp. 85–86.

6 Also spelled Janjula, Anula, Anyula, Yanyula.

7 Deric Thompson, oral history interview transcript, NTRS 226, TS 426; see also David Carment, 'Jose, Roger', *Northern Territory Dictionary of Biography*, vol. 1, *To 1945* (Darwin, 1990), p. 162.

III 'The Surf Upon the Shore'

1 H. M. Cooper, *The Unknown Coast, A Supplement* (Adelaide, 1955), p. 16.

2 Recent tributes include Tim Flannery, *Terra Australis* (Melbourne, 2000); Anthony J. Brown, *Ill-Starred Captains: Flinders and Baudin* (Hindmarsh, SA, 2000); Paul Brunton (curator), *Matthew Flinders: The Ultimate Voyage* (Sydney, 2001) and web site: www.slnsw.gov.au/flinders/; Sarah Thomas (curator), *The Encounter 1802: Art of the Flinders and Baudin Voyages* (Adelaide, 2002); and Gillian Dooley, 'Matthew Flinders as Writer', *Australian Book Review*, March 2002, pp. 45–48.

3 Matthew Flinders to George Bass, 15 February 1800, in Paul Brunton (ed.), *Matthew Flinders: Personal Letters*

from an Extraordinary Life (Sydney, 2002), p. 48; 'Mateship on Flinders' Ship Shown in "Corker of a Letter"', *Sydney Morning Herald*, 4 March 2002.

4 Quoted from Flinders' journal, 14 May 1805, Public Records Office, London, Adm. 55/76; later revised and published as *A Voyage to Terra Australis* (London, 1814).

5 Matthew Flinders, *A Biographical Tribute to the Memory of Trim* (Sydney, 1997), pp. 6–8.

6 James D. Mack, *Matthew Flinders, 1774–1814* (Melbourne, 1966). Also Ernest Scott, *The Life of Captain Matthew Flinders, R.N.* (Sydney, 1914) and Catharine Retter and Shirley Sinclair, *Letters to Ann: The Love Story of Matthew Flinders and Ann Chappelle* (Sydney, 1999).

IV **Border-land and Combo-land**

1 W. E. Harney, *Life Among the Aborigines* (Adelaide, 1957), p. 152.

2 Cheryl Frost, *The Last Explorer: The Life and Work of Ernest Favenc* (Townsville, Qld, 1983).

3 Alan Powell, *Far Country: A Short History of the Northern Territory*, 3rd edn (Melbourne, 1996), p. 96.

4 Alfred Searcy, *In Australian Tropics* (London, 1907, facsimile of 1909 edition, with introduction by C. C. Macknight, Carlisle, WA, 1984), p. 331.

5 Ibid., pp. 139, 142, 159, 163.

6 *Australian National Dictionary* (Melbourne, 1988).

7 David Collins, *An Account of the English Colony in New*

South Wales (1798), ed. Brian Fletcher (Sydney, 1975), vol. 1, p. 491.

8 Alan Powell, *Far Country*, pp. 140, 161.

9 Northern Territory Archives F267, Minute Book for Courts of Summary Jurisdiction held at Borroloola, 1925–1948, no. 1/48.

10 Keith Willey, *Ghosts of the Big Country* (Adelaide, 1975), p. 30.

11 Harney, *Content to Lie in the Sun*, p. 65.

12 W. E. Harney, *Bill Harney's War*, with an introduction by Manning Clark (Melbourne, 1983), p. 10.

13 Harney, *Bill Harney's War*, p. 1.

14 Harney, *Content to Lie in the Sun*, p. 67.

15 Willey, p. 25. For Harney, see Jeremy Long, *The Go-betweens: Patrol Officers in Aboriginal Affairs Administration in the Northern Territory 1936–1974* (Darwin, 1992), pp. 37–43, 62–65, 67–68.

16 W. E. Harney, *North of 23°: Ramblings in Northern Australia* (Sydney, 1946).

17 George Farwell, *Ghost Towns of Australia* (Adelaide, 1965), p. 209.

18 Barry Hill, *The Rock: Travelling to Uluru* (Sydney, 1994), p. 8 and *passim*.

19 Harney, *North of 23°*, p. 74.

20 Harney, *Life Among the Aborigines*, p. 164.

21 Ibid., p. 173.

22 Douglas and Ruth Lockwood (eds.), *A Bushman's Life* (Melbourne, 1990), p. 243.

V **The Revenge of the Oral**

1 Ernestine Hill, *The Great Australian Loneliness* (Melbourne, 1948), p. 214.
2 Harney, *North of 23°*, p. 106.
3 Robin Hardiman, 'The Lost Library of Borroloola', *Barkly News Pictorial,* March 1999; Harney, *Life Among the Aborigines*, p. 158; Hill, *The Great Australian Loneliness*, p. 215.
4 Farwell, p. 208; Lockwood, p. 151; Attenborough, p. 123.
5 J. H. Eedle, *Gaols and Goals* (Darwin, 1981).
6 Les Murray, *The Peasant Mandarin* (St Lucia, Qld, 1978) p. 150.
7 Ted Egan, *Sitdown Up North* (Sydney, 1997), pp. 104–5.
8 Vernon O'Brien, 'Borroloola: A Renaissance', *Northern Perspective*, 8 (2), December 1985, pp. 1–6.
9 Jean Dartnell, 'Borroloola: The Carnegie Library that Wasn't', *Riverina Library File*, 4 (2), 1983, p. 22.

VI **The Fewness of His Needs**

1 Police Journals, Borroloola, NTAS, F268.
2 Franklin James Johns, oral history interview, NTRS 226, TS 68, NTAS.
3 W. McKinnon, Police Station, Borroloola, NAA, Darwin, CRS F1 1943/92.
4 Randolph Stow, 'Epic of Capricorn', *Times Literary Supplement*, 9 April 1975, p. 417; for Herbert's biography and attitudes, Frances de Groen, *Xavier Herbert* (St Lucia, Qld, 1998).

5 Françoise Fromonot, *Glenn Murcutt: Works and Projects* (London, 1995), p. 142.
6 Colin Macleod, *Patrol In the Dreamtime* (Sydney, 1997), pp. 201–2.
7 Farwell, p. 209.
8 Baker, p. 163.
9 Harney, *North of 23°* p. 91.
10 Egan, quoted in Baker, p. 166.
11 Quotations in this section are from Victor C. Hall, *Sister Ruth* (London, 1968), *passim.*
12 Egan, p. 110.
13 Ibid., pp. 113–14. Quoted by kind permission of Ted Egan.
14 Lockwood, p. 151; Attenborough, p. 123; Ernestine Hill, *The Territory* (Sydney, 1951), p. 426; Macleod, p. 201.
15 Alexandra Hasluck (ed.), *Aubrey Tennyson's Vice-Regal Days* (Canberra, 1978), pp. 176, 219; Stella Bowen, *Drawn from Life* (London, 1941, reprinted 1999), p. 10.
16 Arthur W. Jose, *The Romantic Nineties* (Sydney, 1933), pp. 61, 69.
17 Letter, 5 September 1906, A. W. Jose papers, Mitchell Library, CY POS 788.
18 Percival Serle, *Dictionary of Australian Biography*, vol. 1 (Sydney and London, 1949), p. 484; Ross Lamont, 'Jose, Arthur Wilberforce', *Australian Dictionary of Biography*, vol. 9, *1891–1939* (Melbourne, 1983), pp. 523–24; Teresa Pagliaro, 'A. W. Jose and the Nineties: Living, Remembering, Constructing a Decade', in Ken Stewart (ed.), *The 1890s* (St Lucia, Qld, 1996), pp. 313–27.

19 John le Gay Brereton, *Knocking Around* (Sydney, 1930), p. 30.

20 Victoria Laurie, 'Unfinished Business: The Legacy of the Durack Dynasty', *HQ Magazine*, March–April 1998, p. 58.

VII **The Fewness of Their Wants**

1 Quoted in Rosalind Kidd, *The Way We Civilise* (St Lucia, Qld, 1997), p. xvii.

2 Nicholas Jose, 'White Lie Number Ten', *London Review of Books*, 19 February 1998, pp. 27–31.

3 Carpentier, p. 240.

4 Judith Wright, *The Cry for the Dead* (Melbourne, 1981), pp. 190, 106.

5 David Trigger, *Whitefella Comin': Aboriginal Responses to Colonialism in Northern Australia* (Cambridge, 1992), p. 20.

6 *Weekend Australian*, 15–16 December 2001; *Daily Telegraph*, 12 March 2002.

7 John S. Alcorn, *The Jolly Rogers: History of the 90th Bomb Group During World War II* (Temple City, Calif., 1981), pp. 21–26; *Aeroplane Dance*, directed by Trevor Graham (Film Australia, 1994).

8 The epigraph on p. x comes from the version composed by Frank Karrijiji, recorded and translated by John J. Bradley, Martin Duwell and R. M. W. Dixon (eds.), *Little Eva at Moonlight Creek and other Aboriginal Song Poems*, (St Lucia, Qld, 1994), p. 11; the lines quoted here are from the documentary film *Aeroplane Dance*.

9 John Van Tiggelen, 'Everything but the Scurvy', *Good Weekend*, 30 September 2000, pp. 28–32.

10 A. W. Jose, *Builders and Pioneers of Australia* (London, 1928), p. 134.

11 O. H. K. Spate, *Monopolists and Freebooters: The Pacific Since Magellan*, vol. 3 (Canberra, 1983), p. 43.

12 Trigger, p. 21.

13 Walter E. Roth, 'Report on the Northern Territory–Queensland Border, North of Urandangie', 14 August 1901, Gulf Country History File, Australian Institute of Aboriginal and Torres Strait Islander Studies Library, Canberra.

14 Trigger, p. 35.

15 Ibid., pp. 2–4, 11.

16 *Courier Mail*, 5 December 1998; *Sydney Morning Herald*, 9 August 1999; Michael Gordon, *Reconciliation: A Journey* (Sydney, 2001), pp. 51–9.

17 'A Work of Grace', *Doomadgee News*, February 1953, quoted in J. Dymock, 'Nicholson River Land Claim', unpublished report prepared for Northern Land Council, Darwin, 1982, p. 123.

18 Gordon, p. 56.

VIII **Exclusion Zone**

1 Quotations here and below are from reports by L. O. and B. D. Akehurst and Will Sharpe, and later M. and D. Read and P. Talbot, *Australian Missionary Tidings* (Sydney, 1931–69).

2 Carpentier, pp. 70, 209, 233.

3 Matthew, 24: 21–22, 25: 31–32.

4 W. J. Hosier, Protector of Aboriginals, 19 September 1931, Gulf Country History File.

5 Gulf Country History File.

6 Trigger, p. 206.

7 Jeremy Long, *Aboriginal Settlements: A Survey of Institutional Communities in Eastern Australia* (Canberra, 1970), p. 188.

8 Trigger, pp. 2–4.

9 McMillan, p. 286.

10 Alexis Wright, 'A Family Document', in Marion Halligan (ed.), *Storykeepers* (Sydney, 2001), pp. 223–40.

11 Alexis Wright, *Plains of Promise* (St Lucia, Qld, 1997), p. 44 and *passim.*

12 Jenny Pausacker, 'Alexis Wright, *Plains of Promise*', *Melbourne Age*, 19 April 1997.

IX **Gulf Warriors**

1 Neales, p. 42.

2 Quoted in Tim Bonyhady, *Burke and Wills: From Melbourne to Myth* (Balmain, NSW, 1991), p. 281.

3 Cyril Pearl, *Morrison of Peking* (Sydney, 1967), pp. 34–35.

4 Farwell, pp. 194, 199.

5 For documentary footage, *Two Laws* (Australian Film Commission, 1981) by Carolyn Strachan and Alessandro Cavadini.

6 David Trigger, 'Land Rights and the Reproduction of

Aboriginal Culture in Australia's Gulf Country', *Social Analysis*, 41 (3), 1997, pp. 84–106.

X Mine of the Century

1 Gustav Sobin, 'Basso Continuo: The Past as Accompaniment', *HEAT* 1, New Series, 2001, pp. 39–43.

2 Michael Archer, Suzanne J. Hand and Henk Godthelp, with a foreword by Sir David Attenborough, *Australia's Lost World: Riversleigh, World Heritage Site* (Sydney, 1991, reprinted 2000), p. 5.

3 Ibid., pp. 7–9.

4 Chief sources for my discussion of Century are Robert Blowes and David Trigger, 'Negotiating the Century Mine Agreement: Issues of Law, Culture and Politics', in Mary Edmunds (ed.), *Regional Agreements: Key Issues in Australia*, vol. 2, *Case Studies* (Canberra, 1999), pp. 85–135; David Trigger, 'Reflections on Century Mine: Preliminary Thoughts on the Politics of Indigenous Responses', in D. E. Smith and J. Finlayson (eds.), *Fighting Over Country: Anthropological Perspectives* (Canberra, 1997), pp. 110–28; Trigger, 'Land Rights', *passim*; Andrew Chew and Susan Greer, 'The Role of Accounting in Developmentalism: Room for An[Other] View?', University of Technology, Sydney, 1997, pp. 1–24; *Mining Monitor*, 1 (3), 1996; reports in the *North West Star*, the *Courier Mail* and the *Australian* newspapers; Pasminco media releases; High Court of Australia transcripts; James Button, 'Warrior from a Far Country',

Melbourne Age, 13 July 1996; Ian Williams, 'Century Zinc Project', paper presented at the Australian Academy of Technological Sciences and Engineering Symposium 'The Spirit of the Snowy – Fifty Years On', 1999; M. Moran and D. Bergen, 'Gulf and West Queensland Regional Homeland Plan', Gulf Aboriginal Development Company and ATSIC Gulf and West Queensland Regional Council, 2000; Ciaran O'Faircheallaigh, *Process, Politics and Regional Agreements* (Canberra, 1998); David Marr, 'Mad about the Buoy', *Good Weekend*, 18 August 2001; *Century Jabiru Newsletter*, March 2002; and personal interviews.

5 I am grateful to M. J. Detmold for making available to me his unpublished study of this subject, 'Law Like Love', vol. 1, 'A Modern Natural Law' (July 2000).

6 Bob Katter, quoted in *North West Star*, 20 February 1997.

7 John Connell and Richard Howitt (eds.), *Mining and Indigenous Peoples in Australasia* (Sydney, 1991), p. 8.

8 Alexis Wright, 'A Kind People' (from *Carpentaria*), *HEAT* 1, New Series 2001, pp. 51–56.

9 Blowes and Trigger, pp. 85, 115.

10 John Bradley (tr. and ill.), *Yanyuwa Country: The Yanyuwa People of Borroloola tell the History of Their Land* (Richmond, Vic., 1988), pp. x–xi.

Epilogue: **Crankhandles**

1 That's how ex-Warumpi band singer/songwriter Neil Murray sees it in *One Man Tribe* (Darwin, 1999).

2 Nicholas Shakespeare, *Bruce Chatwin* (London, 1999), p. 489.
3 Phillip Toyne, quoted ibid., pp. 412–13.
4 Ibid., p. 413.
5 Geoff Bagshaw, quoted ibid.
6 Ibid., p. 490.
7 Judith Ryan, *Ginger Riley* (Melbourne, 1997), pp. 8, 13, 14, 17.
8 Brenda L. Croft, *Beyond the Pale: Contemporary Indigenous Art* (Adelaide, 2000), p. 88.
9 Dula Njurruwuthun, quoted in Buku-Larrngay Mulka Centre, *Saltwater: Yirrkala Bark Paintings of Sea Country* (Neutral Bay, NSW, 1999), p. 12.
10 Ibid., p. 26.
11 Toni Morrison, 'On "The Radiance of the King"', *New York Review of Books*, 9 August 2001.
12 Shiva Naipaul, *An Unfinished Journey* (London, 1986), p. 21.

BIBLIOGRAPHY

Alcorn, John S., *The Jolly Rogers: History of the 90th Bomb Group During World War II* (Temple City, Calif., 1981).

Andrew, D. and H. Finlay, *Lonely Planet: Northern Territory* (Melbourne, 1999).

Archer, Michael, Suzanne J. Hand and Henk Godthelp, *Australia's Lost World: Riversleigh, World Heritage Site*, with a foreword by Sir David Attenborough (Sydney, 1991, reprinted 2000).

Attenborough, David, *Quest Under Capricorn* (London, 1963).

Australian Missionary Tidings (Sydney, 1931–69).

Australian National Dictionary (Melbourne, 1988).

Baker, Richard, *Land is Life: From Bush to Town: The Story of the Yanyuwa People* (Sydney, 1999).

Blowes, Robert and David Trigger, 'Negotiating the Century Mine Agreement: Issues of Law, Culture and Politics', in Mary Edmunds (ed.), *Regional Agreements: Key Issues in Australia*, vol. 2, *Case Studies* (Canberra, 1999), pp. 85–135.

Bonyhady, Tim, *Burke and Wills: From Melbourne to Myth* (Balmain, NSW, 1991).

Bowen, Stella, *Drawn from Life* (London, 1941, reprinted 1999).

Bradley, John (tr. and ill.), *Yanyuwa Country: The Yanyuwa People of Borroloola Tell the History of Their Land* (Richmond, Vic., 1988).

Brereton, John le Gay, *Knocking Around* (Sydney, 1930).

Brown, Anthony J., *Ill-Starred Captains: Flinders and Baudin* (Hindmarsh, SA, 2000).

Brunton, Paul, *Matthew Flinders: The Ultimate Voyage* (Sydney, 2001) and web site: www.slnsw.gov.au/flinders/.

Brunton, Paul (ed.), *Matthew Flinders: Personal Letters from an Extraordinary Life* (Sydney, 2002).

Buku-Larrngay Mulka Centre, *Saltwater: Yirrkala Bark Paintings of Sea Country* (Neutral Bay, NSW, 1999).

Button, James, 'Warrior from a Far Country', *Melbourne Age*, 13 July 1996.

Carment, David, 'Jose, Roger', *Northern Territory Dictionary of Biography*, vol. 1, *To 1945* (Darwin, 1990).

Carpentier, Alejo, *The Lost Steps*, tr. Harriet De Onis (London, 1956). Originally published as *Los pasos perdidos* (Mexico City, 1953).

Chatwin, Bruce, *The Songlines* (London, 1987).

Chew, Andrew and Susan Greer, 'The Role of Accounting in Developmentalism: Room for An[Other] View?', University of Technology, Sydney, 1997.

Collins, David, *An Account of the English Colony in New South Wales*, vol. 1, ed. Brian Fletcher (Sydney, 1975; originally published 1798).

Connell, John and Richard Howitt (eds.), *Mining and Indigenous Peoples in Australasia* (Sydney, 1991).

Cooper, H. M., *The Unknown Coast, A Supplement* (Adelaide, 1955).

Croft, Brenda L., *Beyond the Pale: Contemporary Indigenous Art* (Adelaide, 2000).

Dartnell, Jean, 'Borroloola: The Carnegie Library that Wasn't', *Riverina Library File*, 4 (2), 1983, p. 22.

de Groen, Frances, *Xavier Herbert* (St Lucia, Qld, 1998).

Detmold, M. J., 'Law Like Love', vol. 1, 'A Modern Natural Law' (unpublished ms, July 2000).

Dooley, Gillian, 'Matthew Flinders as Writer', *Australian Book Review*, March 2002, pp. 45–48.

Duncan, Ross, *The Northern Territory Pastoral Industry, 1863–1910* (Melbourne, 1967).

Duwell, Martin and R. M. W. Dixon (eds.), *Little Eva at Moonlight Creek and Other Aboriginal Song Poems* (St Lucia, Qld, 1994).

Dymock, J., 'Nicholson River Land Claim', unpublished report prepared for Northern Land Council, Darwin, 1982.

Eedle, J. H., *Gaols and Goals* (Darwin, 1981).

Egan, Ted, *Sitdown Up North* (Sydney, 1997).

Farwell, George, *Ghost Towns of Australia* (Adelaide, 1965).

Favenc, Ernest, *Tales of the Austral Tropics* (London, 1894).

Flannery, Tim, *Terra Australis* (Melbourne, 2000).

Flinders, Matthew, *A Biographical Tribute to the Memory of Trim* (Sydney, 1997).

—— *A Voyage to Terra Australis* (London, 1814; facsimile edition, Adelaide, 1966).
Fromonot, Françoise, *Glenn Murcutt: Works and Projects* (London, 1995).
Frost, Cheryl, *The Last Explorer: The Life and Work of Ernest Favenc* (Townsville, Qld, 1983).
Gaunt, C. E., 'The Birth of Borroloola', *Northern Standard*, 13 October 1931, reprinted in J. A. Whitaker, *Borroloola: Isolated and Interesting, 1885–1985* (Darwin, 1985).
Gordon, Michael, *Reconciliation: A Journey* (Sydney, 2001).
Hall, Victor C., *Sister Ruth* (London, 1968).
Hardiman, Robin, 'The Lost Library of Borroloola', *Barkly News Pictorial*, March 1999.
Harney, W. E., *Bill Harney's War*, with an introduction by Manning Clark (Melbourne, 1983).
—— *Content to Lie in the Sun* (London, 1958).
—— *Life Among the Aborigines* (Adelaide, 1957).
—— *North of 23°: Ramblings in Northern Australia* (Sydney, 1946).
Hasluck, Alexandra (ed.), *Aubrey Tennyson's Vice-Regal Days* (Canberra, 1978).
Herbert, Xavier, *Capricornia* (Sydney, 1938).
—— *Poor Fellow My Country* (Sydney, 1975).
Hill, Barry, *The Rock: Travelling to Uluru* (Sydney, 1994).
Hill, Ernestine, *The Great Australian Loneliness* (Melbourne, 1948).
—— *My Love Must Wait* (Sydney, 1941).
—— *The Territory* (Sydney, 1951).

—— 'Wings to Borroloola', *Walkabout*, 1 October 1945.
Jose, A. W., *Builders and Pioneers of Australia* (London, 1928).
—— *The Romantic Nineties* (Sydney, 1933).
—— *Two Awheel and Some Others Afoot in Australia* (London, 1903).
Jose, Nicholas, 'White Lie Number Ten', *London Review of Books*, 19 February 1998, pp. 27–31.
Kidd, Rosalind, *The Way We Civilise* (St Lucia, Qld, 1997).
Lamont, Ross, 'Jose, Arthur Wilberforce', in *Australian Dictionary of Biography*, vol. 9, *1891–1939* (Melbourne, 1983), pp. 523–24.
Laurie, Victoria, 'Unfinished Business: The Legacy of the Durack Dynasty', *HQ Magazine*, March–April 1998, pp. 50–60.
Lawrence, D. H., *Kangaroo* (London, 1923).
Lockwood, Douglas, *I, The Aboriginal* (Adelaide, 1962).
—— *Up the Track* (Adelaide, 1964).
Lockwood, Douglas and Ruth Lockwood (eds.), *A Bushman's Life* (Melbourne, 1990).
Long, Jeremy, *Aboriginal Settlements: A Survey of Institutional Communities in Eastern Australia* (Canberra, 1970).
—— *The Go-Betweens: Patrol Officers in Aboriginal Affairs Administration in the Northern Territory, 1936–1974* (Darwin, 1992).
Mack, James D., *Matthew Flinders, 1774–1814* (Melbourne, 1966).
Macknight, C. C., *The Farthest Coast: A Selection of Writings*

Relating to the History of the Northern Coast of Australia (Melbourne, 1969).
—— *The Voyage to Maregé: Macassan Trepangers in Northern Australia* (Melbourne, 1976).
Macleod, Colin, *Patrol In the Dreamtime* (Sydney, 1997).
Marr, David, 'Mad about the Buoy', *Good Weekend*, 18 August 2001.
Matthiessen, Peter, *In the Spirit of Crazy Horse* (New York, 1983).
McMillan, Andrew, *An Intruder's Guide to East Arnhem Land* (Sydney, 2001).
Moran, M. and D. Bergen, *Gulf and West Queensland Regional Homeland Plan* (Mount Isa, Qld, 2000).
Moriarty, John with Evan McHugh, *Saltwater Fella* (Ringwood, Vic., 2000).
Morrison, Toni, 'On "The Radiance of the King"', *New York Review of Books*, 9 August 2001.
Murray, Les, *The Peasant Mandarin* (St Lucia, Qld, 1978).
Murray, Neil, *One Man Tribe* (Darwin, 1999).
Naipaul, Shiva, *An Unfinished Journey* (London, 1986).
Neales, Sue, *The Gulf Country*, photography by Murray Spence (Terrey Hills, NSW, 2000).
O'Brien, Vernon, 'Borroloola: A Renaissance', *Northern Perspective*, 8 (2), December 1985, pp. 1–6.
O'Faircheallaigh, Ciaran, *Process, Politics and Regional Agreements* (Canberra, 1998).
Pagliaro, Teresa, 'A. W. Jose and the Nineties: Living, Remembering, Constructing a Decade', in Ken Stewart

(ed.), *The 1890s* (St Lucia, Qld, 1996), pp. 313–27.

Pausacker, Jenny, 'Alexis Wright, *Plains of Promise*', *Melbourne Age*, 19 April 1997.

Pearl, Cyril, *Morrison of Peking* (Sydney, 1967).

Powell, Alan, *Far Country: A Short History of the Northern Territory* (Melbourne, 1982; 3rd edn, 1996).

Retter, Catharine and Shirley Sinclair, *Letters to Ann: The Love Story of Matthew Flinders and Ann Chappelle* (Sydney, 1999).

Roberts, Tony, *Rough Justice: Old Days in Borroloola* (in preparation).

Roth, Walter E., 'Report on the Northern Territory–Queensland Border, North of Urandangie', 14 August 1901, Gulf Country History File, Australian Institute of Aboriginal and Torres Strait Islander Studies Library, Canberra.

Ryan, Judith, *Ginger Riley* (Melbourne, 1997).

Scott, Ernest, *The Life of Captain Matthew Flinders, R.N.* (Sydney, 1914).

Searcy, Alfred, *In Australian Tropics* (London, 1907; facsimile of 1909 edition, with introduction by C. C. Macknight, Carlisle, WA, 1984).

Serle, Percival, *Dictionary of Australian Biography*, vol. 1 (Sydney and London, 1949).

Shakespeare, Nicholas, *Bruce Chatwin* (London, 1999).

Shute, Nevil, *A Town Like Alice* (London, 1950).

Sobin, Gustav, 'Basso Continuo: The Past as Accompaniment', *HEAT* 1, New Series 2001, pp. 39–43.

Spate, O. H. K., *Monopolists and Freebooters: The Pacific Since Magellan*, vol. 3 (Canberra, 1983).

Steel, W. A. and J. M. Anthill, *The History of All Saints' College, Bathurst, 1873–1963* (Sydney, 1964).

Stow, Randolph, 'Epic of Capricorn', *Times Literary Supplement*, 9 April 1975, p. 417.

Thomas, Sarah, *The Encounter 1802: Art of the Flinders and Baudin Voyages* (Adelaide, 2002).

Toohey, Paul, 'You Should've Been Here Yesterday', *The Australian Magazine*, 2–3 June 2001, pp. 18–22.

Trigger, David, 'Land Rights and the Reproduction of Aboriginal Culture in Australia's Gulf Country', *Social Analysis*, 41 (3), 1997, pp. 84–106.

—— 'Reflections on Century Mine: Preliminary Thoughts on the Politics of Indigenous Responses', in D. E. Smith and J. Finlayson (eds.), *Fighting Over Country: Anthropological Perspectives* (Canberra, 1997), pp. 110–28.

—— *Whitefella Comin': Aboriginal Responses to Colonialism in Northern Australia* (Cambridge, 1992).

Van Tiggelen, John, 'Everything but the Scurvy', *Good Weekend*, 30 September 2000, pp. 28–32.

Webb, J. C., 'Borroloola Ration Depot: An Appreciation', 28 February 1956, National Archives of Australia, Darwin, CRS F1 1952/770 Part 1.

Whitaker, J. A., *Borroloola: Isolated and Interesting, 1885–1985* (Darwin, 1985).

White, Patrick, *Voss* (London, 1957).

Willey, Keith, *Ghosts of the Big Country* (Adelaide, 1975).

Williams, Ian, 'Century Zinc Project', paper presented at the Australian Academy of Technological Sciences and Engineering Symposium 'The Spirit of the Snowy – Fifty Years On', 1999.

Wright, Alexis, 'A Family Document', in Marion Halligan (ed.), *Storykeepers* (Sydney, 2001), pp. 223–40.

—— 'A Kind People' (from *Carpentaria*), *HEAT* 1, New Series 2001, pp. 51–56.

—— *Plains of Promise* (St Lucia, Qld, 1997).

Wright, Judith, *The Cry for the Dead* (Melbourne, 1981).

LIST OF ILLUSTRATIONS

ACKNOWLEDGEMENTS

I am grateful to the following organisations and their staff for making material available and for assisting me in my research: National Library of Australia; State Library of New South Wales; State Library of South Australia; Northern Territory Library; Australian Institute of Aboriginal and Torres Strait Islander Studies Library, Canberra; Fryer Library, University of Queensland; Mount Isa City Library; South Sydney City Library; Northern Territory Archives; National Archives of Australia; Registrar of Births, Deaths and Marriages, New South Wales; Historical Society of the Northern Territory; Inverell District Family History Group; Picton Family History Society; Old Police Station Museum, Borroloola; Film Australia; Aboriginal and Torres Strait Islander Commission, Cairns; Carpentaria Land Council; Mr Copy, Surry Hills; Alcaston Gallery, Melbourne; Art Gallery of South Australia; Flinders University Art Museum; Museum of Victoria.

Special thanks to all those individuals who helped along the way, including Kathy Bail, Mick Baker, Françoise Barr,

John Bradley, Ian Britain, David Carment, Rob Carroll, Andrew Chalk, Chong Weng-ho, Liz Corbett, Elaine Corrie, Harvey Creswell, Tamsin Donaldson, Ted Egan, Sammy Evans, Pauline Fietz, Peter and Sheila Forrest, Tim Game, Carrillo Gantner, Benjamin Genocchio, Francis Good, Trevor Graham, Jack Green, Roy Hammer, Violet Hammer, Richard Harding, Sam Heard and Merridy Pitcher, Gordon Hookey, Ivor Indyk, Janet Leather and Eddie Webber, Kim Lockwood, Ruth Lockwood, Jeremy Long, Andrew McMillan, David Malouf, Kathy Mawson, John and Ros Moriarty, Michael Neve, Vernon O'Brien, Claire Roberts, Tony Roberts, Nicolas Rothwell, John Thompson, Tracker Tilmouth, David Trigger, Ruth Watson, Alexis Wright, R. B. Wyatt, and the Yanner family.

I also wish to thank Peter Carson, Penny Daniel and their colleagues at Profile Books; Julie Pinkham and Foong Ling Kong and their colleagues at Hardie Grant Books; my copy-editor Trevor Horwood; and my agents Rosemary Creswell and Derek Johns.

INDEX

Page numbers in italics refer to illustrations

Index